THE CHALLENGE

OF DISCIPLESHIP

THE CHALLENGE OF DISCIPLESHIP

A Critical Study of the Sermon on the Mount as Scripture

Daniel Patte

TRINITY PRESS INTERNATIONAL
Harrisburg, Pennsylvania

Trinity Press International, P.O. Box 1321, Harrisburg, PA 17105
Trinity Press International is a division of the Morehouse Group.

Cover art: Elizabeth McNaron Patte
Cover design: Kirk Bingaman

Library of Congress Cataloging-in-Publication Data
Patte, Daniel.
    The challenge of discipleship : a critical study of the Sermon on the mount as scripture / Daniel Patte.
        p.   cm.
    Includes bibliographical references.
    ISBN 1-56338-286-5 (pbk. : alk. paper) ·
    1. Sermon on the mount – Criticism, interpretation, etc.
    2. Christian life – Biblical teaching.   I. Title.
    BT380.2.P265 1999
    226.9'06–dc21   99-16380

Printed in the United States of America

99 00 01 02 03 04   10 9 8 7 6 5 4 3 2 1

For Lauren, Benjamin, and Daniel

Contents

Part 2
ASSUMING RESPONSIBILITY FOR OUR VIEWS OF
SCRIPTURE AND THEIR ROLES IN OUR INTERPRETATIONS
OF MATTHEW 5:17–48 AND 7:12

Preface

In the following pages, I invite you to a critical study of the Sermon on the Mount as Scripture. At the outset, this approach, *scriptural criticism*, might take you aback, although the reasons for your surprise might vary.

First-time readers of the New Testament and lay church members might fear that the use of this critical approach will make this book too technical and/or that it will involve a negative attitude toward their faith-interpretations. I made sure it is not too technical. The few methodological discussions are relegated either to endnotes or to the appendix. Furthermore, from beginning to end, this book respects faith-interpretations of the Sermon on the Mount as Scripture and gives them a central place.

Teachers and scholars might then be afraid that this approach will not be critical enough, since it deliberately takes into account and respects believers' readings of the biblical text as Scripture. Why should this approach be suspect? Is it inappropriate for anthropologists to take seriously the religious views and interpretations of the natives? Actually, without such fieldwork, anthropological studies are often viewed as lacking crucial evidence. Why should we presuppose that Christian believers have inappropriate readings of their sacred Scripture? The central question is: Can a critical study ignore the fact that believers read the Bible as Scripture?

I address this question in two locations. In my earlier book *Discipleship According to the Sermon on the Mount: Four Legitimate Interpretations, Four Plausible Views of Discipleship, and Their Relative Values*, I propose a detailed discussion of a series of scholarly interpretations of the Sermon on the Mount, of their methodologies, and of their interrelations, which shows how each implicitly presupposes a specific type of faith-interpretation. Therefore, in the present book, my comparison of these interpretations can be focused on their most salient features and on their conclusions. Similarly, the detailed explanation and justification for the procedure implemented in this book — scriptural criticism —

is found in the appendix, "Why a Critical Study of the New Testament as Scripture?" There I argue that, since we cannot escape having presuppositions related to our (positive or negative) assessments of faith-interpretations, our vocation as critical scholars and teachers is best fulfilled when we explicitly account for believers' readings of the biblical text as Scripture.

Conscientious preachers might have a feeling of déjà vu. Is not scriptural criticism what they do each week when they prepare their sermons? Indeed! In order to prepare themselves to preach about a text, they strive to integrate three interpretive moments. They carefully analyze the biblical text with the help of critical commentaries in order to identify the range of significant features offered by this text. They also read the biblical text theologically in order to formulate its teaching into a meaningful sermon that will bring their congregations into dialogue with the text about certain theological issues. And, of course, they read the biblical text as Scripture in order to discern the most helpful teaching, the Word of God, offered by this text for believers in a certain context. Most importantly, beyond what they have learned in seminaries where biblical studies, systematic theology, and practical theology are taught separately, the best preachers bring these interpretive moments together in a creative tension, because they know that without this tension their preaching is neither faithful nor responsible. Such preachers, including my pastor, K. C. Ptomey (at Westminster Presbyterian Church in Nashville, Tennessee), are right to have a feeling of déjà vu. I took their practice as a model of what an overall critical study of a biblical text should include. My hope is that, through its systematic presentation of a practice of scriptural criticism, this book will facilitate the emulation of these faithful and responsible preachers.

But scriptural criticism is not merely for preachers. It is for all of us, including first-time readers of the New Testament and/or lay church members, because it gives us the opportunity of standing back and assuming responsibility for our own interpretations. Whoever we are, we need to assess whether or not the interpretation we chose is the best for believers today, because the interpretation of a scriptural text always matters.

The interpretation of the Sermon on the Mount as Scripture matters to you even if you are not Christian, because Christian believers live by this teaching, and because the way they live often has significant consequences for others. Many teachings based on the Sermon on the Mount have strongly positive, and at times, awe-inspiring effects upon others, because they call Christians to a life devoted to the welfare of others. Yet, unfortunately, history shows that discriminatory teachings (promoting, for instance, anti-Judaism and patriarchalism) have also been based upon this text. Thus, from your perspective as an outsider, you might want to point out to Christians how certain teachings of the Sermon on the Mount affect other people, for better or for worse.

If you are a Christian, assuming responsibility for your own interpretation is all the more important. As you commit yourself to live by a teaching of the Sermon on the Mount, you want to be in a position to confess, "*I* believe (*credo*) this teaching is the Word of God for us today." In order to make this confession, you need to recognize that you made a choice among several other interpretations. In so doing you have adopted a critical attitude, which simply requires that you respect other people's interpretations as you wish them to respect yours.

In turn, as I practice scriptural criticism, I will respect your interpretation, even as I try to lead you to assume responsibility for it. Throughout this book I make room for your reading of the Sermon on the Mount, whatever it might be, though I stipulate that it be formulated as a "teaching of this text for believers today." Scriptural criticism brings together believers' faith-interpretations and their contextual concerns, theologians' hermeneutical dialogues with the text about certain theological categories, and biblical scholars' analyses of the textual evidence.

Recognizing the complementary character of these three modes of interpretations and conceiving of a way to integrate them in an overall critical practice is not something that I, a biblical scholar, could have done by myself. Collaboration with a systematic theologian was necessary. Cristina Grenholm and I conceptualized scriptural criticism as a critical approach that strives to make explicit the contextual, hermeneutical, and analytical frames of biblical interpretations, when writing the methodological "overture" for the series "Romans through History and Culture," found in the first volume, *Reading Israel in Romans: Legitimacy and Plausibility of Divergent Interpretations*. In our earlier works, each of us had a partial model. In her studies of the relationship between critical studies and theological interpretations of the Bible — *Romans Interpreted: A Comparative Analysis of the Commentaries of Barth, Nygren, Cranfield and Wilckens on Paul's Epistle to the Romans* and subsequently in *The Old Testament, Christianity and Pluralism* — Cristina Grenholm had

developed a sophisticated model that emphasizes the complementary character of theologians' and biblical scholars' approaches,
tied together by her feminist concerns. For my part, in *Ethics
of Biblical Interpretation: A Reevaluation*, struggling to disentan-
gle my work as a biblical scholar from its androcentricism and
Eurocentricism and their problematic effects led me to reenvision
the relationship between the believer's faith-interpretation and the
scholar's analytical interpretation. I then recognized that the task
of scholarly biblical studies is to "bring to critical understanding
faith-interpretations" — a theological task. With the help of my
structural semiotic perspective, I had envisioned the relationship
between analytical and contextual interpretations, but ignored the
place of theological interpretations and their hermeneutical frame.
When Grenholm's and my approaches were brought together at
the 1997 Society of Biblical Literature Consultation on the Reception of Romans and Exegesis, what we finally called "scriptural
criticism" began to take shape, and was hammered out in the introduction of *Reading Israel in Romans*. This scriptural critical study
of the Sermon of the Mount, which happens to be published before
our co-authored essay, is framed by this approach.

I am also much indebted to the many students at Vanderbilt
University, at the Université de Neuchâtel, at Union Theological Seminary (Dasmariñas and Manila, Philippines), as well as
to members of several adult Sunday School classes of Presbyterian and Episcopal churches in Nashville who patiently (and some
times, not so patiently!) endured my fumbling efforts to develop
this pedagogical approach before having the proper frame for it.
The few who are mentioned in notes, because they contributed a
specific feature of my interpretation, represent literally hundreds
of voices who prompted me to continue this project even as they
constructively questioned aspects of it. There is not a page of
this book that is not shaped by the insights, suggestions, objections, and questions of these students, as they shared their own
interpretations of the Sermon on the Mount with me and their
classmates.

I am particularly indebted to the younger colleagues (many of
whom now have teaching positions around the world) who have
been my teaching assistants during the eight years it took me to develop this approach. They actively contributed to the reorientation
of my conception of critical biblical study as we strove together
to be pedagogically responsible. Thus, I want to thank Professors W. Gregory Carey, Musa Dube, Tat-Siong Benny Liew, Vicki

Phillips, Diane Turner Sharazz, Nicole Wilkinson Duran (who were my teaching assistants from 1992 to 1995), as well as my more recent teaching assistants, who have seen this book progressively take shape and have discussed many of its features with me, Florinel Cimpean, James Grimshaw, Leticia A. Guardiola-Saenz, Laura Hocker, R. Grace Imathiu, Monya Stubbs, Yak Hwee Tan, Revelation E. Velunta.

I owe an important debt of gratitude to several colleagues who have kindly taken the time in their busy schedules to read a draft of this book. My thanks go to Professors Sandra M. Schneiders, Jack L. Seymour, David Odell-Scott, Fred W. Burnett, and Laurence L. Welborn. Each of them, in her or his own way, has helped me improve this book in significant ways through suggestions and comments.

This work has also been fundamentally shaped by and made possible through the faithful support of Aline, my wife, who by her own dedication to the life and ministries of the Presbyterian Church (USA) at the local and regional levels keeps reminding me that biblical studies would become meaningless if divorced from the church. This book is dedicated to three young readers of the Bible — Lauren, Benjamin, and Daniel Wasby — our grandchildren.

THE CHALLENGE

OF DISCIPLESHIP

Introduction

A Critical Study of the New Testament as Scripture

The tempter came and said to [Jesus], "If you are the Son of God, command these stones to become loaves of bread." But he answered, "It is written, 'One does not live by bread alone, but by every word that comes from the mouth of God'" [Deut. 8:3]. Then the devil took him to the holy city and placed him on the pinnacle of the temple, saying to him, "If you are the Son of God, throw yourself down; for it is written, 'He will command his angels concerning you,' and 'On their hands they will bear you up, so that you will not dash your foot against a stone'" [Ps. 91:11–12]. Jesus said to him, "Again it is written, 'Do not put the Lord your God to the test'" [Deut. 6:16]. (Matt. 4:3–7)

The Challenge of Discipleship and Our Readings of the Sermon on the Mount

Reading Matthew 5–7 as Scripture: A Challenge to Discipleship

As the title and subtitle of this book state, its subject matter is the challenge of discipleship that arises from our readings of the Sermon on the Mount as Scripture. The question is: How does the Sermon on the Mount affect Christian believers in the concreteness of their lives?

The general answer is clear: When this text is read *as Scripture* by believers who seek to be faithful disciples, it challenges them to make fundamental changes in their lives. Its teaching transforms the perspectives, attitudes, and/or behavior that govern their daily lives, just as in Matt. 4:4–7, the teachings of Deut. 8:3 and 6:16 corrected the views that Jesus was tempted to have of himself, his needs, and his relationship to God.

Such is the transformative power that a biblical text has each time believers read it as Scripture. As believers know well, this transformative encounter with the text is a recurring event. Again and again they are challenged by the same text, and this in many different ways.

Why is this? Undoubtedly because a text such as the Sermon on the Mount is so rich that it offers believers ever new teachings for their lives. In each instance, it is the transformative power of one dimension of the text (not the entire text) that confronts believers. Yet, believers are not passive. They play a role in formulating their faith-interpretations of this text of Scripture. Consciously or, most often, subconsciously, they allow themselves to be affected by one aspect of the text rather than by another. Perhaps somewhat haphazardly, for one reason or another they select one of the several potentially transformative teachings about discipleship offered by the text.

Where there is choice, there is responsibility. Thus, reading the Sermon on the Mount as Scripture involves another challenge for believers; they are called to assume responsibility for their faith-interpretations. Why did they (consciously or not) select one faith-interpretation rather than another?

There is much at stake in accepting or rejecting the challenge of discipleship formulated in a chosen faith-interpretation of the Sermon of the Mount. The type of critical study presented in this book is aimed at helping you, my readers, to assess the relative value of your faith-interpretations. It invites you to bring to critical understanding your faith-interpretation of the Sermon on the Mount, and especially its teaching about discipleship, so that you might be in a position to explain why you choose a certain faith-interpretation.

Who Needs a Critical Understanding of His/Her Faith-Interpretation of The Sermon on the Mount?

Whoever you are, you might be tempted to think that this critical biblical study is not for you. Everyone has a good reason for excusing himself or herself.

Some might want to say that as Christian believers they do not need critical biblical studies for their devotional readings of Scripture. On the contrary! Christian believers direly need to examine their interpretations in order to assume responsibility for them. Otherwise, how could they confess their faith-interpretations (and their faith!) as their own?

Some who are not Christian believers also read the Sermon on the Mount as a text to live by, and thus as Scripture, even though it is not part of their Scriptures. Mahatma Gandhi, for instance, expressed in his letters to Leo Tolstoy how much he lived by this text.[1] In this case, they might be directly interested by Christian faith-interpretations of this text.

Yet, most of the readers of the Sermon on the Mount who are not Christian believers might want to protest that Christian faith-interpretations do not concern them, because they have merely an academic interest in New Testament texts. On the contrary! In many cases they cannot afford to ignore how Christian believers interpret this text, because the ways in which Christians live their faith might have significant implications for them. Jews, women (including secular women), and many victims of injustice know this only too well. Furthermore, readers of the Sermon on the Mount who are not Christians cannot help envisioning the teaching that this text has for Christian believers. Bringing this teaching to critical understanding is to recognize that the particular faith-interpretation they ascribed to Christian believers is merely one among several possible ones.

Still others who are trained in biblical scholarship — for example, preachers and teachers — might want to object that I inappropriately interrelate critical studies of the Bible and faith-interpretations. Critical studies should be as detached as possible, and thus free from faith concerns, should they not? On the contrary! Critical biblical studies and faith-interpretations are necessarily closely intertwined; in most instances scholarly interpretations presuppose faith-interpretations, at least those interpretations that they want to challenge.

A Practice of Critical Studies of the Bible in Which Believers Have an Important Role

Through this book I seek to promote a practice of critical studies of the New Testament in which all readers can participate because all of them have significant roles in it, whether they are Christian believers or not, ordinary readers or trained biblical scholars. For this purpose, I seek to overcome common misunderstandings that believers have about critical biblical studies, as well as the no less common misunderstandings that biblical scholars have about faith-interpretations.

These misunderstandings are not about faith-interpretations and/or about critical studies in and of themselves. Rather, they concern the relationship of the two, as well as the relationship between believers and scholars. When confusion about these relationships is overcome, believers can recognize what is at stake for them in critical studies; conversely, scholars can recognize that they have everything to gain by a more explicit dialogue with believers.

The first step is to take note that faith-interpretations and critical studies are two distinct practices of interpretation. Then, one can recognize that they are complementary. Faith-interpretations are primarily concerned to discern what the biblical text teaches believers for and about their lives. Critical biblical studies are primarily concerned to assess the legitimacy and plausibility of existing interpretations before proposing their own conclusions about the text.

Against the presuppositions of those believers who fear that critical biblical studies will destroy their faith and their faith-interpretations, I stress that one of the main goals of critical biblical studies is, and has always been, to establish the legitimacy and plausibility of "certain" faith-interpretations, by showing how they can be grounded on textual evidence and formulated in terms of meaningful themes or categories. I simply raise the question: Why should this positive attitude of critical studies be limited to "certain" faith-interpretations?

Conversely, against the scholars' presuppositions that faith-interpretations cannot be legitimate and plausible, I argue that faith-interpretations are much more reliable than is usually thought. Many scholars feel that the main problem with faith-interpretations is that they involve reading into the text parts of the believers' experiences and views. But when one recognizes faith-interpretations as a distinct practice of interpretation, it appears that far from being in and of itself a problem, reading into the text is a necessary component of the reading process; it is a part of the practical dimension of reading, which is particularly apparent when believers read a text as Scripture.[2]

My concern with these phobias — believers' fear of critical studies and scholars' fear of faith-interpretations — is that believers and scholars cannot sit around the same table, read the Bible together, and learn from each other. In this introduction and in the body of this book, my primary goal is to make sure that you, whoever you are, have a place at the table. The scholars have already taken their seats. Therefore, my primary concern is for those of you who feel intimidated by these scholars. Yes, you also have reserved seats around the table — you, who (want to) read the Sermon on the Mount, even though you have not devoted your life to biblical scholarship; you, Christian believers, who read this text as Scripture; as well as, you, non-Christian readers of the New Testament, who are curious about this text that Christians call Scripture. It is your questions I will strive to address, while helping scholars to listen to you. (I address in the appendix other questions that biblical scholars might have.)[3]

I conceive of this book as initiating a discussion. Consequently, I envision myself as one of the participants sitting around the table with you, my readers. Thus, I will have to introduce myself. I am not some faceless mannequin! Like everybody else, I am interpreting the New Testament from a certain context. I will let you know who I am and, whenever it is needed, I will note the implications of the fact that I am a male reading the New Testament, usually in North American and European contexts. But I also want to affirm that I am a Christian believer — a Protestant, a descendant of the Huguenots. Acknowledging the role of my faith in my interpretations does not make them less critical and scholarly. On the contrary! (I will discuss my convictions in more detail in the following pages as well as in the appendix). Thus, in our roundtable discussions, I will readily identify with those of you who are Christian believers (saying "we"), even though I also envision around the table readers who are not Christian believers.

A brief discussion of the process of reading the Bible as Scripture is a good starting point for clarifying the relationship between critical studies of the Bible and faith-interpretations, and thus the important role of critical studies for believers.

Reading the Sermon on the Mount as Scripture: The Text-Life Dimension of Reading

Believers Reading the Bible as Scripture

When we, believers, read the Bible as Scripture, it provides us with the nourishment we need for our spiritual life. It offers us a Word to live by. Thus, in various kinds of devotional readings, we bring our lives to the text, just as, in Matt. 4:4, Jesus brings to Deut. 8:3 his experience of being tempted to change stones into bread when he was hungry. Through the interaction between the biblical text and our lives we perceive a teaching of this text for us today.

Such a faith-interpretation directly affects us in one way or another. We learn something. A transformation takes place. A faith-interpretation might transform our knowledge of the text, because hidden features of the text become visible as we read it in terms of our lives. It might also transform our understanding of the subject matter of the text. But more importantly, our encounter with the text as Scripture transforms the perception we have of our own lives. The text frames our way of perceiving our experience in a certain context, and conversely our context frames our perception of the text, as we read it for a teaching for or about our lives. Thus, in Matt. 4:4, Jesus' reading of Deut. 8:3 is framed by his temptation experience. He gains from his reading of Deut. 8:3 an understanding of his temptation experience, as well as a confirmation and refinement of his view of his relation to God (Matt. 3:15). In this life-context, the teaching of Deut. 8:3 as Scripture is that human life requires both physical bread and spiritual nourishment, both bread and God's Word. In summary, when the dead letters on pages of the Bible are framed by the life-context of certain believers, they become living Word — a Word to live by — that somehow transforms the reader-believers. Faith-interpretations overtly display the practical concerns and interests that govern them. And this is as it should be.[4]

Why Believers Need to Assume Responsibility for Their Faith-Interpretations

Yet, there is a problem with faith-interpretations. Some of the teachings we, believers, formulate or have received are of dubious value. The main problem is not so much that we betray the text (although such misreadings happen), but rather, that the teaching we identified is at times (often?) everything except a Word of God by which we should live.

This is the case in Matt. 4:5–6. The devil's interpretation of Ps. 91:11–12 — that Jesus should throw himself down to demonstrate that he truly trusts God and God's word — is a very plausible faith-interpretation. And yet, Jesus rejects it. Why?

The contextual framing of this reading in terms of Jesus' perilous situation on the pinnacle of the temple is appropriate; it does not betray the text, since this psalm underscores that God is the refuge of those who trust in him when they face adversity. It is also appropriate to read these verses as a Scripture that provides a teaching regarding what Jesus should do in a specific situation; neither in Jesus' words nor in Matthew's do we find a suggestion that Psalm 91 should be excluded from the canon! But for Jesus, this specific teaching is not a word to live by. Far from being a Word of God, it is a temptation; it entices Jesus to adopt a most inappropriate attitude toward God: putting God to the test. In this passage Jesus does not reject the text itself; he rejects a specific (faith-)interpretation of it. What is problematic is the devil's *choice* of an interpretation. Thus, Matt. 4:5–7 presupposes that there are several plausible faith-interpretations and that the devil (as pseudobeliever) made the wrong choice.

This suggestion can readily be verified by taking note that there are many possible faith-interpretations of any given biblical text. Thus, a great variety of sermons are preached on the same text. This multiplicity of faith-interpretations of a given text is to be expected since their contextual frames necessarily vary. Life settings vary; the concerns and interests of reader-believers vary; the features of the text viewed as most significant vary. Therefore, consciously or not, reader-believers make a series of choices that determine the characteristics of each of their faith-interpretations.

We, believers, spontaneously pass a judgment upon faith-interpretations when we affirm that some are Words of God to live by and that others are satanic temptations. The question is: On what basis is this judgment made?

The faith-interpretations that we readily see as inappropriate include those promoting a teaching that, we feel, is theologically problematic (because it challenges or distorts our convictions about God, as is the case in Matt. 4:5–6) and/or ethically problematic (because it calls for attitudes and actions that, we feel, are not helpful and may even be harmful for other people). For instance, from a post-Holocaust perspective, I readily reject as ethically problematic faith-interpretations of New Testament texts that, in my view, promote anti-Judaism, and thus anti-Semitism, as well as those that fail to denounce anti-Judaism — according to the principle that a teaching that is not part of the solution is part of the problem. Similarly, I readily see as ethically problematic faith-interpretations that in my view promote or simply condone injustice and oppression of any kind. By contrast, I generally recognize as morally responsible those faith-interpretations that, I feel, support my theological convictions and promote justice. I anticipate that you, my reader, proceed in similar ways if you are a Christian believer.

In sum, consciously or not, as believers we attempt to assume responsibility for our faith-interpretations. Actually, we are eager to do so, because having faith-interpretations of the Bible also involves affirming our faith. We want to confess that we believe that our faith-interpretation of a biblical text is for us a Word of God to live by, as we also confess our faith. As long as each of us cannot say, "*Credo*, I believe, this is the Word of God for us," we fail to claim our faith-interpretation as our own.

Critical Biblical Studies Help Believers to Assume Responsibility for Their Faith-Interpretations

We, believers, are eager to confess our faith-interpretations, but in most instances we are ill-prepared to do so. Affirming our faith-interpretations as Word of God for us while denouncing other faith-interpretations as satanic is already assuming responsibility for our own interpretations. But we often do so on the basis of "gut feelings," rather than on the basis of a careful assessment of the choices available to us and of the implications of each. Before confessing our faith we must carefully examine it; an authentic faith is a "faith that seeks understanding" (*fides quaerens intellectum*), as Anselm said to describe the process of theological inquiry.[5] Similarly, believers need to assess the relative value of their faith-interpretations of biblical texts. They need to bring to critical understanding their faith-interpretations. The task of critical biblical studies is to help believers in this assessment of their faith-interpretations.

The Role of Critical Biblical Studies for Believers

Critical Biblical Studies Are Always Studies of the Bible as Scripture

A constant temptation in critical studies of the Bible is to forget that this book offers a Word to live by. Ignoring this practical dimension of reading religious texts is a failure to account for their religious character. Whether or not we are believers ourselves, we, biblical scholars, cannot afford this omission. Otherwise how could we claim to offer critical interpretations?

This suggestion should not surprise biblical scholars. It simply presupposes that in order to be critical, studies of the Bible must abide by the two basic commitments that define our task as biblical scholars.[6]

First we, biblical scholars, are committed to strive to account for the main characteristics of each biblical text. Obviously, this includes elucidating the religious experience the text reflects and the religious teaching it offers.

Second we, biblical scholars, are committed to strive to make explicit the way we reached our conclusions. We do so by specifying the goals of each of our studies, by explaining the methods we used, by disclosing the presuppositions behind these goals and methods. Obviously these presuppositions include the awareness that believers read the Bible as Scripture. We, biblical scholars, whether or not we are ourselves believers, cannot ignore this fact. Thus, we necessarily presuppose that believers find in this text some kind of teaching, which our scholarly interpretation either supports or refutes. In this way, whether we, biblical scholars, like it or not, our interpretations always reflect a certain reading of the biblical text *as Scripture*, although it might only be a faith-interpretation we reject. A critical study of the Bible should also make explicit this practical dimension of its reading process.

For us, biblical scholars who are Christian believers, reading a New Testament text as if it were not a text to live by is actually disingenuous. Our "detached" conclusions about what the text is and says, whatever they might be, are always somehow related to our perception of the way in which this text applies or does not apply to our lives in a given context. We cannot avoid reading the text through some kind of contextual frame as we spontaneously envision its teaching for believers today.

Similarly, biblical scholars who are not Christians cannot read the New Testament without some awareness that Christians live by it, even if their goal is to find additional reasons for not believing in it as authoritative Scripture.

In sum, a critical study of the New Testament — that is, a study that makes explicit its interpretive processes — requires from us the acknowledgment that it implicitly or explicitly includes the practical question: What is for believers the teaching of this text as Scripture? This question is too important to be left out of the sphere of critical biblical studies. By refusing to consider that reading the Bible as Scripture is a part of the subject matter of critical biblical studies, we contribute to bibliolatry. Neither believers nor scholars want such a mythologizing of Scripture. It makes impossible the recognition that reading a biblical text as Scripture is a complex and multifaceted process that can become a means of oppression and deprivation as well as a means of liberation and nourishment. Assessing the teaching(s) that the biblical text as Scripture has for believers today is a moral duty.

Believers Do Not Need Critical Biblical Studies to Identify the Teaching of the Sermon on the Mount for Them

A second temptation for us, biblical scholars, is to think that the role of critical studies is to provide the background and textual information necessary for formulating the "correct" teaching of the text for believers today. Furthermore, through our pedagogical attitude we, biblical scholars, have for too long unwillingly convinced ourselves as well as "ordinary" readers that the teaching of a New Testament text for believers is hard to reach: the meat of a nut with a very hard shell; stones needing to be transformed into bread.

Does not one need the help of a biblical scholar — or of a miracle worker! — to ascertain what is the "true teaching" of this text for believers? Should not ordinary readers abstain from reading this text until they have been instructed on how to do so in an appropriate way?

Of course not! But we, biblical scholars — and following us, preachers and pastors — have unfortunately promoted this passive attitude through the way we present our studies. In so doing we show that we have forgotten that for believers biblical texts are readily available bread and nourishment. Thus, there is no need for an intermediary between texts and readers.

Biblical Scholars Are Not in a Privileged Position to Discern the Teaching of the Text for Believers

The question becomes: What is the role of critical biblical scholarship? How is it related to faith-interpretations and their formulations of the teaching of the text for believers? How should I conceive of my relationship as a biblical scholar with the other readers of the Bible around the table?

First, negatively, I need to emphasize that, as a biblical scholar, I am not in a privileged position to discern what is the teaching of the Bible for believers. On the contrary! I am constantly tempted to withdraw into the world of the text or archives of the past, and thus to forget that this text has a teaching for me and my life as a believer. Ordinary readers are in a better position to ascertain the teaching of a biblical text for believers in given situations because, unlike scholars, they do not isolate the Bible from the ways in which it challenges the convictions and other habits of the heart by means of which we negotiate daily life. After all, the teaching of a scriptural text for believers is nothing other than the way in which it affects them in the concrete contexts of their lives by challenging one or another of their views, by requiring or motivating them to do or not to do something, and/or by calling them to adopt a different kind of behavior.

Biblical Scholars Know the History of Interpretations of the Bible

Because biblical scholars, and I among them, have emphasized the elucidation of what the text says and is (an appropriate task!), we tend to forget that our true expertise comes from our knowledge of the history of the interpretations of the Bible. With our awareness of many possible interpretations of each given text, an essential part of our role is to help ordinary readers, and especially believers, to become aware that they have chosen one interpretation among several plausible ones.

Consequently, in this book as elsewhere, my role as a biblical scholar is that of a facilitator. This role does not begin in the ivory tower of my study or of the library; rather, it begins by reading along with ordinary readers by means of interactive studies. Then, I am in a position to help them assume responsibility for their interpretations by bringing into the discussion my scholarly knowledge of a diversity of interpretations and of the ways in which these have been developed around certain themes (or categories) and on the basis of textual and contextual evidence. My goal is to foster the recognition by all of us involved in such interactive studies that, whatever might be our respective interpretations, each of us has a choice among several legitimate possibilities. Thus, each of us is confronted with the question: Why did I/we choose a given interpretation rather than another one?

Reading the Sermon on the Mount with Others

An Interactive Study

Our study of the Sermon on the Mount will be interactive. Reading a book is by nature an interactive process — almost as interactive as the use of a Web page. Why would we continue reading a book if its subject matter did not engage us and if we did not respond to its prodding? This interactive engagement is magnified in the case of a book about another text. Thus, as I write this book on the Sermon on the Mount, I assume that you are interested in this biblical text, that you already know much about it, and that you will want to reread it. Otherwise, why would you want to read this book on the Sermon on the Mount? I also assume that, even if you did not personally choose this biblical text, you are interested in it, because you have at least a general feeling that directly or indirectly its teaching affects you and your life. This is one of the reasons you want to reread this text with me.

Reading with You Rather Than for You

My awareness that you have a prior knowledge of the Sermon on the Mount and a prior understanding of its teaching clarifies my role as your guide in this study. First, I do not need to read this text for you, that is, instead of you, as if you did not know how to read. Instead of reading this text for you, I propose to read it with you. I will read along with you, respecting your interpretation and its conclusions about the teaching of this text for Christian believers. I will present my own interpretation, but not as the one that you should substitute for yours. My goal is to foster a dialogue between our respective and distinctive interpretations, which will soon become a "multilogue" as more readers join us.

Reading with Others

Reading the Sermon on the Mount in an interactive way, and thus discovering the different interpretations of those with whom we read, is useful for non-Christians, so as to help them discover the diversity of plausible teachings offered by a text; this knowledge might also call their attention to and protect them from harmful Christian readings. Recognition of this diversity of interpretations is even more important for readers who are Christian believers. As long as we are not confronted with other people's different readings, we are in no position to discern whether the teaching we found in the text is truly a Word of God for us, rather than a comfortable teaching that muffles this Word. This discernment can take place only when we are in a position to address the question: Why did I choose this interpretation rather than another one? In order to conceive of the fact that we made choices in interpreting, we need to listen to other people's interpretations and to acknowledge their legitimacy, although we might question their value. This is what happens when one reads with others.

Reading with You through the Printed Medium

Reading with other people is one thing in a live dialogue around a table, and quite another in writing a book. Obviously, I cannot literally read with you, since I do not know who you are and what your interpretation of the Sermon on the Mount is. As a medium, the printed words initially separate us.

Yet, the printed pages can also bridge the distance between us, if we use them appropriately with a clear understanding of our respective roles. In this setting, reading with you means helping you to think about your own reading, to understand it, and to evaluate it. My role is to help you to understand how you read the Sermon on the Mount, what choices you made among several available options, and why you made those choices. You will need to play your role, which involves rereading the Sermon on the Mount and formulating your own conclusions about the teaching of this text.

In order to entice you to do so, each chapter opens with a quotation from the Sermon on the Mount and asks you to take the time to write down in a few lines your answers to the questions: According to you, what is the teaching of this passage about (one aspect of) discipleship for believers today? What do believers learn from this text for their lives or about their lives? In the rest of the chapter, I help you reflect upon your interpretation of this passage, by suggesting several of the options available to you and by discussing the implications of choosing one rather than another of these options.

Reading with You the Sermon on the Mount for Its Teachings about Discipleship: A Contextual Choice

The medium of the printed page requires that I take the initiative in our dialogue. This involves asking you to reread the Sermon on the Mount with a certain focus. As the title of this book signals, I ask you to focus your attention on the teaching of the Sermon about discipleship. In the three parts of this book, we will successively ask three questions.

First, regarding the beatitudes (as related to their context in Matt. 5:1–16 and 7:13–29): What is the teaching of this text about discipleship for believers today? Here the concern is with the overall conception of discipleship and what it entails. We will find that there are at least five types of answers given to this question (and possibly six, counting yours) by readers of the Sermon on the Mount.

Second, regarding Matt. 5:17–48: What is the teaching of this text for believers today about fulfilling the Scriptures as disciples? The diverse interpretations of the role of the Scriptures according to this text will clarify one of the central reasons for the plurality of conclusions regarding the teaching about discipleship of the Sermon on the Mount.

Third, regarding Matt. 6:1–7:11 and its teaching about basic convictions about the disciples' relationship to God and prayerfully seeking God's kingdom and justice: Why did you choose one interpretation rather than another? At the end of this study, believers cannot but ask themselves: Among all these interpretations of the

Sermon on the Mount's teaching about discipleship, which one is the best for us today?

By choosing these three topics I have somewhat restricted the scope of your readings. You might have wanted to focus on other issues that I might have sidelined because, in my cultural, socio-economic, and religious context, they are not as interesting and significant as discipleship is. I can only read from the perspective of the context in which I find myself. My reading and this study are those envisioned by a Protestant male European-American who teaches in a private university in the southern United States of America and often visits other parts of the world where he learns much and teaches some. I do not say this as an apology. By this brief identification of the complex context from which I read the Sermon on the Mount, I simply signal my awareness that my reading is necessarily focused upon certain aspects of this biblical text by the interests, concerns, and views that emerge from my relations with people in diverse situations. Being aware of my own limitations leads me to expect that you, my readers, will have different interests, concerns, and views, reflecting the specific contexts from which you read. Therefore, I anticipate that, even as I hope to help you see aspects of the Sermon on the Mount you have never perceived, you yourself have different insights into the teaching of the Sermon that I need to learn from you.

I hope it becomes clear that I do not want to diminish in any way the value of your interpretation by implicitly or explicitly suggesting that my own is necessarily better. Rather, I want to engage with you in a multilogue over which of the many different interpretations of the Sermon on the Mount is the best for Christian believers today, that is, in the concrete situations in which we find ourselves. This discussion is urgent, because interpretations of biblical texts always matter.

The Legitimacy and Plausibility of a Diversity of Interpretations

It does not take long to recognize that the Sermon on the Mount is read in very different ways by different people. This is well documented by the history of the reception of this text through the centuries and by the large number of books on the Sermon found in our libraries.[7] I also witness this diversity of interpretations each time I ask the members of a group to write down what is, according to them, the teaching of this text for believers. Even if the group is fairly homogeneous, I am always astounded by the range of readings.

Does this mean that most of the members of such groups are inept readers who misinterpret the teaching of the Sermon on the Mount? By no means! Actually, in most cases their diverse conclusions about the teaching of the Sermon have been advocated and supported by various biblical scholars, who, in their commentaries, used one critical approach or another. Of course, interpretations by ordinary readers do not have the sophistication of those proposed by scholars, who have spent a lifetime in research. Yet, despite a lack of familiarity with the original linguistic, historical, literary, and cultural context in which the Sermon on the Mount was written, ordinary readers reach practical conclusions about the teaching of the text for believers today that are readily comparable to those implied by the diverse scholarly interpretations. When their practical conclusions are not comparable to those implied by existing scholarly interpretations, I believe that they call the attention of scholars to a dimension of the text that has been neglected. A new scholarly investigation, possibly using a new analytical method, is needed to elucidate the textual features that believers have found to be significant for their faith-interpretations.[8]

By these general observations, I want to underscore two related issues.[9] As the scholarship shows, there is a diversity of legitimate and plausible interpretations. This is not surprising. A text as rich as the Sermon on the Mount can be expected to have different specific teachings for reader-believers in various concrete situations. Conversely, this means that critical biblical studies do not determine the universally true teaching of the text, as they too often imply. Rather, they elucidate the legitimacy and plausibility of choosing diverse options as one reads the Sermon on the Mount. A new scholarly interpretation does not dismiss previous ones, but shows the legitimacy and plausibility of other reading options. Then, despite the differences, one can treat each scholarly interpretation with the respect due to it.

Basic Legitimacy and Plausibility of Authentic Practical Interpretations

I strongly believe that each practical interpretation proposed by ordinary readers — including you, my reader — must also be treated with due respect. Though it seems at first a dubious suggestion, I am ready to claim that most practical interpretations are basically legitimate and plausible, even though they might need refinements.

Before dismissing this affirmation as fanciful, note that it applies only to truly practical readings — for instance, to readings through which Christians seek to discern the teaching of the Sermon on the Mount for themselves as believers. Since such practical readings include elucidating a teaching that transforms certain of the views, beliefs, and convictions by which they live, the reader-believers instinctively make sure that their conclusions are properly grounded on textual evidence and make sense. The potential problem is not their lack of reading abilities, but rather their lack of awareness that there are other legitimate and plausible interpretations or their mistrust of other interpretations, which serves as an excuse for ignoring them.

Assuming Responsibility for Our Interpretations

My point is that each time we read as Scripture a text such as the Sermon on the Mount, we choose one interpretation from among several legitimate and plausible ones. This is why I suggested above that my task, as a biblical scholar aware of the existence of several of these interpretations, is ultimately to help you to raise the question: Why did I/we choose this interpretation rather than another one? Then we will be in a position to ask: Among the diverse existing interpretations, what is the best choice for believers today?

In order to help you address these questions, I need to show you: (1) that you have a choice among several plausible interpretations, (2) that you made this choice by legitimately selecting one option among those offered by the text, and (3) that you had practical reasons for the choice you made.

Recognizing That We Have a Choice among Several Legitimate Interpretations

Recognizing that there are several legitimate and plausible interpretations of any given text is counterintuitive. A primary reason is that we are unaware that each biblical text has several meaning-producing dimensions and that each reading focuses on one of these textual dimensions. Because our attention is focused totally upon one dimension, the others are hidden from us.

Reading a text is similar to "reading" the accompanying images,[10] which are actually simple texts. In the first one, a well-known cognitive test, when we perceive the vase (candlestick), our attention is focused on features of the drawing that hide the two faces (persons) looking at each other, which are nevertheless represented by the same image.

This point is even clearer when we consider the less familiar drawing below in which people see a cross (when the focus is on the center of the black drawing) or four flowerlike designs (when the focus is on the periphery of the black drawing) or doves (when the focus is on the white drawing).

The multiplicity of meaning-producing dimensions in a text is even more apparent when we consider the following simple text-drawing asking ourselves, "How many squares do I see?"[11]

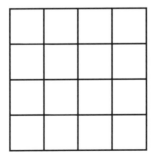

The answer can vary from 1 to 30 squares. We can focus on the largest square (1), or on the smallest squares (16), or on the squares composed of four smallest squares (9), or on the squares composed of nine smallest squares (4) — without speaking of combining squares of different sizes!

In order to overcome the counterintuitive perception that a text is one-dimensional, we need to learn to see it with the eyes of other people. As we change the frame through which we look at the text, we perceive different textual designs. The legitimacy of identifying in the text-drawing one meaning-producing dimension (the vase or the cross) or another (the faces or the doves) can be explained to those who do not see it, by pointing out the features that express it in the text-drawing. Similarly, biblical scholars make explicit the features of the text that justify the legitimacy of their focus upon a specific meaning-producing dimension of the text. Though scholars too often do so in order to dismiss other interpretations, I am convinced that the different critical methods and the several textual meaning-producing dimensions they focus upon are distinctive interpretations that need to be respected. Each time, they involve reading the text through a particular frame and therefore seeing something that is hidden when one reads through other frames.

Assessing the Relative Value of Diverse Interpretations of the Teaching of the Sermon on the Mount for Christian Believers

In the following chapters I will progressively show that the works of diverse scholars demonstrate — at times against their will — that it is appropriate to ground one's interpretation on any one of the several meaning-producing dimensions of a text. In the process, we will see that any interpretation involves a series of interpretive choices. As we become aware of this, we spontaneously ask ourselves, "Why did I choose this interpretation rather than another one?" This question is at first a matter of curiosity. Yet, it soon becomes an essential question that each of us needs to ask, since believers and nonbelievers alike live by their interpretations of such texts.

Why Non-Christians Also Need to Read the Sermon on the Mount as Scripture for Believers

I presuppose here and throughout our interactive study that our interest in the Sermon on the Mount is not simply casual, as might be the case with a thriller or a modern novel. Whether we acknowledge it, resist it, or reject it, this text is a part of the Christian Scriptures. If you are a Christian believer, you will, of course, want to read the Sermon on the Mount as Scripture. But, as I repeatedly noted, I do not assume that you necessarily are a Christian believer. From an outsider's perspective, whether as a participant in another religious tradition or as a secular person, you cannot help taking into account that the Sermon on the Mount is part of the Scriptures by which Christian believers live. Your interest remains focused upon the religious teaching of this text for believers, even if you do not want any part in it because you find it abhorrent and dangerous. In so doing, from your outsider's perspective, you associate yourself with many Christian believers who find that they have to practice a *hermeneutic of suspicion* toward this part of their Scriptures and toward the interpretations of it by diverse groups of believers.

Caution! The Stakes Are High When Reading the Bible as Scripture

After the Holocaust, which could not have taken place without Christians at least tacitly condoning anti-Judaism and anti-Semitism, many of us Christians are cautious. Before committing ourselves, we feel that, for the sake of the gospel, we must closely examine the religious teachings believers find in the Sermon. Unfortunately, recent history has shown that it is appropriate for us to suspect that several of these teachings might, in a subtle or not so subtle way, excuse or even advocate anti-Judaism.

Another reason for being suspicious is that several of the teachings that believers find in the Sermon have been, in a subtle or not so subtle way, used to justify the exploitation, subordination, and oppression of other peoples. How can we not raise questions regarding the choice of such teachings as interpretations of the Sermon on the Mount, when this very text calls believers to adopt the meekness of those who do to others as they would like others to do to them? How could we not be suspicious of teachings that subtly promote spouse battering by conceiving of forgiveness as inscribed in a cycle of violence, rather than breaking open this cycle? Of teachings that promote patriarchalism, rather than a discipleship of equals in the family of God? Of teachings that call for a triumphalist rejection and condemnation of all those who did not receive "the" truth from us, rather than for a welcoming acceptance of others, because the will of God is already inscribed on their hearts?

In view of the plurality of interpretations, as cautious Christian believers we want to verify that the teachings of the Sermon on the Mount by which we will live do conform to the gospel in which we believe.

Whether we approach the Sermon on the Mount with the full

confidence we have as Christian believers, or with the cautious suspicion of a faith that must constantly discern between false and
true teachings, or with the detached perspective of outsiders, all of
us must ask: Why did I/we choose this interpretation of the teaching about discipleship of the Sermon on the Mount? Whoever we
are, we cannot afford to bypass this question. Assessing whether or
not we have chosen the best interpretation for believers in a given
context is the challenge of discipleship with which our readings of
the Sermon on the Mount confront us.

Part 1

The Beatitudes
as Scripture
*The Teaching about Discipleship
of Matthew 5:1–16 and 7:13–29*

Chapter One

"Blessed Are the Poor in Spirit"

The Beatitudes and Discipleship Today,
Matthew 5:1–16 and 7:13–29

Your Reading of the Beatitudes as Scripture

What Do Christians Learn from the Beatitudes
for Their Life as Disciples Today?

Please reread the beatitudes (Matt. 5:3–12) and their context in
the Sermon on the Mount, especially its introductory (5:1–16) and
concluding (7:13–8:1) parts. Keep in mind the question: What
is the beatitudes' teaching about discipleship for believers and/or
would-be believers today?[1]

As you ponder the text, take the time to reflect on the needs of
would-be disciples in a concrete situation. Are any of these needs
addressed by the beatitudes? Or is this text addressing the needs
of people whom disciples are to serve in a given context? Though
it will take some reflection, I expect that you will reach clear conclusions about this teaching of the beatitudes for believers today.
Envisioning a specific situation in which this teaching applies often
helps in formulating this teaching.

I encourage you to write down your conclusions in a few sentences (in the space provided on p. 31). Here is the text of the New
Revised Standard Version, into which I introduce in brackets a few
elements of alternative translations.

**5:1When Jesus saw the crowds, he went up the mountain; and after
he sat down, his disciples came to him. 5:2Then he began to speak,
and taught them, saying:**

**5:3"Blessed [Happy, Helped][2] are the poor in spirit, for theirs is
the kingdom of heaven [for them God reigns].**

5:4"Blessed [Happy, Helped] are those who mourn, for they will be comforted.

5:5"Blessed [Happy, Helped] are the meek, for they will inherit the earth [land].

5:6"Blessed [Happy, Helped] are those who hunger and thirst for righteousness [justice],³ for they will be filled [eat their fill].

5:7"Blessed [Happy, Helped] are the merciful [compassionate], for they will receive mercy [compassion].

5:8"Blessed [Happy, Helped] are the pure [open, clear of shame]⁴ in heart, for they will see God.

5:9"Blessed [Happy, Helped] are the peacemakers, for they will be called children of God.

5:10"Blessed [Happy, Helped] are those who are persecuted for righteousness' [justice's] sake, for theirs is the kingdom of heaven [for them God reigns].

5:11"Blessed [Happy, Helped] are you when people revile you and persecute you and utter all kinds of evil against you falsely on my account. 5:12Rejoice and be glad, for your reward is [wages are] great in heaven, for in the same way they persecuted the prophets who were before you.

5:13"You are the salt of the earth [land]; but if salt has lost its taste [has become foolish], how can its saltiness be restored? It is no longer good for anything, but is thrown out and trampled under foot. 5:14You are the light of the world. A city built on a hill cannot be hid. 5:15No one after lighting a lamp puts it under the bushel basket, but on the lampstand, and it gives light to all in the house. 5:16In the same way, let your light shine before others, so that they may see your good works and give glory to your Father in heaven.

7:13"Enter through the narrow gate; for the gate is wide and the road is easy that leads to destruction, and there are many who take it. 7:14For the gate is narrow and the road is hard that leads to life, and there are few who find it.

7:15"Beware of [take heed of, be on the look out for] false prophets, who come to you in sheep's clothing but inwardly are ravenous wolves. 7:16You will know [recognize] them by their fruits. Are grapes gathered from thorns, or figs from thistles? 7:17In the same way, every good tree bears good fruit, but the bad tree bears bad fruit. 7:18A good tree cannot bear bad fruit, nor can a bad tree bear good fruit. 7:19Every tree that does not bear good fruit is cut down and thrown into the fire. 7:20Thus you will know them by their fruits.

7:21"Not everyone who says to me, 'Lord, Lord,' will enter the kingdom of heaven, but only the one who does the will of my Father in heaven. ⁷:²²On that day many will say to me, 'Lord, Lord, did we not prophesy in your name, and cast out demons in your name, and do many deeds of power [miracles] in your name?' ⁷:²³Then I will declare to them, 'I never knew you; go away from me, you evildoers [doers of lawlessness].'

⁷:²⁴"Everyone then who hears these words of mine and acts on them will be like a wise man who built his house on rock. ⁷:²⁵The rain fell, the floods came, and the winds blew and beat on that house, but it did not fall, because it had been founded on rock.

⁷:²⁶"And everyone who hears these words of mine and does not act on them will be like a foolish man who built his house on sand. ⁷:²⁷The rain fell, and the floods came, and the winds blew and beat against that house, and it fell — and great was its fall!"

⁷:²⁸Now when Jesus had finished saying these things, the crowds were astounded at his teaching, ⁷:²⁹for he taught them as one having authority, and not as their scribes. ⁸:¹When Jesus had come down from the mountain, great crowds followed him.

Reading the Bible Is Not a Spectator Sport

On the basis of my experience with groups, I anticipate that you resist formulating your own conclusions about the teaching of the beatitudes for believers and/or would-be believers. Am I wrong in suspecting that you are ready to bypass this step in order to go directly to my comments on these verses? You have glanced at the well-known text quoted above, with the feeling that a cursory reading is enough to remind you of what it includes before reading the commentary on it. I know. I often do this.

But, unlike traditional biblical studies for which an awareness of the content of the text is sufficient, for our present purpose this broad knowledge is not enough. The forthcoming discussion of teachings of this text for believers today will be more meaningful for you if you formulate your own interpretation. Let me remind you that, as discussed in the introduction, much is at stake in your involvement in this interactive study. Reading the Bible as Scripture is not a spectator sport.

Of course, I cannot prevent you from bypassing this step. But we at least need to understand why we are so often reluctant to formulate our conclusions about the teaching of biblical texts for believers today. While there are some legitimate reasons for this reluctance, in two cases it arises out of misunderstandings.

The Teaching of This Text for Believers
Can Be Formulated by Nonbelievers

One possible reason for your reluctance might be that you are not a
Christian, or at least not a Christian who practices devotional readings of the Bible. But this is not a valid excuse. I did not ask you to
formulate the teaching of this text for you, but rather, its teaching
for believers today. One does not need to be a believer in order to
assess what a person who believes in the authority of this text as
Scripture should learn from it. Of course, you will have envisioned
a particular kind of believer. But Christians do the same. Actually, in a sense, nonbelievers are in a better position than believers
to formulate this teaching, as will become clear below. Thus, for
everyone the question remains: Why are you reluctant to formulate
the teaching of the beatitudes for believers today?

The Teaching of This Text for Believers Is Not the Same
As What the Text Says

A second reason for your reluctance could arise from your feeling that you do not have the expertise required for formulating the
teaching of this text. This kind of reluctance involves confusing the
teaching of this text for believers today (our present concern) with
"what the text says" — its themes and topics. It is indeed important to know that this text includes the beatitudes (5:3–12), the
(so-called) teaching about being salt of the earth and light of the
world (5:13–16), as well as the teachings about the narrow gate
and the hard road (7:13–14), about false prophets being recognized by their fruits (7:15–20), about the last judgment (7:21–23),
and the parable of the house builders (7:24–27). Even though we
commonly call them teachings, the contents of these verses are
what the text says, and not its teachings for believers, that is, what
believer-disciples learn for or about their lives from the text.

Descriptions of what the text says (as briefly summarized above)
are necessary and have their place in our study. But here I propose to start with a discussion of the teaching of the text for
believers, so that from the beginning all readers and hearers of
the text — including you, my reader — might become involved in
this interactive study. While a precise study of the nature of the
text and of what it says often requires the expertise of scholars, all
Christians and persons who can observe Christians are potentially
authoritative informants regarding the teaching of the beatitudes
for believers today.

The Teaching of the Text Is New for the Believer-Reader

What Christians learn from the beatitudes for or about their lives as disciples is an authentic teaching of this text for believers today if they live by this teaching. Consequently, if you are a Christian there is no difficulty in formulating your conclusions about such a teaching; it is simply a matter of reporting how these verses (and their context in the Sermon on the Mount) affect you, or should affect you if you were a faithful disciple. If you are not a Christian, it is simply a matter of envisioning how these verses should affect believers who hold them as Scripture. In doing so, keep in mind that, by definition, a teaching transforms the person who is taught, or brings something new to her or him. Thus, the questions are: How do the beatitudes transform the believers' understanding of what life as disciples entails? Does this text demand from them a change of behavior? Does it call them to a new life? How does it challenge their beliefs and convictions as Christians? How does it transform their perception of what is happening around them in life?

I am aware that such questions stopped you in your tracks. Even if these verses are well-known, one can no longer run through them. Reading this text as Scripture requires from Christian believers to ponder from its perspective their views, beliefs, and convictions, as well as their concrete experience. Today, in the believers' particular circumstances, which teaching does this familiar text have for them? What new light does it cast upon them as believers, upon would-be believers around them, and upon the concrete situations of their lives?

Reason for Our Reluctance: Christian Believers Feel Compelled to Live by the Teaching Found in Their Scripture

Christian believers find these questions difficult to answer. But it is not because we are unable to identify the teaching of this text for us. In most instances, we can readily do so, if we take the time to consider our views and our experience in light of the text. The proof is that secular or agnostic readers have no difficulty formulating such a teaching, as they point out how this text should challenge the current views and/or the behavior of Christians around them, or how this text proposes a new way of looking at the present situation. So it is also for us, Christian believers. But we who affirm the Scriptural authority of this text have a problem!

Unlike non-Christians, we feel compelled to accept and live by the teaching we identified. We Christians do not have the luxury of adopting a detached perspective. Thus, we hesitate to formulate our conclusions about its teaching, because we might have to change our lifestyle or our beliefs. This teaching might even challenge our convictions about the Bible as Scripture — for instance, if we find that this text contradicts beloved convictions established for us by other Scriptural texts. In sum, our initial claim that we have difficulties identifying the teaching of this text may be nothing other than a reluctance to formulate conclusions that might change our life.

This reluctance is a sign of appropriate and healthy caution. Changes and transformations at the core of our identity and life are matters to be taken most seriously. It is appropriate to calculate the cost of such changes (see Luke 14:28–29), so as to assess the way in which they affect other aspects of our life and other people around us. This is what Bonhoeffer reminds us to do by entitling his study of the Sermon on the Mount *The Cost of Discipleship* and by paying with his life for his commitment as a disciple.[5] As Christian believers committed to loving both God and neighbors, we also want to make sure that this teaching and the changes of attitudes and behavior it implies do not hurt other people, but in fact benefit them.

Formulating the Teaching for Believers Today While Suspending Commitment to It

In this spirit I suggest, even if you are a Christian who diligently searches the Scriptures for God's Word for you today, that you give yourself some distance from this teaching. At least for the moment. This is why I do not ask you to express what the teaching of the beatitudes is for you. This would be a teaching that you would have to adopt in your life. Rather, I ask you to formulate the teaching of the beatitudes for believers today. Although what you will formulate is the teaching of this text for believers who are like you, because they are in similar situations and circumstances, I ask you to suspend any commitment to it. For the moment, adopt the perspective of a non-Christian observing the ways in which Christians interpret their Scripture. This will give you the opportunity to assess the teaching you identified, to calculate its benefits and liabilities, and to consider whether there are alternative teachings that might offer better possibilities in these circumstances. Then, if you are a Christian believer, you will be in a position to assume responsibility for the teaching to which you will commit yourself, as you indeed should.

Questions for Our Readings

In sum, whether or not you are a Christian, you should have no difficulty formulating your conclusions about the teaching of the beatitudes for believers today, especially their teaching about discipleship (or the life of Christian believers as disciples). One or more of the following questions might help you in this process.

- Do the beatitudes transform the understanding Christians have regarding what life as disciples entails? If so, how? What are the implications for discipleship in the present situation?

- Do the beatitudes demand that Christians change behavior in their lives as disciples in the present situation? If so, what kind of changes are required?

- Do the beatitudes challenge the beliefs and convictions of Christians? If so, which ones?

- Do the beatitudes transform the perception that Christian believers have of the concrete situations in which they are? If so, how?

In order to help you keep your distance from this teaching while holding it before you, I suggest that you now take the time to write down a brief summary of your conclusions in the space provided below.

_____

_____

_____

_____

_____

_____

_____

_____

_____

_____

Comparing Your Conclusions
with Five Other Interpretations

I am aware that I did not leave much space for you. I do not mean
to limit you. You can always write down your conclusions elsewhere. Yet a few lines should be sufficient for expressing the main
characteristics of your conclusions about the teaching of the beatitudes for Christian believers today. In the five examples below, I
summarize this teaching in one line (the five subtitles).

Each of these readings (which I identify with capital letters for
future references) represents a type of interpretation that might
have different emphases in various settings. Since your own conclusions refer to your concrete situation, I expect that they are more
specific. Nevertheless, you should have no difficulty comparing
your conclusions with those of the five readings presented below.

The purpose of this comparison should be clear. It is to bring
to light the distinctiveness of your own interpretation. I do not
suggest that you should adopt one of the five readings I propose.
There are many other interpretations of the teaching of the beatitudes for believers today that are as legitimate as these. Of course,
you might discover that your interpretation is relatively close to
one of those presented. Fine. But the most important thing for you
is to note what is distinctive about your interpretation. Assuming
responsibility for our interpretation involves not only verifying that
our conclusions are properly grounded in the text (as I will invite
you to do below) but also becoming aware of the ways in which
they differ from other interpretations, and thus recognizing that we
chose among several possibilities. Then we can evaluate our choice.

Now you understand why I urged you to write down your own
interpretation: to preserve its distinctiveness, which, otherwise, you
might overlook when considering other interpretations.

In order to begin to identify the distinctiveness of the five readings I present, I keep in mind that, in each case, formulating the
teaching of a biblical text for believers today necessarily involves
envisioning the following:

- *The Problem:* the needs that must be addressed so that certain
  people might be faithful disciples in a specific context;

- *The Solution:* the teaching of the beatitudes that addresses
  these needs; what is new for or about the believers' lives;

- *The Transformation:* the transforming effect of this teaching upon the believer-readers' lives; the process through which the problem is overcome and the solution implemented.

As we go along, you might want to think about what your own interpretation implied about each of these three points.

Reading A1: The Beatitudes Provide Rules for One's Life as a Christian[6]

The Problem: People who live according to the secular values of a Western capitalist culture or according to the values of a non-Christian culture have lost any sense of the will of God; in such cultural settings, Christian believers are confused by conflicting moral teachings.

The Solution: For such people, the beatitudes teach the basic precepts (about being poor in spirit, meek, merciful, peacemakers, etc.) that believers should implement in their lives.

The Transformation: The transforming effect of this teaching upon such people is that, instead of following the easy road of the world (7:13–14), they become true members of the community of people under God's rule (the kingdom, 5:3, 10) and can be light of the world (5:14–16).

Reading A2: The Beatitudes Provide Rules for the Community of Christian Believers

A second Reading A focuses on the needs of the community of believers rather than on those of individual believers.

The Problem: A Christian community struggles to find its place and role in a secular culture (and possibly in a non-Christian culture).

The Solution: The beatitudes teach the way of life that should distinguish the community of disciples from the rest of society.

The Transformation: The transforming effect of this teaching upon such a community is that it provides basic rules with which to decide who may enter (7:13) the community of people under God's rule (the kingdom), and who does or does not belong to the community (7:15–23).

More Specific Teaching of the Beatitudes
According to Readings A1 and A2

In both cases, the teaching of the beatitudes for believers takes the form of admonitions and commands that, as expressions of God's will, demand that reader-believers abandon the norms and ways of life of the secular capitalist Western world or of the non-Christian world. This is clear when one notes that true disciples are lowly in spirit, humble people ("poor in spirit," 5:3) who submit to God's will; grieve over the world or over their sins ("mourn," 5:4); have a humility demonstrated in kindness ("meek," 5:5; about Jesus, 11:29); strive to behave righteously ("hunger and thirst for righteousness," 5:6); are "merciful" (5:7); fulfill the demand of righteousness with a good conscience ("pure in heart," 5:8); are "peacemakers" (5:9); and are persecuted because of their righteous behavior (5:10) or because they follow the "way of righteousness" (21:32) taught by Jesus ("persecuted . . . on my account," 5:11–12). By adopting this way of life, disciples demonstrate that they belong to the sphere of God's rule, and no longer to the world.

Reading B: The Beatitudes Are a Call to Discipleship[7]

The Problem: People are totally devoted to worldly pursuits even though they know there are alternatives, and Christian believers are tempted to backslide. They lack any motivation to be disciples.

The Solution: The beatitudes are a call to discipleship, that is, an invitation aimed at convincing people to become disciples. For believers, they are a renewed call, motivating them to continue being disciples and enticing them to be more fully devoted to a life of discipleship.

The Transformation: The transforming effect of this teaching upon such people is that they are enticed to abandon their ordinary lives in order to become disciples by being made aware of the rewards and goals of discipleship. These rewards and goals are emphasized in the text: for the disciples themselves, present and future blessings (5:3–12); for the world, the "salt" and "light" of humble, loving acts that promote the radical justice-righteousness of the kingdom and demonstrate God's love (5:13–16); for God, praises (5:16). The repeated promises of blessings in the beatitudes (and the warnings that one might be deprived of them, 7:13–27) are strong motivations for devoting one's life to God's kingdom and its righteousness-justice — the ministry begun by Jesus.

More Specific Teaching of the Beatitudes According to Reading B

The effect of the beatitudes upon readers who are like the crowds (5:1–2) is that of a call to discipleship. Of course, they want to receive the blessings of the kingdom that are promised to them. Thus, they should want to identify themselves with the blessed ones, by adopting the behavior demanded of disciples; they should want to become disciples, even if, from the perspective of outsiders, this is a foolish, costly decision (5:11). For believers (already committed disciples), the beatitudes are a call to a more permanent and more complete commitment to this radical way of life. In sum, becoming disciples involves committing oneself to be, in all kinds of circumstances, now and in the future, poor in spirit, meek, hungry and thirsty for righteousness, merciful, pure in heart, peacemakers, and persecuted for righteousness' (justice's) sake.

Reading C: The Beatitudes Provide a Vision of the Kingdom and of God's Loving Care[8]

The Problem: People are "harassed and helpless, like sheep without a shepherd" (Matt. 9:36), without hope and vision for their lives because traditional cultures have disintegrated; Christian believers always need to share the hope and vision that gather them as a community of disciples.

The Solution: The beatitudes offer a vision of God's loving care and of life in the kingdom, which has been fully manifested in Jesus' ministry (including cross and resurrection) and is partially manifested by his true followers, who, from the perspective of this vision, can be recognized by their fruits.

The Transformation: The transforming effect of this teaching upon such people is that they become aware that in order to share in this vision-faith and have meaning and purpose for their lives they should imitate Jesus (who through his deeds and attitudes manifested God's loving care and life in the kingdom) and the blessed ones (models of discipleship, even if they embody only one of the beatitudes).

More Specific Teaching of the Beatitudes According to Reading C

The beatitudes provide a vision for the reader-believers' life that includes both an eschatological horizon: the promises of the coming kingdom (e.g., "for theirs is the kingdom of heaven," 5:3, 10;

"for they will be comforted," 5:4); and a theological horizon: the expression of the loving care of God as our heavenly Father expressed by the repeated declarations of blessing ("blessed"). As a religious word of blessing uttered by Jesus as Lord, such a blessing has the power of positing a new reality (as a curse also does, see 7:23). Such persons are blessed by God, and thus are in a special relationship with God (as in Exod. 19:4–5); they are chosen of God — God's own. Furthermore, since the blessed ones are people with an ideal kind of behavior ("poor in spirit," "merciful," etc.), by describing them, the beatitudes invite the reader-believers to identify and imitate those who display one aspect or another of this behavior of God's chosen. In this way, the beatitudes invite the reader-believers to identify certain characters in the Gospel of Matthew as models to be imitated — including first, Jesus, who embodies all the beatitudes, but also the little ones, children, women, Gentiles, and other characters who embody in the Gospel one or another of the beatitudes. The teaching of the rest of the Sermon gives the readers the vision they need in order to distinguish true models of discipleship from "false prophets" (7:15–20).

Reading D: The Beatitudes Provide Eyes to See Manifestations of the Kingdom and God's Will among Us[9]

The Problem: People, including Christian believers, are constantly lured to follow and imitate false prophets — persons whom we take to be worthy leaders, be they in the social, political, economic, cultural, or religious realms.

The Solution: The beatitudes provide the necessary eyes of faith to discern those who truly manifest God's will in their lives, by imitating the way in which Jesus recognized blessed ones in the poor in spirit, etc.

The Transformation: The transforming effect of this teaching upon such people is that they can now wisely discern those they should emulate. Eyes of faith are necessary because the identity of the blessed ones is far from obvious. They are found among those we readily despise, because of their poverty in spirit, their meekness, etc. When reader-believers have identified such models, they are like the wise housebuilder; they are in a position to build their lives on solid foundations (7:24–27).

More Specific Teaching of the Beatitudes According to Reading D

In this case, the beatitudes teach reader-believers how to discern not only who is doing God's will (7:15–20), but also what God's will is (the solid foundation for one's house, 7:21–27). By proclaiming these beatitudes, Jesus exemplifies such moral discernment. In each beatitude, the description of the behavior (being poor in spirit, mourning, meek, etc.) is a description of doing God's will (7:21). At first, for the reader-believers, choosing these kinds of behavior as expressions of God's will is counterintuitive. Yet the description of the eschatological blessing (e.g., "theirs is the kingdom," "they will be called children of God") reveals the wisdom of this choice.

Through the beatitudes used as lenses, reader-disciples are invited to look around and identify those who are blessed, that is, those whom they should imitate as models of discipleship. The impersonal form ("they") of the beatitudes suggests that one can expect to find such models of discipleship anywhere in society, not only in the church. Imitating Jesus means that reader-believers identify blessed ones among the "poor in spirit" (5:3). Those who lack the self-confidence to assert their own will are despised by the world as indecisive weaklings. Yet, following Jesus, reader-believers should recognize that among such people are some who have this attitude because inwardly they have made God's will their own will (cf. 7:21). They submit to the yoke of heaven, and thus belong to the kingdom of heaven: "theirs is the kingdom of heaven." Similarly, for all the beatitudes: by imitating Jesus' discernment, reader-believers should learn to recognize among those people whom they despise, people who have inwardly made God's will (righteousness) their own will, no matter what the consequences might be — theirs is the kingdom. To sum up, the beatitudes help reader-believers to develop their moral discernment by providing them with a series of exemplary cases of people who perform outward actions that, despite the appearances, are solid foundation (rock) chosen with true moral discernment.

Reading E: The Beatitudes Empower Reader-Hearers to Be Disciples and the People of God[10]

The beatitudes have a slightly different empowering effect for two kinds of readers: (1) the poor and oppressed; (2) other members of the church.[11]

(1) *The Problem:* People, including Christian believers, have no control over their own lives; they are deprived (of justice and the bare necessities of life); they are oppressed and powerless; they suffer (mourn) and thirst for justice.

The Solution: The beatitudes are effective and efficient performative words that empower such people (as a community) to become agents of the kingdom and of God's justice.

The Transformation: The transforming effect of this teaching upon oppressed-deprived people is their empowerment because the beatitudes affirm that "for them God reigns," show them the way God acts for them (consoling them, giving them justice and land), and reveal to them who they are (children of God) and the reasons for their being persecuted (for the sake of justice). Thus, they are helped by these powerful and liberating words; they recognize that their oppression is neither a fate nor a punishment, but an injustice that contradicts God's justice and kingdom and against which, as children of God, they can and should struggle, even if this involves being persecuted.

(2) *The Problem:* The existence of poverty. All other Christian believers should be aware that, as disciples, they "always have the poor with [them]" (Matt. 26:11).

The Solution: The beatitudes are a call to solidarity with the poor and the oppressed.

The Transformation: Through the first set of beatitudes (5:3–6), which show that God reigns for the poor and oppressed (God's preferential option for the poor), other Christian believers are empowered for such a solidarity, that is, for being compassionate (5:7), unashamed of this solidarity (being "pure in heart," 5:8), being peacemakers (5:9), and accepting persecution for justice's sake, 5:10).[12] Thus, the disciples are empowered to share the poverty and oppression of the poor and oppressed, as they join them in the struggle for the kingdom and God's justice, and then are in a position to proclaim to them the beatitudes as good news of the kingdom.

More Specific Teaching of the Beatitudes According to Reading E

In both cases, the affirmation that the hearers are blessed or happy is also and primarily heard as an affirmation that they are empowered by God, "helped" by God (a most appropriate translation proposed by Alice Walker).[13] How? As Bravo Gallardo emphasizes, "These persons are not promised an inversion of their situation whereby the poor would be rich and the persecuted become persecutors."[14] Rather, the poor are helped because "for them God reigns" (Bravo Gallardo's translation of "theirs is the kingdom").

This affirmation and assurance that God reigns in favor of the poor does not glorify poverty, as if it were a virtue or a blessing. This is at least clear in 5:3, which adds "in spirit" to qualify "poor" and identifies the "poor in spirit" with those who are "persecuted for justice's sake" (and who receive the same promise, "theirs is the kingdom," 5:10). Who are the poor? In brief, those who suffer, because they are dispossessed of the promise and of their identity as people of God. They are comforted because they can now be confident that the promise is for them and that they are part of the people of God (5:4). They are those who seem unable to defend themselves; but their nonviolence is no longer the passive submission of victims, but the quiet confidence of children of God who know that God will give them back the land that is their inheritance (5:5). They are those who are desperately seeking justice for themselves and others, but now are assured that they will be satisfied as God makes real the new justice and new social relations (5:6). They are those who through their compassion (empathy) readily identify with other poor and oppressed, and thus act on behalf of their neighbors (5:7). They are those who are not ashamed of their identity as children of God and of their association and solidarity with God's other children, the poor and the oppressed (5:8). They are those who are creating the possibility of peace, which, as Gallardo says, "is the result of justice and law, and of right relationship with God, with others, with the world, and with oneself" (5:9). Such people are "helped," even as they are poor in spirit and persecuted as the result of their participation in the struggle for the kingdom and God's justice (6:33; 5:10). All those involved in this struggle are affected by the oppressive systems they seek to overcome. In sum, as Bravo Gallardo concludes, "To those who are *poor and persecuted*, therefore, discipleship is being revealed: who God is and how God acts in their favor, who they are, why they are persecuted, and what their destiny is *both today and in the future*."[15]

Your Reading: Identifying Problem, Solution, and Transformation Presupposed by Your Interpretation

How does your own interpretation of the teaching compare with these five readings? What are some of the distinctive features of your own reading?

Of course, the five kinds of conclusions about the teaching of the beatitudes for believers in different situations as presented above do not form a comprehensive list of possible interpretations of this text. They merely include the kinds of conclusions that (1) I have encountered in my limited experience (somewhat expanded by the reading of books and articles), and that (2) make sense for me because, from my cultural perspective, I can envision how readers/believers could be affected in these ways by the beatitudes. I am fully aware that, despite its complexity and its hybridity, my cultural perspective also hides from me other possibilities. Consequently, while I anticipate that in some instances you might find that your own interpretation is closely related to one of the readings I presented, I expect that you also find that it does not neatly fit any of them. At a minimum, your reading is a variant of one of the five, with differences reflecting the specificity of your concrete situation. But in many instances, your interpretation might belong to a completely different kind of reading, especially if you are from a culture different from mine. Our respective conclusions about the teaching of the beatitudes for believers today depend not only on the concrete situations of the believers we envisioned, but also on the cultural categories we used.

In order to clarify the distinctiveness of your own interpretation, you might want to take the time to identify the problem you envisioned (that is, the needs that must be addressed so that certain people might be faithful disciples in a specific context) and your understanding of the solution that the beatitudes offer for resolving the problem, as well as the transformation brought about by this teaching for the believer-readers, that is, what in this teaching is new for or about their lives. Summarizing these characteristics of your interpretation of the teaching of the beatitudes about discipleship for believers today might be helpful, before we proceed to bring to critical understanding your faith-interpretation in the next chapter. I provide the space to do so below.

According to your interpretation,

The Problem (the needs that must be addressed so that certain people might be faithful disciples in a specific context) is:

_____

_____

_____

The Solution (the teaching of the beatitudes that addresses these needs) is:

_____

_____

_____

The Transformation (the effect of this teaching upon the believer-readers' lives, that is, what in this teaching is new for or about their lives) is:

_____

_____

_____

Assessing the Plausibility of Our Perception of the Believers and Their Needs

Whether or not we, the interpreters, are believers, when we formulate the teaching of a biblical text for believers today (and/or for would-be believers), we implicitly envision certain believers who would develop such a faith-interpretation in terms of their needs. Following the preliminary analysis of our faith-interpretations, we can begin to verify whether our presuppositions are plausible or not. Do the believers (or would-be believers) we envision truly exist around us? Are the needs that we attribute to them actual needs in our specific context?

These questions allow us to verify whether our interpretation presents an actual teaching of the text for believers today or whether it merely repeats what the text says — some "timeless teaching," which is not a teaching at all, because it does not affect believers in any way. We might also find that the teaching of the text we identified is not for the believers (or would-be believers) we envisioned, because it only affects people who are in very different situations.

For instance, many readers readily conclude that the teaching of the beatitudes for believers today is that this text reveals the will

of God that believers should implement in their lives. As we noted
in our discussion of Readings A1 and A2, this is a potential teaching for people in a secular or non-Christian world. But this is not
the teaching of this text for those members of Christian communities who already know what the will of God is! There is nothing
new for such believers in this interpretation. Such a message does
not affect them in any way. The real teaching of this text for such
believers might be one that emphasizes the way in which the beatitudes overcome a lack of will, a reluctance to do God's will (as in
Reading B), a lack of faith-vision of the kingdom (as in Reading C),
a lack of discernment (as in Reading D), or a powerlessness to do
the will of God (as in Reading E). A teaching of the beatitudes is
plausible and realistic only insofar as it addresses actual needs of
believers in a specific context.

Thus, bringing to critical understanding our interpretations requires us not only to verify that their teaching is properly grounded
in the text, but also to make explicit how the interpretation relates
the biblical text and contemporary reader-believers.

Chapter Two

Assuming Responsibility for Our Faith-Interpretations

In the previous chapter I presented five types of interpretations of the teaching of the beatitudes for Christian believers today. To these should be added your own interpretation as a sixth, and possibly several others.

I affirmed that I would take seriously each of these interpretations. I assume they are legitimate and plausible until proven otherwise. Actually, I will show that the five interpretations I have presented are equally legitimate and plausible. I anticipate this is also true of your own interpretation.

For Christian believers, this plurality of interpretations with their different conclusions regarding the teaching of the beatitudes for believers is troubling. What happens to the authority of Scripture when one affirms the legitimacy of different conclusions about the teaching of a text? This question needs to be addressed without delay.

For those of you who are not Christian believers, addressing this question is also important. It will help you understand how, in your interpretation of the teaching of the text for believers, you envisioned the role of the authority of Scripture for these believers.

Another set of questions arises from the recognition that in faith-interpretations, believers bring to the beatitudes their concerns (a contextual problem) and their expectation that these verses somehow will address these concerns (providing a solution). How can I claim that these interpretations are legitimate and plausible until proven otherwise? Is it not clear that they "read something into the text"? For critics who observe from the outside how Christian believers interpret their Bible as Scripture, such practices are suspect. But are they really?

As we ponder these questions,[1] keep in mind your interpretation of the teaching of the beatitudes for believers. How is it related to the other interpretations? What is the significance of the fact that it does not stand alone, but is one among several existing interpretations? Finally, what are the consequences of ignoring these questions?

I will emphasize in this chapter that neither Christian believers nor critics can afford to pretend that this plurality of interpretations does not exist. All of us need to recognize that this plurality signals that any given interpretation results from a series of choices. Assuming responsibility for our interpretations involves acknowledging that we have made these choices and being ready to justify them to ourselves as well as to others.

Acknowledging the Existence of a Plurality of Interpretations

This Study Does Not Advocate a Multiplication of Readings

Some of you might have hastily concluded that this critical study advocates the multiplication of interpretations. It does not. It simply observes that a plurality of interpretations exists and seeks to deal with this fact. Believers constantly produce new interpretations as they read a biblical text as Scripture. Scholarly commentaries often seem to produce new interpretations, but, in fact, they primarily reflect the believers' multiple interpretations, assessing them positively or negatively. At any rate, this study does not multiply the readings of the Sermon on the Mount. For me, it is not the role of biblical scholars to produce new interpretations.

The plurality of interpretations originates with believers. Accordingly, as a Christian believer I developed my own interpretation of the teaching of the beatitudes for believers today (Reading D). But as a biblical scholar, my role is to facilitate the recognition that each existing interpretation represents a series of choices among options offered by the text. Ultimately I seek to make it possible for each of us to assume responsibility for our choice of one interpretation rather than any of the others.

Why Are Christian Believers Disturbed by the Plurality of Interpretations?

The plurality of interpretations of the beatitudes discussed in chapter 1 is surprising for us, Christian believers, simply because we easily pretend that this plurality does not exist. Of course we are aware that, beside ours, there are other so-called interpretations.

But we dismiss these as if they had no legitimacy and plausibility. Since they differ from our interpretation — which we are confident is well grounded on the text — these other readings must be misinterpretations.

The absurdity of this attitude appears as soon as we recognize that it is reciprocal. Other believers view our interpretation as a misinterpretation, even though we are confident it is legitimate. Do we want to make the arrogant claim that we alone know how to read? Or that none of us has a legitimate interpretation?

Why do we have this strange inclination to suppress the truth that believers legitimately interpret a given text in many different ways? Why do we resist so much the idea that there might be several legitimate and plausible interpretations of a biblical text?

I suspect that the main reason is that as Christian believers we lack the confidence to assume responsibility for our faith-interpretations and to trust in the power of the gospel. One of the goals of this critical biblical study is to help Christian believers to overcome their reluctance to assume responsibility for their faith-interpretations. This involves exploring the reasons for their reluctance and showing them the choices they make as they formulate their interpretations. Conversely, this critical biblical study calls attention to the diverse ways in which believers are powerfully affected by the biblical text. Thus, against the suspicions of critics, this study also clarifies that, far from simply reading something into the text, faith-interpretations are fundamentally shaped by the text.

Overcoming Believers' Reluctance to Assume Responsibility for Their Faith-Interpretations

Christian Believers Live by One Authoritative Teaching of the Text

When believers read a biblical text, they do so in order to identify an authoritative teaching by which they will live: the Word of God that this text has for them in a particular situation.

Of course, a believer cannot live by several different teachings of a given text at the same time. This would amount to trying to serve different masters. Then the believer would "either hate the one and love the other, or be devoted to the one and despise the other" (Matt. 6:24). It is therefore appropriate for a believer to identify "the" teaching (singular!) of this text for her or him at a given time.

Thus, I do not dispute that Christian believers should end up with one single teaching of the beatitudes for their life today. The goal of this critical study is to help reader-believers to decide which interpretation offers the best teaching to live by. But I reject the frequent presupposition and claim that this single teaching is dictated by the text. Identifying the teaching of a text for believers today necessarily involves choosing to focus on certain of its features by viewing them as more significant than others. The more believers claim their reading is "literal," the more selective it is, as will become clear when I present some of the specific choices involved in the five (six) interpretations of the beatitudes.

Yearning for Absolute Certainty in Interpreting Scripture: A Lure

Yet as believers we resist the suggestion that we made a choice, because it raises a fundamental question regarding the value of our interpretations. How can we still view this teaching as Word of God if *we* chose it, either individually or collectively? As believers, we would like to keep this teaching fully anchored in an objective reality (in a "textual object" or in another concrete authority) outside of ourselves, so that it might have authority over us. We are indeed reluctant to assume responsibility for our faith-interpretations!

I understand this yearning for certitude, for seeing face to face, rather than seeing dimly in a mirror. The less control we have over our lives — because of natural constraints (e.g., disease, death) or social and economic forces that keep us under their sway — the more we seem ready to submit to authorities who promise absolute certainty and the more we relinquish control over our own lives as believers. Thus, we are ready to relinquish responsibility for our interpretations of Scripture to the text of Scripture itself, denying that we interpret it, or to an authoritative, infallible interpreter (a pastor, a prophet, a pope, a professor) who provides us with "the" true interpretation. Then, we believe that we have an absolute certainty upon which we can build a more secure life. (Is this absolute certainty of an authoritative interpretation the rock mentioned in Matt. 7:24?) Yes! I yearn for such a certitude, for seeing face to face.

Yet, as Christians we should know better. As Paul emphasized, for the time being we merely see dimly in a mirror. Consequently, we have to live by faith and hope (see 1 Cor. 13:8–13). This means that all interpretations, including those by so-called authorities and by ourselves, are at best partial, because all human beings have to concede with Paul, "Now I know in part" (1 Cor. 13:12). By definition, faith-interpretations are partial, and not absolutely certain. Yet, it remains that they present the teaching of Scripture — the Word — by which believers should live. Living by faith demands that we assume responsibility for our faith-interpretations and confess our faith saying, "*I* believe (*credo*) this is the Word of God for us today."

Assuming Responsibility for Our Faith-Interpretations Involves Acknowledging the Role of the Text

The confusion remains. We, Christian believers, want to confess our faith-interpretations and say, "*I* believe." Yet, we are reluctant to do so. We are ready to confess that a certain teaching has the authority and power to govern our lives, and is thus a Word of God for us. But we are reluctant to confess it as a *faith*-interpretation, as a leap of faith, as a personal decision. We would prefer to pledge allegiance to the Word of God. To submit to its authority. To relinquish all responsibility. But we are reluctant to say, "*Credo, I* believe." To assume responsibility for our faith-interpretations. To acknowledge that on the basis of faith we made a choice among several potential teachings of a given biblical text.

We need to overcome this confusion. For this, let me first underscore that assuming responsibility for our faith-interpretations requires that we acknowledge the role of the text.[2] Otherwise, how could we truly elucidate our own role in the interpretive process?

Interpreting a biblical text as Scripture, that is, reading the text for its teaching for believers today, requires the participation of both the text and the believer-readers. Confessing that this text is Scripture includes acknowledging that it has some kind of power over us as believers. Somehow the text affects us. It marks us and our lives. It makes us see our lives in a new light. It molds our way of life. In sum, for us believers, the Scriptural text teaches us something about and/or for our life today.

But, of course, the text cannot have these effects as long as it does not interact with the believer-readers' lives. The teaching of Scripture is not the content of a "dead letter" disconnected from life. It is the result of a two-way interaction between text and life and life and text.

The teaching of a text is determined by the way the text powerfully marks the parts of life it touches and/or by the way the text "reads the readers" and the parts of their lives they expose to it. Consequently, in order to assume responsibility for our inter-

pretations we need both to acknowledge the diversified power of
the text and to elucidate the specific *contextual frames* and *bridge-
categories* through which we, as believer-readers, relate text and
life. We need to consider how, through such contextual frames and
bridge-categories, reader-believers shape the effect of the text upon
their lives by exposing only parts of their lives to the text.

The teaching of a text is also determined by the way reader-
believers understand the text by seeking to discern its views on
certain topics — such as discipleship, the subject matter of this
study. Understanding the text's views on a theological subject we
have chosen amounts to entering into a dialogue with the text
about this subject. Consequently, in order to assume responsibility
for our interpretations we need to elucidate the specific *hermeneutical frames* and *theological categories* we used, including the
view of Scripture that presided over this dialogue and the way we
defined the subject matter of this dialogue (here, discipleship).

Finally, the teaching of a text is determined by the characteristics
of the text itself, which can be recognized by analyzing the text. In
order to assume responsibility for our interpretations we need to
acknowledge that a specific textual dimension is the focus of each
of our interpretations, because it is through this dimension that
the text affects our lives and that we understand the text's views
of a topic (here, discipleship). The specific textual dimensions that
played this central role in our respective interpretations can then
be identified by elucidating the specific *analytical frames* and *critical categories* that, consciously or not, we have used to ground on
textual evidence our conclusions regarding the contextual teaching
of this text about a theological category such as discipleship.

In sum, in order to assume responsibility for our interpretations
of the Sermon on the Mount for believers today we need to acknowledge that we have made three kinds of choices — contextual,
hermeneutical, and analytical — that frame the way the biblical
text affects us as Christian believers and transforms us by offering us a Word of God to live by. An analogy might help us better
understand the threefold framing involved in each interpretation.

Reading a biblical text is somewhat like taking a picture. As
we take a picture, consciously or not (automatic cameras do much
of this by themselves), we frame it in three different ways: (1) we
select a subject (a flower, a group of persons, a landscape) by locat-
ing it through the viewfinder, and in the process we exclude many
other things that are also in front of us; (2) we focus the lens on
the subject, making sure that all its details (the petals, the faces,

the trees) are clear, even though the foreground or the background might become blurry; (3) we adjust the speed of the shutter (or use a flash) in order to take into account the specific contextual situation — day or night, sunny or cloudy, indoors or outdoors, etc. Similarly, any reading frames the text in a threefold way by choosing (1) a *hermeneutical frame*, through which we identify the subject matter of the reading (here, specific theological views of discipleship and of Scripture function as hermeneutical frames for different interpretations); (2) an *analytical frame* (which brings in sharp relief the most significant textual features regarding disciple-ship according to a given view of it); and, as we noted earlier; (3) a *contextual frame* (which bridges the gap between text and life by taking into account the specific situation of the reading process).

A discussion of each of these framing choices will further clarify how we can identify the specificity of each of our interpretations.

The Legitimacy of Bringing Our Lives to the Text: The Contextual Frame of Our Interpretations

Framing Our Interpretations of Biblical Texts with Our Concerns and Interests: A Necessity

Perhaps a lingering suspicion remains. In the preceding chapter I tried to help you identify some of the distinctive features of your interpretation of the teaching of the beatitudes for believers today. You might still have the feeling that by leading you to acknowledge the contextual character of your interpretation, I discredited it. But I did not. Let me explain.

I have indeed suggested that the distinctiveness of a faith-interpretation is directly related to the concrete situation of the believers who would live by this teaching. Since by definition this teaching is new for the reader-believers and is about or for their particular lives, it cannot be the same for everyone. As I suggested, the teaching of the beatitudes is not the same for people who live according to the secular values of a Western capitalist culture, be-cause they do not know any other values (Reading A); for people who are totally devoted to worldly pursuits, even though they know there are other possibilities (Reading B); for people who are without hope and vision for their lives (Reading C); for people who (are tempted to) follow false leaders (Reading D); or for people who are oppressed and powerless (Reading E). When the problem changes, the solution that the beatitudes bring to this problem also changes.

Consequently, I expect that your own interpretation of the teaching of the beatitudes for believers is framed by the specific kind of believers and situation you envision. You spontaneously bring to the text your own concerns, or those you imagine a believer would have in a specific context. Yet, let me emphasize: these contextual features of your interpretation do not discredit it. On the contrary. By referring to the way in which the five other interpretations conceived of the problem and of the solution offered by the text, I hoped to make it plain that all interpretations of Scripture relate biblical text and life, even when all the attention is focused upon other aspects of the interpretive process (as in scholarly study). There is nothing wrong with this. But pretending that we do not do so is not only disingenuous, but also uncritical and unethical.[3]

Believers cannot reach conclusions about the teaching of a text for their lives today without bringing their lives to the text. Acknowledging this is not confessing a sin! It is confessing one's faith that the text is revelatory.

Identifying the Characteristics of the Contextual Frames of Our Interpretations: Reading the Beatitudes and Being Read by Them

Believers gain from the text a new perspective on their lives through an ongoing two-way process. Believers read the biblical text with the expectation that, in turn, this scriptural text will "read them." The believer-readers' true needs, problems, concerns, and interests are brought to light when they allow the biblical text to read their life-situations. A contextual frame is posited.

To come back to our analogy between reading and taking a picture with a camera, here the text is the camera by means of which we take a picture of our lives. Through the viewfinder of the camera-text we see most clearly what is happening in our lives, the nature of our needs, and the way in which our concerns need to be addressed. The text frames our lives, bringing to the forefront aspects of our situation that we felt were not particularly significant, then focusing our attention on these features; and challenging us to transform our way of life (or to allow for its transformation).

Conversely, when believer-readers read the biblical text through this contextual frame, they find in the text the teaching that meets their needs, addresses their problems and concerns, or satisfies their interests.

In order to recognize the characteristics of the contextual frame of our faith-interpretations, we need to identify the bridge-categories we chose to relate life and text. In the preceding chapter, we began doing so by identifying for each of our six interpretations (including yours): the problem (the needs that the text addresses), the solution (the teaching that addresses these needs), and the transformation (what in this teaching is new for or about the lives of the reader-believers). This preliminary comparative analysis helped each of us to become aware that we had actually chosen a certain view of the problem, solution, and transformation among other possible views. The clearer these options are, the easier it is for us to assess whether or not our specific choice of bridge-categories is the most appropriate in our situation. Thus it is helpful at this point to list the major types of bridge-categories we have identified, with the awareness that this list is certainly partial and that each type can take many concrete forms.

The easiest way of presenting these four types of bridge-categories through which life and text are related is to list the four main problems for which the text is expected to provide solutions as it transforms the reader-believers' lives. In a specific context, the believers (or would-be believers) might have:

- A *lack of knowledge* or a *wrong knowledge* (regarding aspects of their lives, what is true or false about life; or regarding issues that are important for life, what is good or bad to do). In this case, identifying the life-text contextual frame involves elucidating the specific lack of knowledge or wrong knowledge that the teaching of the text overcomes.

- A *lack of will* (not wanting to do something) or a *wrong will* (wanting to do the wrong thing). In this case, identifying the life-text contextual frame involves elucidating the specific lack of will or wrong will that the teaching of the text overcomes or reorients.

- A *powerlessness* (resulting from one's personal mental or physical limitations, or from a situation where one is overpowered and/or oppressed by external forces, be they natural, social, political, economic, or religious). In this case, identifying the life-text contextual frame involves elucidating the specific way in which the teaching of the text empowers the powerless.

- A *lack of faith* or a *wrong faith*, which can be either (1) communal faith, that is, the faith or symbolic world shared by all the members of a community under God; or (2) personal faith, that is, the faith through which individuals conceive of their relationship to God and others. In both cases, identifying the life-text contextual frame involves elucidating the specific way in which the teaching of the text conveys faith to the reader-believers, and which specific faith is conveyed.

Clearly, these four bridge-categories are broad. Each of them potentially encompasses many different ways of relating life and text, since lives and texts are variables. Yet, this partial listing of bridge-categories helps us in two ways.

First, it helps us identify important characteristics of the relationships between life and text in our interpretations, including when our particular interpretation does not fit any of the suggested categories (then a new category needs to be added to the list). Can you identify in a tentative way which bridge-category you used in your interpretation to relate life and text? Is it one of those mentioned above? Or another one? Or a combination of several bridge-categories? In this latter case, which one is predominant?

Second, this listing further clarifies why the same text can legitimately have very different contextual teachings, that is, different ways in which the reader-believers are transformed. For instance, through their many different features, the beatitudes can convey to readers a certain kind of knowledge, or entice them to do the right thing (i.e., to have the right will), or empower them, or convey faith to them. Whatever might have been the original purpose of these words (either in Jesus' ministry or in Matthew's time), the beatitudes have many edges through which they actually mark the believer-readers in their concrete lives.

The Legitimacy of Bringing Our Theological Views to the Text: The Hermeneutical Frames of Our Interpretations

Understanding a Biblical Text and Entering into Dialogue with It

Similarly, there is nothing wrong with bringing to the text our theological views, our conceptions of any of the aspects of a believer's life under God. We cannot help doing this, because understanding a biblical text requires being in dialogue with it. Yet, as in any true dialogue, we have to expect that our views will be somehow altered and at times radically transformed.

As in the case of a live conversation with another person, entering into dialogue with a text involves finding an issue, a topic, a matter about which both of us are interested, though we might have different levels of knowledge about it. This involves learning about the text and its views on the topic, or learning about the person and her or his views. But beyond this small first step, true dialogue is intersubjective and thus reciprocal.

True dialogue with someone requires that I "learn this person"[4] with full respect for his or her mystery as an Other, who always surprises me with new views, new insights, new perspectives. As I enter into dialogue with someone, I must anticipate that this other person will challenge my conceptions. Conversely, this intersubjective learning requires that I bring my own views, insights, perspectives into the conversation, with the confidence that they will be respected and affirmed in their differences. Through the trusting relationship of such a dialogue, I gain a new knowledge of the subject matter. But this is not because my earlier conception of it has been rejected, as would be the case in a polemical relationship. Rather, in the trusting relationship of a true dialogue, my new knowledge arises from the fact that I perceive my conception of the subject matter from the perspective of the other person. We now understand each other about the subject matter of our dialogue.

Similarly, reading meaningfully is understanding each other about a subject matter, although our dialogue partner is a text. Understanding a biblical text, especially when it is read as Scripture, involves respecting its mystery, expecting that it will surprise us and challenge our views. Yet, this understanding of a biblical text also entails coming to the text with the confidence that it will affirm and respect us as persons with our own ever-changing views and perspectives. Respecting the mystery of a biblical text entails recognizing that each time we read this text we need to make sense of it anew, because the subject matter of our reading-dialogue is in constant flux. Conversely, a trusting dialogic relationship with a biblical text is the relationship that a specific view of the Bible as Scripture establishes between the text and the believer-readers.

In sum, we make sense of a biblical text by dialoguing with it. Our understanding of a text is necessarily framed by (1) our choice of a subject matter for this dialogue, and (2) our choice of

a particular view of the Bible as Scripture that governs our trusting relationship with the text. Conversely, the understanding of the
subject matter of the dialogue that we brought to the text is necessarily framed by (1) what the text has to say about this subject
matter, and (2) the extent to which this particular text can actually fulfill the functions assigned to it by the view of Scripture with
which we approached it.

Choosing a Subject Matter for Our Dialogue with the Text: Framing Our Interpretations with Our Conceptions of Discipleship

I choose discipleship as the subject matter of our reading-dialogue
with the beatitudes. This choice may seem self-evident. Yet, it is
not. Let me explain.

This choice is not demanded by the text. Instead of discipleship,
I could have chosen another theme — for instance, God, kingdom, eschatology, Jesus, righteousness, justice. My interests (which
I hope you share) are determinant in my choice of topic. Nevertheless, the text delimited the range of possibilities; the dialogue
would stop abruptly if the text had nothing to say on the topic I
have chosen. Thus I simultaneously verified that the text has something to say about discipleship. How? Simply by making sure that
the text made sense when read in terms of my view of discipleship.

Determining whether this text offers a teaching about discipleship is not simply a matter of identifying the textual features (e.g.,
words, phrases) about this topic. If that were the case, I would not
have found much about discipleship in the Sermon on the Mount!
Beyond Matt. 5:1, there are no words explicitly referring to discipleship. Discipleship is not an actual content of the text. Rather, it
is a conception, a semantic construct, that provides a hermeneutical frame within which we can make sense of this text as we
dialogue with it.

Discipleship (or another subject matter) functions as a hermeneutical frame when it delimits a semantic space within which we
can position a text in order to make sense of it. For instance, if I
define discipleship as "the life of Christian believers as disciples"
(a very general definition that we will refine below), discipleship
can be viewed as a semantic space delimited by four corners: disciples (of Jesus' time), (present-day) believers, Christ, and life (and
many other things, as we will see). By positioning the beatitudes
within my conception of discipleship as hermeneutical frame, I can
explore whether or not it makes sense to say that this text offers a
teaching about discipleship. In effect I asked: Does the text inter-

relate disciples, believers, Christ, and life? I concluded that it did. Disciples are mentioned in the preceding verses. The blessed ones can be viewed as believers. The beatitudes are words of Christ. And life-situations are described in each beatitude.

Clearly, the fit between the text and my conception of discipleship as frame is not perfect. Disciples are not directly mentioned in the Sermon on the Mount itself (though the "you" of 5:11–12 and beyond might be read as a reference to disciples). Blessed ones are not exactly believers. Yet, this fit is good enough for me to make sense of this text by reading it for its teaching about discipleship. That the fit is not perfect simply suggests that the text's view of discipleship is not exactly the same as mine. Thus, I can expect to learn something about discipleship from this text.

Broadening these observations, the five (or six) interpretations of the beatitudes made sense of this text in quite different ways, as is clear from their diverse conclusions about the teaching of the text for believers today. Why? In part because each made sense of the text by framing it with its own conception of discipleship (as I hope you did). Even though each defined discipleship within a somewhat different kind of semantic network, each found some kind of fit between the text and the proposed hermeneutical frame.

Is this an illegitimate way of reading? Is this forcing the text into the framework of our conceptions? Not at all. This is the only way of entering into dialogue with the text concerning a subject matter, in order to make sense of this text.

This point is readily illustrated by considering once again a simpler kind of text, the black-and-white cognitive test image that we saw in the introduction. We noted that according to the way we look at it, we see one of two designs. Let us focus on one of the two: the white shape in the middle of it, rather than the black shape (the two faces looking at each other).

Now the question is: What do you see in this white shape? My students answered: A vase. A candlestick. A table. A martini glass. A bird bath. A chalice.

In order to make sense of this white shape (an actual feature of this text), each student has spontaneously positioned it within a specific hermeneutical frame. When it is envisioned within the semantic space of a home, the white shape is a vase (further associated with flowers), or a candlestick (further associated with a fireplace, an altar, or a dinner setting), or a table (possibly beside an armchair). Envisioned within a bar or a New Year celebration in North America, it is a martini glass. Envisioned in the backyard of a North American house, it is a bird-bath. Envisioned within a church setting and the Eucharist (Lord's Supper), it is a chalice. Each student made sense of the white shape by positioning it within a specific hermeneutical frame.

References to disciples in Matt. 5:1, to Jesus as speaking these words, to blessed ones, and to their life-situations are textual features like the white shape. As the white shape is one of the designs that can be perceived and described as belonging to the diagram, so these textual features can be perceived and described as belonging to the beginning of the Sermon on the Mount. Yet, in and of themselves these features do not make sense. They become meaningful only when read in terms of our own views — here, our conceptions of discipleship. But we make sense of this text and its features in different ways because we frame them with different conceptions of discipleship.

After the dialogue with the text is initiated in this way, our conception of discipleship is in turn challenged by the text. Wherever the fit between our conception and the textual evidence is not quite perfect, the text challenges an aspect of our view of discipleship. For instance, that believers are presented in the text as blessed ones has the potential to challenge a significant aspect of my conception of discipleship.

In most instances, what the text teaches us about discipleship is related to some aspect of the original conception of discipleship with which we framed our reading of the text. A critical study multiplies these possibilities of learning from the text something new about discipleship by allowing us to become aware that we used as a hermeneutical frame one among several plausible views of discipleship. We gain this critical perspective by comparing our interpretations with others and taking note of the different options for defining discipleship. Once again, a listing of some important options facilitates this comparison.

The diverse conceptions of discipleship can first be separated into two broad groups: those that give priority to doing God's will and those that give priority to imitating Jesus. Then, in each group, the several kinds of conceptions of discipleship can be distinguished by their particular emphases. As you consider these different options, think about your own interpretation. Which one did you choose?

- Discipleship as Doing God's Will

    — with emphasis on learning from Jesus what God's will is

    — with emphasis on being enticed and exhorted by Jesus to do God's will

    — with emphasis on being empowered by Jesus to do God's will

- Discipleship as Imitating Jesus

    — with emphasis on learning from Jesus how to act as he did and how to follow him by prolonging his ministry (Jesus as a model for acting)

    — with emphasis on learning from Jesus how to discern those who manifest the kingdom today, as the blessed ones did, and are models to be followed by believers, as the disciples followed Jesus during his ministry (Jesus as a model for discerning)

Each of these five conceptions of discipleship is plausible. Of course, to a certain extent each involves all these features. Yet, as we will see, it makes a great deal of difference to give priority to one or another of these features, so much so that the conceptions of discipleship can be shown to exemplify quite dissimilar ethical theories. All of these conceptions of discipleship, and certainly others, can be found among existing interpretations of the Sermon on the Mount as theological categories that frame readers' dialogues with the text.

Can you identify in a tentative way which conception of discipleship you used as a theological category to make sense of the text in your interpretation? Is it one of those mentioned above? Or another one? Or is your view of discipleship a combination of several of these options? In this latter case, which one is predominant?

Choosing a View of the Bible as Scripture: Framing the Believers' Dialogue with the Text

For believers, making sense of a biblical text by dialoguing with it entails not only choosing a subject matter (discipleship, in the present case), but also establishing a trusting relationship with the text. Otherwise, true dialogue between the reader-believers and the text is impossible. This trusting relationship is established for believers by viewing the biblical text as Scripture.

It is self-evident for believers that the Sermon on the Mount is to be read as Scripture. Similarly, it is self-evident for them that reading this text as Scripture involves being in a special, trusting relationship with the text. Believers therefore rarely raise questions regarding the nature of this trusting relationship, as if there were only one way of conceiving of it. In fact, believers construct it in several ways. Thus, any given interpretation reflects the choice of one kind of Scripture-believers relationship among several plausible options.

Acknowledging that we have chosen a specific view of Scripture-believers relationship as part of our hermeneutical framework is another step toward assuming responsibility for our interpretations. A listing of some important options might facilitate this process, even if the view of Scripture we choose is not found on this partial list.

I represent each view of Scripture by a more-or-less traditional metaphor and then briefly describe the relationship between Scripture and believer-readers as represented by this metaphor.

- Scripture as *Lamp to My Feet* (Ps. 119:105): a compass for life; a law believers should use as a guide for their own lives —

    Relationship: Scripture teaches believers what they should do, step by step, because they lack direction for their lives and do not know what is good and evil.

- Scripture as *Canon:* a measure for assessing behavior and life; a law for a community of believers —

    Relationship: Scripture shapes the believers' moral life as implementation of God's will, so that the community-church might fulfill its mission; it provides a means to recognize who does or does not belong to the community of believers.

- Scripture as *Good News:* loving word of a parent —

  Relationship: Scripture reveals God's love and thus speaks a comforting, encouraging, merciful word that helps believers to experience God's love, grace, and mercy.

- Scripture as *Family Album* —

  Relationship: Scripture establishes and reinforces one's identity and vocation as a member of the family of God (God's people); it gives believers a true sense of relationship to others and to God.

- Scripture as *Corrective Glasses:* promise/prophecy being fulfilled; incarnated word —

  Relationship: Scripture allows believers to see their lives/experiences with the eyes of faith, discerning in the midst of evil "what is good and acceptable and perfect" (Rom. 12:2) and what God is doing.

- Scripture as *Empowering Word* —

  Relationship: Scripture conjures a new reality (e.g., preliminary manifestations of the kingdom and of God's justice) in the present situation of otherwise powerless believers, thus empowering them to struggle for the kingdom and God's justice.

- Scripture as *Holy Bible* —

  Relationship: Scripture confronts believers with the holy; goosebumps experience resulting from a sense of awe, mystery, and wonder because Scripture shatters all the expectations of the believers and eventually confronts them with something radically different and awe-inspiring.

Each of these views of the relationship between Scripture and believers-readers can establish a trusting relationship and thus can contribute to framing the process through which believers make sense of a biblical text. Yet it should be clear that the roles of Scripture mentioned above are neither exclusive of each other nor a complete list of such roles. In any religious tradition, Scripture (whatever it might be) plays several roles in the life of believers.

One or another of these roles becomes predominant according to the circumstances and according to the believers' convictions. Yet, the other roles are never completely absent. For instance, an interpretation that emphasizes the role of Scripture as lamp to my feet does not exclude its roles as canon, good news, family album, corrective glasses, empowering word, and holy Bible. Furthermore, these metaphors do not account for several other roles of Scripture. We would need other metaphors to represent, for example, its healing role (bringing back wholeness to the broken heart),[5] its role in mystical experiences ("holy Bible" might be appropriate here),[6] its role in the women-church (at times represented by the traditional metaphor of Scripture as "bread"),[7] its role as "talking book" in the spirituality of Asian women,[8] or its role as conjuring a new reality in African-American traditions (I will associate the latter two with "empowering word").[9]

Thus, keeping in mind that you might have to propose your own metaphor, can you identify in a tentative way which view of Scripture you used in your interpretation to relate the biblical text and the believer-readers? Is it one of those mentioned above? Or another one? Or a combination of metaphors? In this latter case, which one is predominant?

According to the view of Scripture used in the interpretation, one ends up with quite different conclusions about what the text teaches about discipleship. Furthermore, as we will see, each view of Scripture is closely related to a given conception of discipleship. Nevertheless, as I repeatedly argued, it is legitimate to use any of these potential hermeneutical frames for one's reading of the text, *as long as the textual evidence warrants it.* This is to say that a critical study must also assess the textual evidence and how it is apprehended during the process of interpretation.

Grounding Our Interpretations on a Specific Dimension of the Text: The Analytical Frame

As we consider the five (or six) interpretations of the teaching about discipleship of the beatitudes (see chapter 1), we also need to take note of the different ways in which each reading is grounded in the text. As already illustrated by the example of the black-and-white diagram of the cognitive test, whenever we look at a text, at first we perceive only one of its dimensions; yet, when we change perspective, we can see other dimensions of it. In other words, the grounding of our interpretations in textual evidence is always selective. Thus, once again, being critical and assuming responsibility for our interpretation requires that we acknowledge our choice to focus our reading upon one specific textual dimension, which can eventually be analyzed by the use of a specific critical method. A listing of some important options might facilitate this process, even if the textual dimension we choose is not found in this partial list.

A reading of a text can be focused upon its:

- *Window dimension* — what is "behind" the text, be it the historical Jesus, early traditions, or the redactor's intention, is most significant (studied by different kinds of historical methods).

- *Story dimension* — the development of the plot, the characters, their interrelations are most significant (studied by methods of narrative criticism).

- *Symbolic message* — metaphors, symbols, their constructions as coded features, and the symbolic organization as conveying a religious vision are most significant (studied by redaction criticism in a history of traditions perspective, by the history of religions approach, and by certain literary approaches).

- *Transformative thrust*[10] — narrative and rhetorical transformations of characters and implied readers in thematic organization are most significant (studied by methods of structural and rhetorical criticisms).

- *Subversive thrust*[11] — social, economic, political, and religious structures of authority presupposed, advocated, or rejected by the text, as well as the traces of struggles for justice behind and within the text, are most significant (studied by methods of social, economic, political, feminist, and postcolonial critical studies).

- *Voices from the margin*[12] — the voices that reflect a different social and cultural construction of reality are most significant (studied by methods of postcolonial and cultural criticisms).

Can you identify in a tentative way the textual dimension in which you have grounded your interpretation? Is it one of those mentioned above? Or another one? A combination of several dimensions? In this latter case, which one is predominant?

Questions for Our Critical Study

I hope that this chapter has addressed some of your questions. Yet, it has not done so by providing answers. Rather it has helped us formulate three sets of new questions that we need to raise about our interpretations in order to assume responsibility for them. To sum up, we need to become aware of the specificity of the frames and categories we implicitly or explicitly used by asking:

- What are the characteristics of the contextual frame we used to relate life and text? Which bridge-categories did we use? Did we presuppose that the reader-believers lack knowledge? Lack will? Are powerless or oppressed in some way? Or lack faith?

- What are the characteristics of the hermeneutical frame we used to make sense of the text? Which theological categories did we use?

  — Did we conceive of discipleship as doing God's will? If so, how does Jesus' teaching of the Sermon on the Mount help believers to do God's will? Or did we conceive of discipleship as imitating Jesus? If so, is Jesus a model through his way of acting or of discerning?

  — Did we conceive of Scripture as lamp to my feet? As canon? As family album? As good news? As corrective glasses? As empowering word? As holy Bible?

- What are the characteristics of the analytical frame we used to ground our interpretations in textual evidence? Which critical categories did we use? Did we focus on the window dimension of the text? On its story dimension? On its symbolic message? On its transformative thrust? On its subversive thrust? On its voices from the margin?

These are the questions I will ask in the following chapters about each of the five interpretations that I presented earlier and that, I hope, you have begun asking about your own.

Chapter Three

Discipleship as Doing God's Will and Our Faith-Interpretations of the Beatitudes

Assuming Responsibility for Our Faith-Interpretations
Because Our Lives Depend upon Them

Assuming responsibility for our faith-interpretations of the beatitudes — that is, for the conclusions we reached regarding the teaching of this text for believers today, whether or not we are ourselves Christian believers — requires that we have a good grasp of the characteristics of our interpretations. For this, we need a clear understanding of the particular frames and categories we chose for each of our interpretations and of the implications of these choices.

Identifying the types of contextual, hermeneutical, and analytical frames we used is an important step in this direction. As you read the preceding chapter you should have already done so, at least in a tentative way. It is helpful, and even necessary, to recognize that we used a certain bridge-category between life and text as a contextual frame, that we made sense of the text in terms of certain views of discipleship and of Scripture, and that we grounded our interpretation on a certain textual dimension by implicitly or explicitly using an analytical frame. But in and of itself, this would be useless labeling.

To assume responsibility for our interpretations we need to see more concretely what difference it makes to choose certain types of frames rather than others. After all, for us believers, it is a matter of deciding whether or not we want to live by the teaching identified by our interpretations. Such life-decisions require more than an abstract and general knowledge of the options mentioned in chapter 2. The lists of options for each frame are helpful as simplified maps of the region; they allow us to identify landmarks and to recognize the significance of guideposts. Yet they hardly replace the firsthand knowledge gained from actually touring the countryside. Deciding to settle down and live in an area exclusively on the basis of map information is a less than ideal approach, and often results in deep disappointments. Thus, before settling down and saying, "This is the best interpretation for me/us today," it is important to use the lists of options as a map to tour the countryside and compare our initial choice with other possibilities, carefully weighing the pros and cons of each one. Our life (or, at least our way of life) depends upon our choice of interpretation.[1] Yet, you will have to make this essential decision for yourself (as is discussed in the concluding chapter). There is no universal best choice, because believers' situations vary all the time.

How Do We Decide Which Interpretation Is Best for Believers in a Given Situation?

A comparison of different interpretations in terms of their key features clarifies the implications of choosing one option rather than another. For this purpose, as we consider each interpretation we will ask three sets of questions.

(1) *What kind of teaching does the text offer to believers today according to this interpretation?* In order to elucidate the specificity of the teaching for believers today of each interpretation, we need to consider how life and text are interrelated through the contextual frame and its bridge-categories. The relative value of this aspect of the interpretation depends upon the way the bridge-categories are appropriately anchored in life and in the text (forming a solid bridge over the gap that separates text from life). Thus, we ask two questions (which we have already began to answer in chapter 1).

- To what extent does the text actually offer a solution for the problem (in a life context) brought to the text by the believer-readers? If the text does not offer a solution, the interpretation is inappropriate, and a better interpretation needs to be found.

- To what extent is this interpretation proposing a real teaching for the believer-readers (something new about or for their life)? Or do they already have the solution? In this latter case, there is no teaching for these believers. One might find a better interpretation. Yet this text might not have a teaching for such believers.

(2) How do believer-readers make sense of this text according to this interpretation? In order to elucidate the particular way believers and text enter into dialogue with each other, we need to consider closely which theological categories are the subject matter (one or another conception of discipleship) of this dialogue and its facilitator (one or another view of Scripture). The relative value of this aspect of the interpretation depends upon the way these categories actually form a hermeneutical frame through which the theological views of the reader-believers are somehow transformed. In this chapter and the following one, our concern will be exclusively with the subject matter, discipleship.

- What is the specific view of discipleship that believer-readers choose as subject matter of the dialogue with the text? Why does it make sense for them? How is it related to their cultural-religious background?

- To what extent does the dialogue with the text alter or transform the believer-readers' conception of this subject matter?

(3) What is the textual evidence on which the conclusions of this interpretation are grounded? The relative value of this aspect of the interpretation depends upon the way the interpretation actually grounds its conclusions about the teaching of the text for believers today regarding discipleship upon a dimension of the text. Because "prooftexting" is a potential signal that no actual interpretation of the text took place, we need to identify the analytical frame and the critical categories that implicitly or explicitly ground the interpretation upon certain characteristics of the text as a whole.

- What kinds of textual features are particularly significant? That is, what textual features serve as a basis for the conclusions about the teaching of the text for believers today regarding discipleship?

- To what extent do these features belong to a textual dimension characterizing the text as a whole?

In the present chapter, I invite you to compare your interpretation with Reading A and Reading B on the basis of each of these three points. In the next chapter the comparison will be made with the other three readings.

Comparing Your Reading with Reading A: Discipleship as Doing God's Will Requires Knowing God's Will — Matthew 5:3–12 as Window

What Kind of Teaching Do the Beatitudes Offer to Believers Today According to Reading A?

If your interpretation is closely related to Reading A1 or to Reading A2, you came to the text with the concern that, in the present secular society, people lack (true) knowledge of God's will. Assessing the value of adopting this contextual frame will involve asking ourselves whether or not this is the main problem in secular societies today. Yet, before raising this question in a meaningful way we need to examine other options.

To what extent do the beatitudes offer a solution for this problem? Since the beatitudes and the rest of the Sermon on the Mount are proclaimed by Jesus, who is presented in the Gospel according to Matthew as the Messiah, Son of God, and the Lord (the risen Lord who will be the eschatological judge, 7:21–23), it is quite plausible to anticipate that his words are a reliable expression of God's will. Thus, it is appropriate for believers to read the beatitudes and the rest of the Sermon on the Mount with the expectation that they will learn from this text the precepts and ways of life that express God's will for their lives as individuals (Reading A1) or as a community of disciples (Reading A2).

It soon becomes clear that the precepts and ways of life commanded by this text as God's will can be actual teaching for secular people since, as we will presently see, they systematically contradict the secular way of life in present Western societies.

How Do Believer-Readers Make Sense of the Beatitudes According to Reading A?

The Views of Discipleship and of the Moral Life Used to Make Sense of the Beatitudes

If your interpretation is closely related to Reading A1 or Reading A2, you implicitly defined discipleship as "doing God's will that was revealed by Jesus, the Messiah."

From this perspective, the beatitudes present God's will in the form of general principles that should govern the life of disciples. At the very least, being meek, merciful, and peacemakers (5:5, 7,

9) can be read as appropriate attitudes toward others, as the disciples' obligations toward others. Being poor in spirit (having a humble relationship with others, 5:3), mourning (for the world we abandon to serve others, 5:4), being hungry, thirsty, and persecuted for righteousness (the proper attitude toward others, 5:6, 10), and having a pure heart (a condition for having the right attitude toward others, 5:8) are also read here as basic principles of proper behavior. People need to know these basic ethical principles (together with those expressed in the rest of the Sermon on the Mount) in order to have a good life, that is, a life in proper relationship with others.

If you have chosen such a reading, you implicitly made sense of this text and of its teaching for believers by understanding discipleship in terms of general principles and rules that reflect obligations toward others and are expressed in laws, codes, and regulations. Many people in Western cultures have such a view of the moral life (this is a *deontological* view of the moral life, such as the one formulated in eighteenth-century Europe by Immanuel Kant).[2] If you hold such a view, Reading A (in either of its forms) is plausible. It makes sense to read the beatitudes as providing a knowledge of the general principles that disciples should implement in their lives because of their obligations toward others and toward God.

How the Beatitudes Transform the Common View of the Moral Life

Adopting Reading A1 or Reading A2 involves, therefore, making sense of the beatitudes in terms of a view of the moral life as implementation of basic moral principles, a view that is commonly found in modern Western cultures. This interpretation is appropriate, provided that, conversely, the beatitudes enter into dialogue with the reader's views and conceptions and transform them. This readily happens in the process of interpretation. If you read the beatitudes for the general principles of the moral life they teach, the beatitudes have certainly transformed your presuppositions about these general principles.

In secular Western culture, the principles and rules that should govern the moral life are universal and foundational because they are *rational* (that is, they are derived from the use of reason). The beatitudes directly challenge these views. From their perspective, these principles and rules are universal, not because they are rational, but because they are the (eternal) will of God revealed by Jesus, the Christ-Messiah, the Lord (7:21–23) who has "all authority" (28:18) to do so.

Then, if you have adopted this reading, it is appropriate to conceive of discipleship as implementing in your personal and/or communal life the general principles of God's will by deriving from it laws and rules adapted for particular circumstances (as one does with this view of the moral life). For instance, as we will see below, meekness (5:5) can be implemented as not resisting evil (5:38–39), which, in turn, according to the circumstances, involves either turning the other cheek (5:39), or giving your shirt to the one who sues you for your coat (5:40), or walking another mile with the person who forced you to walk one mile (5:41), or giving money to someone who begs or wants to borrow from you (5:42). In the "sphere of God's eschatological rule" (Kingsbury's phrase interpreting "kingdom of heaven"), disciples submit to God by obeying Jesus' authoritative revelation of God's will, as transmitted by the eleven disciples whom Jesus commissioned to make other disciples (28:16–20).

In sum, from this perspective, all the attention is on obeying God's will as revealed by Jesus, and therefore on the disciples' need to know God's will in the form of basic principles. Among these principles are instructions regarding the way to implement God's will in specific circumstances by reinterpreting it as required by the situation.

Thus, if you have chosen an interpretation more or less like Reading A, you can be reassured: it is plausible and meaningful for many believers in Western cultures in which one finds such a view of the moral life; conversely, it transforms secular views of the moral life into theological ones. Furthermore, as we will now see, it is easy to verify that this interpretation is grounded on appropriate textual evidence, though as with any interpretation, it is focused upon the aspects of the text that are viewed as most significant.

What Is the Textual Evidence on Which the Conclusions of Reading A Are Grounded?

The Beatitudes as Window upon Matthew and His Church

This teaching is most directly supported by the beatitudes when they are read as window allowing us to see the situation in which Matthew wrote his Gospel. From the perspective of this analytical frame, scholars (such as Strecker) consider Matthew a redactor who rewrote the tradition he received in order to express the message that, in his view, his community needed to hear. The beatitudes through all of their features are a window upon the intention of the redactor, and particularly Matthew's concern with ethical issues and the need of the community for a clear knowledge of God's will (the problem for Matthew, according to this reading). The beatitudes are also a window upon the church in Matthew's time, here, upon the ethical "self-consciousness of the community,"[3] as well as upon its needs at a time when its members are reviled and persecuted.

The Significance of the Beatitudes as Window upon Matthew and His Church

A comparison of Matt. 5:3–12 with the beatitudes found in Luke 6:20–23 shows that Matthew has "moralized" the beatitudes.[4] "Blessed are you who are poor" (Luke 6:20, referring to people suffering from actual poverty) becomes "Blessed are the poor in spirit" (Matt. 5:3, interpreted here as an ethical attitude); "Blessed are you who are hungry now" (Luke 6:21, referring to people with actual hunger) becomes "Blessed are those who hunger and thirst for righteousness" (Matt. 5:6, interpreted here as referring to hunger for the right kind of behavior). Furthermore, those beatitudes that are found exclusively in Matthew refer to ethical attitudes or behavior. According to this interpretation, for Matthew, true disciples are people with a specific, ethical way of life: they are lowly in spirit, humble ("poor in spirit," 5:3);[5] grieve over the world[6] or over their sins[7] ("mourn," 5:4); have a humility demonstrated in kindness ("meek," 5:5; of Jesus, 11:29);[8] strive to behave righteously ("hunger and thirst for righteousness," 5:6);[9] are "merciful" (5:7; obviously, an ethical behavior); "fulfill the demand of righteousness" with a good conscience ("pure in heart," 5:8);[10] are "peacemakers" (5:9; again, an obviously ethical behavior); are persecuted because of their righteous behavior ("persecuted for righteousness' sake," 5:10),[11] or because they follow the "way of righteousness" (21:32) taught by Jesus ("persecuted . . . on my account," 5:11–12).[12] The description of the blessed ones, the "indicative," is simultaneously an "imperative," an admonition, a command.[13]

As window upon Matthew's church, the beatitudes are what the intended readers, the members of his church, should have perceived as a realistic description of their historical situation. They were reviled and persecuted by people who "utter all kinds of evil against" them (5:11). They were in need of admonitions to be faithful disciples (as is shown by the very fact that the beatitudes are moralized).

Nevertheless, they were those to whom these blessings were addressed, because, despite their imperfection, they strove to obey these admonitions. They already belonged to "the sphere of God's eschatological Rule."[14] So it is also for present-day disciples.

In this window dimension, the promise that "theirs is the kingdom of heaven" is not understood as the promise of a glorious future to the poor, the hungry, and the mourning (as it is in Luke; and in Reading E, see chapter 4). With its strong ethical connotations, kingdom is understood as "the reign of heaven." Being part of the kingdom means submitting to the kingly authority of God and of his will. "Just as the rabbis admonish people to carry already now the yoke of the reign of God, it is decisive for Matthew to live in the present in agreement with the [reign of heaven] so that the community will be granted at the end the entrance into [it]."[15] Thus, the members of the church viewed themselves as disciples, because "they had taken upon themselves [Jesus'] yoke and were 'learning' from him."[16] For them, God's eschatological Rule (or "reign") is already partly realized in the community of disciples who strive to fulfill God's eternal will revealed by the eschatological Lord.[17]

Even though such disciples are still longing for the complete fulfillment of these promises (rewards "in heaven," 5:12), they are already comforted (5:4; by the very declaration that they are and will be blessed);[18] they already obtain mercy (5:7, as they pray, "forgive us our debts, as we also have forgiven our debtors," 6:12); they are already called "children of God" (5:9; cf. 5:45).[19] By submitting to the commands of Jesus and being "poor in spirit" etc., the disciples submitted to God's Rule and entered its sphere.

A Step in the Process of Assuming Responsibility for Our Interpretations

Whether or not our conclusions about the teaching of the beatitudes are similar to Reading A, our study of it helps us take a step in our quest for assuming responsibility for our own faith-interpretations.

Proponents of Reading A: Gaining a Critical Perspective on Their Faith-Interpretations

For those of you with interpretations similar to Reading A, the preceding pages have clarified many aspects of your interpretation.

The elucidation of main characteristics of the contextual frame (the problem in our context is a lack of knowledge of God's will), of the hermeneutical frame (discipleship as doing God's will entails fulfilling the principles of our obligations toward others as formulated by Jesus), and of the analytical frame (the beatitudes as window upon Matthew and his community and their ethical concerns) of your interpretations has helped you to become self-conscious about the interpretive process of your own reading. You have gained a measure of critical understanding of your faith-interpretations.

For you, the proponents of Reading A (in either of its forms), the overall interpretive process is primarily shaped by the tension between what the text meant and what the text means, and the effort of overcoming this gap. The ethical teaching that Matthew addressed to his community (what the text meant) is now addressed to present-day believers both as individuals and as communities. For such believers, what the text means is that as disciples they should submit to God's Rule and enter its sphere, as Matthew's church did. Thus, the analytical frame presenting what the text meant is transposed upon the contextual frame presenting what the text means for today. This transposition is facilitated by the view of discipleship as doing God's will understood from the perspective of a view of the moral life that emphasizes basic principles and rules (a deontological view). In the different situations in which present-day believers find themselves, the overall obligation to submit to the authority of God and to God's will remains. Yet, as is clear in the beatitudes, the admonitions and commands addressed to Matthew's church in the Sermon on the Mount are to be interpreted as basic principles, which need to be implemented in somewhat different ways according to the circumstances.

For Proponents of Other Readings:
A Step toward Assuming Responsibility
for Their Faith-Interpretations

For those of us who have faith-interpretations quite different from Reading A, the preceding pages also play an important role in our efforts to assume responsibility for our interpretations.

First, be reassured: I will proceed with other readings as I did with Reading A. That you reached different conclusions does not mean they are wrong (implausible and illegitimate). You probably focused your attention on another teaching of this text for believers (reading with another contextual frame), used another appropriate view of discipleship to make sense of this text (reading with another hermeneutical frame), and have grounded your interpretation upon another textual dimension (reading with another analytical frame). Thus, as you certainly expect by now, I will show that the other four Readings are also plausible and legitimate. Even if your faith-interpretation is unlike any of the five discussed here, more likely than not it can be shown to be plausible and legitimate, provided it offers a genuine teaching of the text for believer-readers (something new for or about their lives).

Of course, you do not need me to tell you that your faith-interpretation is legitimate and plausible. You are already convinced of this. Yet, by showing that Reading A is plausible and legitimate, the preceding pages might have shaken your absolute confidence in the legitimacy and plausibility of your own interpretation. I hope they did! An important step toward assuming responsibility for your interpretation involves recognizing that it is not the only possible one. It involves recognizing that, when you chose another interpretation, you (consciously or not) rejected Reading A. More specifically it involves acknowledging the three-fold basis of your rejection. You have judged that, in your context, Reading A does not offer an appropriate teaching for believers, even though it apparently does in another context, where a lack of knowledge of God's will is prevalent and where the text offers a sensible solution to this problem. You have judged that there is another way to make sense of the text, even though it is also plausible to do so in terms of Western views of discipleship and of the moral life as implementation of general principles and rules (a deontological view), since these cultural views are in turn altered by the text. You have judged that your conclusions could be grounded on another kind of textual evidence, even though it is now clear that an interpretation, such as Reading A, has appropriately grounded its conclusions on the window dimension of the text.

Such acknowledgments are an important step in assuming responsibility for our own interpretations. Now it becomes clear that we need to make explicit the contextual, hermeneutical, and analytical frames of our interpretations, as we will do now for Reading B. Ultimately, after a broad range of options has been elucidated, we will be in a position to raise in a meaningful way the question: Why did I choose this interpretation rather than another one?

Comparing Your Reading with Reading B: Discipleship as Doing God's Will Requires Wanting to Do God's Will – Matthew 5:3–12 as Story

What Kind of Teaching Do the Beatitudes Offer to Believers Today According to Reading B?

If your interpretation is somewhat related to Reading B, you came to the text with the concern that, in today's secular society, people need to be convinced to do God's will, because they are totally devoted to worldly pursuits or, if they are Christian believers, because they are tempted to backslide. In this case, your assessment of the problem that needs to be addressed in the present context is quite different from that of Reading A.

Reading B raises an important question for the proponents of Reading A, especially if both readings are developed in the same context: contemporary secular societies in Europe and North America. Is it really true that, in such a context, people do not know God's will? Do they not know what constitutes the good moral life, as expressed in the Sermon on the Mount? Is it really true that people do not know all this in a culture that in its public discourses constantly refers to Christian values, even though they are not implemented?

This is a very practical issue. By adopting Reading B, you are in effect saying loud and clear to the proponents of Reading A, "The problem for people today in our context is *not* a lack of knowledge of God's will." Therefore, an interpretation (Reading A), and following it, all the sermons emphasizing that the beatitudes teach God's will for believers' lives, completely miss the mark. It is not an actual teaching — something new — for these people, because they already know it. At least, this is the case for most church members.

For you who adopt Reading B, the problem is that people do not want to do God's will. Why? Possibly, because they have different priorities, that is, because they prefer to do something else. Or because they find it too costly.

Therefore for you who follow Reading B, the beatitudes seek to convince the readers to do God's will and to become disciples; or, for the believers themselves, the beatitudes reinforce the decision to become disciples.

How Do Believer-Readers Make Sense of the Beatitudes According to Reading B?

The Views of Discipleship and of the Moral Life Used to Make Sense of the Beatitudes

If your interpretation is closely related to Reading B, you implicitly adopted a voluntary, intentional view of discipleship.

From this perspective, the beatitudes call the hearers and readers to adopt the kind of behavior described. This is why the beatitudes emphasize that those who adopt this attitude or perform these deeds will receive the best rewards: "for theirs is the kingdom of heaven . . . for they will be comforted . . . for they will inherit the earth . . . for your reward is great in heaven." Therefore, those who will be the beneficiaries of these promises are blessed. They have made the right choice, even though it might seem difficult at first. Conversely, from this perspective 7:13–27 also makes sense: it includes warnings that one might be deprived of these rewards or even punished if one takes the "easy road" (7:13).

Thus, the beatitudes call hearers to discipleship. They entice them to abandon their ordinary lives with promises of rewards for a life of discipleship and, in the following verses, with a description of the goals of discipleship. Who would not want to receive for oneself these present and future blessings (5:3–12)?

Yet, this is not simply selfish calculation. When one is a faithful disciple, one has a mission for the world. One provides the "salt" and "light" of humble loving acts that promote the radical justice-righteousness of the kingdom and demonstrate God's love (5:13–16). Furthermore, such actions also bring good consequences for God, namely praise: "Let your light shine before others, so that they may see your good works and give glory to your Father in heaven" (5:16).

Who would not want to devote one's life to God's kingdom and its righteousness — the ministry begun by Jesus — especially if it also means that there will be rewards for oneself?

If you have chosen such a reading, you implicitly made sense of this text and of its teaching for believers by understanding discipleship as a voluntary or intentional commitment that involves responding to a call and making an ongoing series of decisions, constantly assessing the relative value (the worth) of each step of the process of discipleship. More specifically, you have understood discipleship in terms of a view of the moral life that is very common in Western secular life: the *consequentialist* or *utilitarian* view.

The view of the moral life focused on an anticipation of the consequences of actions governs business and many other under-takings of modern Western life. According to this view, we choose to perform one kind of action rather than another because we de-termine that it would be the most profitable or the most rewarding, or at least the less costly. Our choice of behavior is based on an assessment of the consequences we anticipate. More formally, we can note with Ogletree that consequentialist views of the moral life "call attention to the fact that our actions are in our power and that we are answerable for their consequences."[20] Thus, following John Stuart Mill, one can say that from this perspective one is most self-conscious about one's value commitments.[21] The focus is on the ways individuals act, that is, on the ways they move from be-ing interested in a potential action, to formulating a project to act, and actually deciding to act. In sum, "consequentialist theories of the moral life presuppose and articulate the intentional structure of human action."[22]

For people who in their daily life (including business life) com-monly use a consequentialist view of the moral life, Reading B is most plausible. It makes sense to conceive of discipleship as vol-untary and intentional, and to read the beatitudes as calling and enticing people to do God's will.

How the Beatitudes Transform the Common View of the Moral Life

Adopting Reading B involves, as in the case of Reading A, mak-ing sense of the beatitudes in terms of a view of the moral life commonly found in contemporary Western cultures. This is appro-priate provided that, conversely, the beatitudes enter into dialogue with the reader's conceptions and transform them. If you brought to the text the view of the moral life that governs your business activities, through the interpretive process the beatitudes have cer-tainly transformed it. The values affirmed by the beatitudes directly challenge those of the business world and of most of contempo-rary society, at least in Europe and North America. The behavior scorned in the world as that of losers is praised as blessed in the beatitudes. In the world, self-confidence, self-affirmation and self-promotion — not poverty in spirit, humility, and meekness — are rewarded by success, recognition, and possessions. Furthermore, from the perspective of modern secular business, the consequences posited as good by the beatitudes are at best unrealistic, because they are related to participation in the kingdom of heaven.

By reading the beatitudes and the Sermon on the Mount in terms of the pattern of a consequentialist view of the moral life, believers are invited to refute these objections step by step, by showing the problematic character of the values used in contemporary societies, and by showing that the goals and rewards posited by the Sermon on the Mount are not as unrealistic as they might first seem.

Actually, consequentialist views of discipleship and their reading of the beatitudes promote a radical, countercultural way of life: in communities that are viewed from the outside as utopian, because of their refusal to abide by the norms of contemporary Western societies, and/or in radical movements that actively challenge some aspect of life in such societies.

Such radical interpretations of the beatitudes have been found throughout the history of the church, and since the Reformation in the so-called Anabaptist movements that radicalized Luther's and Zwingli's approach to the Bible. Present-day Mennonites, Moravians, and Hutterites are heirs of this tradition, to which Eberhard Arnold belonged. This leader of the Bruderhof movement resisted the Nazis in Germany because of the Sermon on the Mount's profound influence upon him. His interpretation emphasizes both the urgency of the mission of the communities of disciples as *Salt and Light*[23] of the world and the need to "show the world what Arnold calls the 'alternate reality' of the gospel in a viable, concrete way — a way that demonstrates 'true unity among believers who are ready to live a life of unlimited, active love.' "[24]

Dietrich Bonhoeffer's interpretation of the Sermon on the Mount, *The Cost of Discipleship*, and Clarence Jordan's "cotton patch" version and commentary belong to this same line of interpretation.

Though in very different contexts, these three authors were not content to provide interpretations of the Sermon; they also lived its teaching in a radical way of life in community — the communelike Hutterite *Bruderhof* for Arnold; the outlawed Church Training College in Nazi Germany for Bonhoeffer, and Koinonia Farm in rural Georgia for Jordan.

The consequentialist view of discipleship is apparent throughout Arnold's efforts to underscore that the way of life advocated and presented in the beatitudes can be adopted only by those who are convinced of its goodness. The radical life of love can be seen as a "burden," indeed, as a very demanding way of life, because

it "oppose[s] outright the present order of society" at both the social and economic levels. This, continues Arnold, "quite naturally
will bring us into conflict [with the world]. We cannot put this burden on anybody else unless he or she prizes the greatness of God's
kingdom above everything else and feels inwardly certain that there
is no other way to go."[25] Drawing attention to the kingdom as
blessing for the present as well as for the future is therefore the
beatitudes' primary teaching, aimed at convincing people to adopt
its radical way of life. Recognizing God's love and goodness as
manifested among us and in Jesus' teaching is the necessary step
that will lead us to want to be disciples, that is, to want to become
fully human and fully dedicated to all.[26]

It follows that discipleship is a matter of the heart, an intentional commitment. It is a response to a call most directly
expressed by the beatitudes, as Bonhoeffer underscores.[27] The hearers are blessed because of the call and promise of Jesus involved
in the beatitudes, and not because they have performed the right
kind of behavior. "All are called to be what in the reality of God
they already are." The disciples and the people as a whole (the
crowd) "are called blessed . . . because they are heirs of the promise. But will they now claim their heritage by believing in Jesus
Christ and his word?" Each beatitude is a "call to come forth from
the people," and as they do so "these meek strangers are bound
to provoke the world to insult, violence and slander" (referring to
5:10–12). From this perspective, as Jordan emphasizes, the beatitudes open the Sermon on the Mount in order "to present the good
news of the kingdom so clearly and convincingly that the people
would repent and make *the great decision*." The purpose of the
Sermon is "to convince [people] of the rightness of the new way,
the result being a commitment of life to life and for life."[28]

Yet, this transformation of people into disciples is not instan-
taneous; it is a long process. Thus, the beatitudes represent a first
series of steps in the process of becoming disciples — a "stairway
to spiritual life."[29] The challenge to the common consequentialist
views of daily life in the Western world is best summarized in Jordan's conclusions about the teaching of the first three beatitudes:

> We found that the Beatitudes were steps into the kingdom,
> or we might call them stages in the "naturalization" of the
> kingdom citizen. First, in forsaking one's old country, "the
> world," the spiritual immigrant must feel a deep dissatisfac-
> tion with the old citizenship and sense a real need for the

new. Second, while recognizing that citizenship is a gift which could never be obtained on one's own, the spiritual immigrant knows that it is crucial to be concerned enough to leave the old and make the journey to the new land. Third, when the immigrant gets there he or she must renounce all former allegiances and make a commitment of complete loyalty to the will and way of the adopted country. In the words of the Sermon, the kingdom citizen must be "poor in spirit," then a "mourner," and then "meek."[30]

In sum, if you have chosen an interpretation similar to Reading B, you can be reassured: you are in good company! It is a plausible interpretation that, for believers, lays out steps leading to a radical life devoted to the kingdom. Of course, there is appropriate textual evidence to establish the legitimacy of this interpretation, provided we take note of the textual dimension upon which it is grounded.

What Is the Textual Evidence on Which Reading B Is Grounded?

The Beatitudes as a Part of Matthew's Story of Jesus and the Disciples

This teaching of Reading B is readily grounded upon the text when the beatitudes and the Sermon on the Mount are read as parts of the story told by Matthew. It is clearly legitimate to read the Sermon in this way; the Gospel according to Matthew is, among other things, a story with a plot, of which the Sermon is a part. The story dimension of the Sermon on the Mount is explicit in its narrative framework (5:1–2 and 7:28–29).[31] The proclamation of the Sermon by Jesus to certain characters — the disciples and the crowds — is very much a part of the plot. By preaching or teaching this sermon to novice disciples (the four fishers, 4:18–22) and would-be disciples (the crowds, 4:23–25), Jesus begins the process of making fishers of people (full-fledged disciples) out of them. Of course, by the end of the Sermon, the hearer-characters are not yet fully transformed into disciples. The hearing of the Sermon represents but one stage of this process. The narrative transformation of the hearers into disciples will be complete only when they actually go into mission, at the very end of the Gospel (28:16–20).[32]

The Sermon on the Mount also represents an ideal story of the disciples: how the hearers of the Sermon (including people from the crowds) should become disciples and carry out their mission, from the perspective of the preacher on the Mount. Though this ideal story does not form a linear plot, it is presented as a series of story segments organized for the sake of the rhetorical strategy of a Sermon that contributes to make disciples out of its hearers.

The Significance of the Beatitudes as a Part of Matthew's Story of Jesus and the Disciples

To understand the role of the beatitudes in the story of Jesus making disciples, we note that from its beginning (4:18–25) this story leaves open the composition of the collective character "disciples." It presents two groups of followers as potential disciples: "novice disciples," the four fishers who, as a result of Jesus' call, want to be made "fishers of people"; and "would-be disciples," the crowds who follow Jesus because of his fame as a healer. The Sermon is addressed to both groups, but especially to the crowds, as is suggested by its framework. While 5:1–2 could be read as addressed to the disciples in the presence of the crowds, 7:28–8:1 makes it clear that the Sermon is also addressed to the crowds — it is its effect *on the crowds* that is described.

In this part of the story Jesus is presented as a preacher who addresses to the crowds a call similar to the one he addressed to the four fishers. Jesus' role is to convince his hearers (establish their will) to be made disciples. For this, he promises them blessings and shows them that his promises are trustworthy. There is no unconditional command and no extraordinary authority here.[33] Jesus convinces his hearers by drawing them into the Sermon through the use of an impersonal style both in the introduction (the beatitudes, 5:3–10) and the conclusion (the warnings to those who do not do these words, 7:21–27). For instance, we do not read "Blessed are *you* poor, for *yours* is the kingdom" (Luke 6:20), but "Blessed are the poor in spirit, for *theirs* is the kingdom" (Matt. 5:3). Similarly, in the conclusion, we read, "*Everyone* who says to me, 'Lord, Lord...'" (7:21). Consequently, the promises of the beatitudes are for everyone who wants to listen, and thus for the crowds. The impersonal conclusion (7:21–27) confirms this observation. It is addressed to everyone who claims to be a (novice) disciple by calling Jesus "Lord" (7:21–23). This group includes all those who follow Jesus for the wrong reasons, as some in the crowds might be tempted to do (see 8:18–22). This concluding section does not prevent the Sermon from being a call to discipleship. It makes it a genuine call, which might or might not be successful.

The personal part of the Sermon — its central part, 5:11–7:20, addressed to "you" — is for those who have heard and truly responded to this call and decided to make God's will as taught by Jesus their own will, unlike those who call him Lord but only pretend to be his followers (7:21–23). In sum, from the perspective of the story, disciples are those who respond to Jesus' call, the beatitudes, and thus those who commit themselves to continue Jesus' ministry by manifesting the kingdom in which they have joined him. As such they are salt and light of the world, people with, as Jordan says, "a commitment of life to life and for life."

From the perspective of the story-analytical frame, the descriptions of the blessed ones in the first two beatitudes (5:3–4) are related to the beginning of the story of the former fishers.[34] They were "poor in spirit" (5:3), since they immediately obeyed Jesus' command (4:20, 22), trusting his promise, rather than calculating the pros and cons of this decision, as would people who believe they know how to make such decisions on their own (people "rich in spirit"). James and John are mourning (5:4), because of their separation from their father, Zebedee (4:22). Then the rest of the descriptions (the blessed ones as meek, thirsty and hungry for righteousness, merciful, pure in heart, peacemakers, and persecuted, 5:5–10) specify what following Jesus to become fishers of people will entail beyond leaving one's family and abandoning the activity one was pursuing according to the values of the world. Discipleship involves having a specific spiritual attitude (being meek, pure in heart), acting in a specific way toward other people (being thirsty and hungry for justice, being merciful and peacemakers), and being persecuted for righteousness' sake. As a consequence of their behavior (thus, at a later stage of their story), disciples will receive immediate blessings (they are declared blessed) and the confidence that they are citizens of the kingdom of heaven (5:3, 10). As such, they can be assured that they will receive additional blessings (in the kingdom): they will be comforted, inherit the earth, be satisfied, obtain mercy, see God, be called children of God (5:4–9). These are rewards — positive consequences for faithfully carrying out their mission — that refer to the ultimate stages of the story of the disciples. In sum, according to the story dimension of the beatitudes, many are called to become disciples. Albeit in an impersonal style, Jesus addresses a verbal call, not to a few individuals only, but also to all the individuals who form the crowds.

A Step in the Process of Assuming Responsibility for Our Interpretations

Once again, whether or not our conclusions about the teaching of the beatitudes are similar to those of Reading B, our study of this Reading helps us take a step in our quest toward assuming responsibility for our own faith-interpretations.

Proponents of Reading B: Gaining a Critical Perspective on Their Faith-Interpretations

For those of you with interpretations similar to Reading B, the preceding pages should have clarified many aspects of your interpretation. The elucidation of main characteristics of the contextual frame (the problem in our context is not wanting to do God's will), of the hermeneutical frame (a voluntary, intentional view of discipleship as doing God's will while constantly assessing the consequences of one's actions for oneself, for others, and for God — a consequentialist view of the moral life), and of the analytical frame (the beatitudes as part of Matthew's story of Jesus and the disciples) of your interpretations has helped you to become self-conscious about the interpretive process of your own reading. You have gained a measure of critical understanding of your faith-interpretations.

For you, the proponents of Reading B, the overall interpretive process is primarily shaped by the call (or invitation) to become disciples that Jesus addressed through the beatitudes to both the disciples and the crowds in Matthew's story, which is now also addressed to contemporary believers and nonbelievers. It is a call to enter the story of Jesus and his disciples and to prolong this story in the present. This prolongation of the Gospel story is facilitated by the hermeneutical frame with its emphasis on the voluntary character of discipleship and a consequentialist view of the moral life that is constantly concerned with the way in which one's actions unfold into a story with good or bad consequences. The promises of the Gospel — blessings for oneself, for others, and for God — are strong motivations to adopt a life of discipleship, even though one knows in advance it will be costly, since discipleship entails a radical way of life that clashes with the values of contemporary Western cultures (and of many other cultures, I presume).

For Proponents of Other Readings: A Step toward Assuming Responsibility for Their Faith-Interpretations

For those of us, including the proponents of Reading A, who have faith-interpretations different from Reading B, the preceding pages also play an important role in our efforts to assume responsibility for our interpretations. As explained in the concluding remarks of our analysis of Reading A, it is now clear that our interpretation, whatever it might be, is not the only plausible and legitimate one. It is also clear we have made a choice — an important step toward assuming responsibility for our own interpretation.

Furthermore, for the proponents of Reading A, who by now are aware of the particular contextual, hermeneutical, and analytical frames of their interpretations and are in a position to contrast them with the frames of Reading B, the specific choices they made become clearer, as is also the case for the proponents of Reading B. As a consequence, critical understanding of the interpretive process is sharpened. We can now address some questions.

What is at stake when we choose a historical-critical method (Reading A) rather than a narrative-critical method (Reading B), or vice versa, as the analytical frame through which we ground our interpretation on textual evidence? Both methods are equally critical, provided that those who practice them acknowledge that they deal exclusively with but one of several dimensions of the text. Yet, in order to have a sharp picture of the significance of the story dimension of Jesus and the disciples told by Matthew, it is essential to maintain this focus, and thus provisionally to block out the other textual dimension, the text as window. Remember that in order to have a clear picture of the white design (the vase, the candlestick, the chalice) we needed to focus on it, and thus to block out the black design, and that doing so self-consciously helped us to sharpen the focus. Likewise, knowing what the text as window refers to (the situation of Matthew's church; the ethical concerns of Matthew as redactor; see Reading A) does not help us to recognize the significance of the unfolding of the story of Jesus making disciples (believers today are also called to be disciples). On the contrary, any attention to the window dimension would confuse the issues and make it more difficult to see the story clearly.

What is at stake when we choose a view of discipleship and of the moral life focused on the implementation of basic principles and rule (Reading A) rather than a consequentialist view (Reading B), or vice versa, as the hermeneutical frame for entering into dialogue with the text and making sense of it? As we saw, both frames can help make sense of the text. Here the issue is making sure that the text and its interpretation are really understood by reader-believers. For this, the necessary condition is that we interpret the text in terms of our cultural views, so that these views might be altered or transformed through their encounter with the text. But the cultural situation in Europe and especially in North America is quite confused. While consequentialist views govern business and most of public life in these societies, and consequently in the daily life of most people, for many (especially in North America), deontological views govern family and private life. Proponents of Reading A passionately emphasize that discipleship and church membership are matters of fulfilling obligations in private and family life (e.g., consider the Promise Keepers movement), and that the other reading politicizes the gospel. Conversely, proponents of Reading B passionately emphasize that the gospel and discipleship encompass all spheres of life. The divorce between daily life and religious life is a scandal because it denies the very core of the gospel; Jesus, had he led that kind of religious life, would not have been crucified! We will further explore the implications of choosing one or the other of these views in the complexity of the European and North American cultural situation (and elsewhere) when we have a more complete picture of the range of choices before us (chapter 7).

Finally, what is at stake when we choose, as the problem that this text addresses, lack of knowledge of God's will (Reading A) rather than not wanting to do God's will (Reading B), or vice versa? This is a genuine choice between two realistic contextual frames, since the text offers solutions for both problems. Therefore the choice really depends upon one's analysis of the situation, regarding the primary needs of people around us, and also regarding our own primary needs. Theoretically, there is no teaching if the text does not address actual problems of reader-believers (as mentioned above). Yet, the situation is more complex, because in most instances there are several levels of interpretation. For instance, a sermon on a biblical text is the preacher's interpretation, which is in turn interpreted by the parishioners. The interesting and complex situation is that parishioners often hear from the sermon a teaching that meets their actual needs, even when the pastors have totally missed the mark by wrongly presupposing that their parishioners had other needs. For pastors this is at times reassuring. Despite their flaws, the sermons reached people. Yet, it is also frightening, because the teaching that they receive through their interpretation might be greatly unexpected. As we will see later, it is through irresponsible interpretation that, too often, anti-Semitic and oppressive teachings are conveyed in the name of the gospel.

This is another reason to pursue our comparative critical investigation, because each time we compare our interpretation to another one we are taking another step toward assuming responsibility for our interpretations. This is why we need to compare (in chapter 4) our interpretations to Readings C, D, and E.

Chapter Four

Discipleship as Imitating Christ and Struggling for the Kingdom and Our Faith-Interpretations of the Beatitudes

The systematic comparison of our interpretation of the teaching of the beatitudes for believers today with Reading A and Reading B has helped us to progress in our efforts to assume responsibility for it. The preceding chapter has also shown that with each new faith-interpretation encountered we learn more about our own, whether it is closely related or totally different. Indeed, we often seem to gain more insight about our interpretation when we contrast it with dissimilar readings. Assuming responsibility for our own interpretation requires recognizing and affirming the legitimacy and plausibility both of our own interpretation and of the differing interpretations of other readers.

As we compare our respective interpretations to Readings C, D, and E, we will follow the same pattern as in chapter 3. Readings C and D differ from Readings A and B, in part because they relate the beatitudes much more closely to the rest of the Sermon on the Mount. In Reading A, the analytical frame focuses attention on individual injunctions as windows, and on what is behind these windows; thus, the order of the precepts in the text does not matter, and the beatitudes can be interpreted by themselves. In Reading B, the analytical frame focuses upon the story that encompasses the Sermon on the Mount; thus, the beatitudes are read in terms of what precedes and follows the Sermon. Here, in Readings C and D, the interpretation is grounded on significant relationships within the Sermon: the relationships of the beatitudes either to the Lord's prayer at the center of the Sermon (Reading C) or to the judgment scene at the end (Reading D). Yet, this visible shift in analytical frame is not isolated. It reflects a comparable shift in hermeneutical frame (discipleship is now viewed as imitating Christ, though in two different ways) and in contextual frame (the basic problem is now lack of faith, though the main characteristic of faith varies).

Similarly, Reading E differs from all the preceding ones, in part because of its contextual frame: the very concrete problem for believers and would-be believers is powerlessness, and the teaching for believers concerns struggling for the kingdom and for God's justice. Yet, there are comparable shifts in analytical frame (the most significant features of the text are its allusions to struggles for economic and social justice) and in hermeneutical frame (discipleship is now viewed as struggling for, or seeking, the kingdom and God's justice, 6:33).

Comparing Your Reading with Reading C: Discipleship as Imitating Christ Requires Being Resocialized – Matthew 5:3–12 as Symbolic Message

What Kind of Teaching Do the Beatitudes Offer to Believers Today According to Reading C?

If your interpretation is somewhat related to Reading C, you came to the text, as we saw in chapter 1, with the concern that, in the present secular society, people lack hope and vision for their lives because traditional cultures have disintegrated. Being secular is lacking this faith-vision. Similarly, Christian believers always need to share in the hope and vision that gather them as a community of disciples. When read in terms of this contextual frame, the beatitudes offer a vision of life in the kingdom ("theirs is the kingdom," 5:3, 10).

Assessing the value of adopting this contextual frame involves asking ourselves whether or not this is the main problem in secular societies today rather than a lack of knowledge of God's will (Reading A) or not wanting to do God's will (Reading B). A general observation suffices here, taking the case of North American societies. While a lack of vision for life does not characterize all segments of the population, it is quite apparent among at least two groups. On the one hand, there are the disenfranchised African-American and Mexican-American young people described by William Finnegan (in a book where he tells of his experience living with four families for extended periods),[1] who struggle to make sense of life in the constant presence of systemic violence and hostility, and whose muted quest for meaning and identity is ignored. On the other hand, the so-called Generation X — the middle-class, educationally successful European-American young people (born between 1960 and 1980) whose experience is strongly influenced by the images and values of television and popular music — is engaged in what one of them, Tom Beaudoin, calls an "irreverent spiritual quest" in which pop culture is the primary source of and catalyst to a "virtual faith" that keeps in tension real spiritual journeys and institutional religion (viewed with suspicion).[2] For people in such quests for a spiritual vision of life, this reading of the beatitudes is potentially helpful. Yet, other segments of the population can be viewed as desperately needing a spiritual vision of life. I allude to those who totally absorb themselves in the numerous activities of busy lives in pursuit of a blurry vision of life that remains unexamined. In sum, a contextual frame shaped by a lack of vision of life or improper visions of life (from the standpoint of the gospel) is appropriate in many circles of North American societies, and possibly in other sociocultural settings.

There is no difficulty in recognizing that the beatitudes offer a solution for this problem. They can easily be read as offering a vision of life in the kingdom ("theirs is the kingdom," 5:3, 10), where "those who mourn...will be comforted" (5:4), "the meek ...will inherit the earth (5:5)," those who hunger and thirst for righteousness...will be filled" (5:6), "the merciful...will receive mercy" (5:7), "the pure in heart...will see God" (5:8), and "the peacemakers...will be called children of God" (5:9). We need to understand more clearly the nature of this vision before assessing its potential effectiveness in overcoming the lack of vision discussed above.

The use of such a contextual frame is potentially appropriate. It is not simply read into the text. Yet, as we will see, contemporary quests for a vision of life are quite distinct from the vision proposed by the beatitudes.

How Do Believer-Readers Make Sense of the Beatitudes According to Reading C?

The Views of Discipleship Used to Make Sense of the Beatitudes: Faith-Vision Shared with a Community as a Prerequisite for Imitating Christ

If your interpretation is closely related to Reading C, you brought to the text a view of discipleship quite different from those discussed in chapter 3. Readings A and B conceive of discipleship as doing God's will, since they emphasize either the implementation of basic ethical principles revealed by Christ (Readings A1 and A2) or the commitment of oneself to continue Jesus' ministry by doing what he taught his disciples to do (Reading B). By contrast, Reading C presupposes that discipleship involves sharing in a vision of the kingdom — participating in it — as one lives with Jesus, imitating the one who manifested the kingdom in his ministry. Then the community of disciples is gathered together by a shared vision of life in the kingdom. In turn, this community conveys this vision to its members; its true leaders ("prophets," cf. 5:12 and 7:15–20, who can be recognized "by their fruits") are also models of discipleship, as they exemplify how to imitate Christ.

When the Sermon on the Mount is read through this hermeneutical frame, it calls for a practice of discipleship by believers who share in a particular symbolic world, namely, the vision of the kingdom offered by the beatitudes as the perspective from which everything in human experience must be understood. This practice of discipleship requires a "faith shared with the community" as a prerequisite.[3] It is a faith through which one holds onto the vision of the kingdom and sees oneself in this world, with an identity that is also a vocation: discipleship.

This vision of the kingdom involves a twofold symbolic horizon, as each of the beatitudes expresses. The eschatological promises ("for theirs is the kingdom of heaven," 5:3, 10; "for they will be comforted," 5:4; etc.) present the eschatological horizon, the coming kingdom. The declarations of blessing ("blessed") depict the present theological horizon, namely, the present manifestations of God's care for us.[4] Then, the descriptions of the blessed ones (e.g., "the poor in spirit") are read in this twofold horizon. By fulfilling all the beatitudes, Jesus has already manifested what life in the kingdom will be. People who imitate Jesus in turn r this kind of behavior in their life, possibly in only one a their experience. They should also be viewed as models pleship. The reader-hearers are thus invited to identify, as blessed ones whom they should imitate, certain characters in the Gospel — Jesus, in particular — and certain persons in the present community of disciples (those who embody this vision as they imitate Jesus).

The descriptions of those who are blessed provide a means of identifying the blessed ones as people to be imitated. For instance, in 5:3, "poor in spirit" points to "the religious state of poverty,"[5] and thus to "the ethical attitude of humility"[6] exemplified by the actual poor who will be comforted, as prophesied in Isa. 61:1–2 (cf. Matt. 11:5). Thus, people who can be identified as being in the religious state of poverty are blessed ones whom one should imitate, even though it might not be otherwise apparent that they belong to the eschatological kingdom. Conversely, through the lens of Matt. 7:13–27, readers are urged to identify among the characters of the Gospel and, primarily, among the people in their daily life, those antimodels of discipleship whom they should distrust: "Beware of false prophets, who come to you in sheep's clothing but inwardly are ravenous wolves. You will know them by their fruits" (7:15–16).

This conception of imitation embodies the ambivalence of a symbolic world that keeps in tension an ideal eschatological future (the kingdom) and a flawed, mixed present in which God's loving care is nevertheless manifested. Since religious leaders are models of discipleship who should be followed (imitated) by the other disciples, they represent "the new, better human being in the coming of the kingdom of God;"[7] they are models of "higher righteousness."[8] Yet, in the present these models are not themselves perfect and are found side by side with false prophets. Before the advent of the kingdom, no one, except Christ, can display all the kinds of behavior described in the beatitudes. Thus, discipleship remains an "imitation of Christ" (*imitatio Christi*), even if there are other people who are partial models of discipleship despite their imperfections.

Imitating the one who embodies the beatitudes (Christ and, secondarily, other models) does not mean acting exactly as Christ does (his behavior is not a norm to be implemented, as in Reading A). It means being both like him and unlike him. Disciples should follow Jesus (thus, continuity), but at some distance — following implies being behind (thus, some discontinuity). As is clear when the model of discipleship is God ("Be perfect, therefore, as your heavenly Father is perfect," 5:48), models are ideals whom one strives to imitate by duplicating their behavior without ever fully succeeding.

The higher righteousness presented in the Sermon on the Mount is an ideal vision of life in the kingdom. Before the eschatological time, we are limited to striving toward this perfection. We are limited to imitating, as we share in the vision of the kingdom with the community of disciples.

The View of the Moral Life Presupposed by This Understanding of Discipleship

This understanding of discipleship as imitating Christ reflects a *resocialization-perfectionist* view of the moral life. Perfectionist theories stress that values (upon which any action is based) are constructs; they are parts of the *symbolic world* in which we live.[9] This world, which might seem natural and/or factual to us, is itself a construct (as cross-cultural studies show); it interrelates the various features of concrete human experience in specific ways and attaches values to each of them.

Perfectionist theories also stress that to be a moral agent is to have "character" (*ēthos*) and "practical wisdom" (according to Aristotle). Acquiring practical wisdom is not simply a matter of intellectual learning — learning about virtues as abstract moral notions, instead of learning virtues by being trained "to do one's functions well."[10] Learning virtues is a matter of practice; virtues are attitudes that one cultivates, as one acquires culture. Thus acquiring practical wisdom is learning to perform well one's function, as apprentices hone their woodcarving skills. A virtue (good woodcarving skill), and, a fortiori, practical wisdom as a series of virtues, cannot be gained by oneself in isolation, although individual effort is demanded. Apprentices need to learn in an actual workshop (with tools and benches) from a master cabinetmaker, and learning involves observing (discerning the useful gestures) and imitating the expert.

Similarly, Christian virtues, as virtues of practical wisdom, are learned in the concreteness of human experience by imitating the way in which "experts" perform them in a specific realm of human experience, namely, the community of disciples who share a symbolic world. Then, one develops moral discernment, through which one distinguishes in the ambiguities of concrete life how one should act as a member of that community by conforming in one's behavior to the community's symbolic world and by imitating models found in this community. Imitating is being conformed and conforming oneself to the community and its symbolic world.

In sum, if your conclusions about the teaching of the beatitudes are framed by the traditional understanding of discipleship as imitation of Christ as in Reading C, they clearly make sense of the text, including what is for many its excessive ethical demands (as spelled out in Readings A and B). From the perspective of this hermeneutical frame, the beatitudes do not demand that disciple-believers be perfect, but that they strive toward perfection by imitating Christ.

How the Beatitudes Transform a Perfectionist View of the Moral Life

Adopting Reading C involves making sense of the beatitudes in terms of a hermeneutical frame characterized by a perfectionist view of the moral life and of discipleship as imitation. This is appropriate because the beatitudes force us to rethink what imitating Christ entails and what a perfectionist view of the moral life involves.

After reading the beatitudes we can no longer envision imitating Christ as the simple performance of acts of love following Jesus' example — as we would according to a traditional perfectionist view focused upon character formation in the concreteness of daily life. By squarely stating that, even in the present, the people to be imitated belong to the eschatological kingdom,[11] the beatitudes make clear that those whom disciples are to imitate manifest this eschatological kingdom. More specifically, believers are to imitate Jesus Christ, the eschatological Lord (as 7:21–23 makes explicit), rather than Jesus of Nazareth. This fundamental eschatological outlook of discipleship according to the beatitudes contrasts with traditional perfectionist views. Disciples look beyond the mixed and flawed present situation toward the perfect, eschatological kingdom, in which there will be justice, peace, and no tears; yet they also believe that there are preliminary manifestations of this kingdom in the present. As members of a community framed by this eschatological symbolic world, disciples pray together: "Our Father in heaven, hallowed be your name," an address that acknowledges God's present loving care; and "Your kingdom come," a petition with an eschatological outlook (6:9–10).

What Is the Textual Evidence on Which Reading C Is Grounded?

The Beatitudes as a Symbolic Message about the Kingdom

This teaching is readily grounded upon the text of the beatitudes and of the Sermon on the Mount when they are read as eschatological religious texts, i.e., as *symbolic messages*. From the perspective of this analytical frame, the symbolic message of the Sermon is most directly expressed in two of its basic characteristics: (1) its artistic arrangement — its symbolic organization — that brings readers to interpret each part in terms of the whole; (2) its symbols and metaphors that invite readers to compare its subject matter with something else — for instance, a well-known tradition or text to which the text alludes.

(1) The ringlike symbolic organization of the Sermon on the Mount[12] accentuates both the parallelism between the ministry of Jesus and that of the disciples (imitation of Christ) and the centrality of the eschatological faith-vision shared in prayer by the disciples.

First, one can note that ringlike inclusions between 4:23 and 9:35 (almost identical summary descriptions of Jesus' teaching-preaching and healing ministry) encase the presentation of both aspects of Jesus' ministry: the Sermon on the Mount (chap. 5–7) and a series of miracle stories (chap. 8–9).[13] These ringlike inclusions call attention to the fact that immediately preceding and following this twofold description of Jesus' ministry the focus is on the ministry of the disciples, called to follow Jesus in order to be made fishers of people (4:18–22) and sent in mission to the crowds, who, without hope and vision, are "harassed and helpless, like sheep without a shepherd" (9:36–10:42). It is striking that the disciples' ministry is described as imitating (duplicating!) that of Jesus: proclaiming the good news of the kingdom (10:7) as Jesus did (4:23a; chap. 5–7) and duplicating his healing ministry (10:8; 4:23b; chap. 8–9). In sum, this ringlike symbolic organization expresses most vividly that discipleship is imitating Christ; the disciples' ministry should be like Jesus' twofold ministry.

A similar ringlike organization is found in the narrative framework of the Sermon between the opening scene (4:23–5:2) and the closing scene (7:28–8:1),[14] as well as in the Sermon itself, which can therefore be represented as a series of concentric triadic groupings: introduction (5:3–16), main body (5:17–7:12), conclusion (7:13–27);[15] and at the very center, the Lord's Prayer (6:9–13).

This organization calls the readers' attention to the Lord's Prayer, with its twofold vision of God's loving care ("Our Father in heaven," 6:9) and of the coming kingdom ("Your kingdom come," 6:10), as a key in terms of which the rest of the Sermon on the Mount is to be interpreted.

In sum, the symbolic organization of Matthew and of the Ser-

4:23–5:2		7:28–8:1
Followed by crowds		Jesus climbs down
Jesus climbs up		the Mountain
the mountain		followed by crowds
	5:3–7:27	
	The Sermon on the Mount	
5:3–16		7:13–27
Introduction		Conclusion
	5:17–7:12	
	Main Body	
5:17–20		7:12
Introit of body		Conclusion of body
5:21–48		6:19–7:11
Antitheses-Torah		Social Issues
	6:1–18	
	Cult	
6:2–4		6:16–18
Almsgiving		Fasting
	6:5–15	
	Prayer	
6:7–8		6:14–15
Not as Gentiles		Forgiveness
	6:9–13	
	LORD'S	
	PRAYER	

Symbolic Structure of the Sermon on the Mount (Reading C)

mon on the Mount already provides ample evidence upon which to ground the perfectionist teaching of the beatitudes regarding discipleship as imitating Christ and as providing a vision of God's love and of the kingdom.

(2) The symbols of the Sermon on the Mount provide further evidence for the ambivalence of this teaching. Saying that Jesus is a symbol or model of discipleship and that his activities are models of the disciples' activities[16] means that the disciples are like Jesus and unlike Jesus.[17] Jesus' ministry is unique because of its special character as manifestation of God's loving care — as God with us, Emmanuel.[18] Thus, the very model calling disciples to imitation posits Jesus as an ideal, who gives them a vision of God's loving care.

Similarly, Jesus is presented as a Moses-like figure in the introduction and conclusion of the Sermon. Jesus climbing up and down the mountain (5:1, 8:1) and delivering a discourse concerning the law and God's will have to be understood as allusions to Moses climbing up and down the mountain (Sinai; see Exod. 19:3, 12; 24:15, 18; 34:1–2, 4). Thus, Jesus is "the mosaic Messiah" "delivering messianic Torah" upon the Sinai-like mountain of revelation.[19] Once again, this symbol involves ambivalence: Jesus is like Moses and unlike Moses, and his teaching is like and unlike the law and the covenant revealed by Moses on Mount Sinai, because he is the eschatological fulfillment of Moses on Mount Sinai.[20] The eschatological, messianic figure of Jesus as the New Moses posits the *eschatological horizon* against which readers are expected to envision themselves as disciples, who together pray, "Your kingdom come."[21]

The Significance of the Beatitudes as Symbolic Message

When read from the perspective of the Lord's Prayer (in terms of the symbolic organization of the Sermon) and of Jesus as a Moses-like model of discipleship, each beatitude directly reflects the twofold symbolic horizon of God's present loving care and of the coming kingdom. The eschatological promises (e.g., "for theirs is the kingdom of heaven," 5:3, 10) express the eschatological horizon, the coming kingdom. The declarations of blessing ("blessed") express God's present care; they are like the blessings and beatitudes in cultic and wisdom texts of the Hebrew Bible (more exactly, its Greek translation, the Septuagint). The persons described in the beatitudes ("the poor in spirit," etc.) *are* blessed by God, and thus are in a special relation with God (as in Exod. 19:4–5); they *are* chosen of God, God's own; they *are* people to be imitated.[22] Thus, each beatitude is to be read as offering a model of discipleship, which allows the readers to identify people they should imitate.

Of course, the beatitudes primarily point to Jesus as the one to be imitated, because he is the only one who embodies all the beatitudes, as Davies and Allison note: "Jesus was himself meek (11:29; 21:5). Jesus mourned (26:36–46). Jesus was righteous and 'fulfilled all righteousness' (3:15; 27:4, 19). Jesus showed mercy (9:27; 15:22; 17:15; 20:30–1). And Jesus was persecuted and reproached (26–27)."[23]

A Step in the Process of Assuming Responsibility for Our Interpretations

Whether or not our conclusions about the teaching of the beatitudes are similar to Reading C, our study of it helps us to progress in our quest to assume responsibility for our own faith-interpretations.

Proponents of Reading C: Gaining a Critical Perspective
on Their Faith-Interpretations

For those of you with interpretations similar to Reading C, the preceding pages have made explicit aspects of your interpretation that
you might have only implied. The elucidation of main characteristics of the contextual frame (the problem in our context is a lack of
hope and true vision for life), the hermeneutical frame (a view of
discipleship as imitating Christ with a faith-vision about the kingdom and God's love as a prerequisite — a perfectionist view of
the moral life), and the analytical frame (the beatitudes as a symbolic message) of your interpretations has helped you to become
self-conscious about the interpretive process of your own reading.
You have gained a measure of critical understanding concerning
your faith-interpretation. From your perspective, the teaching of
the beatitudes for believers today is an invitation to recognize
blessed ones — Christ, but also other Christlike people — as models of discipleship, with the understanding that believers can do so
only insofar as they share in the liturgical life (the praying of the
Lord's Prayer) of the church as community of disciples, and as they
view Jesus' ministry as well as their own experience in terms of
the twofold horizon of the eschatological kingdom and of God's
present loving care.

For Proponents of Other Readings: A Step toward Assuming
Responsibility for Their Faith-Interpretations

For those of us, including the proponents of Readings A and B,
who have faith-interpretations different from Reading C, the elucidation of the main characteristics of Reading C makes even clearer
than before that our interpretation, whatever it might be, is not
the only plausible and legitimate one. We have to acknowledge
that when we chose an interpretation we excluded the options
represented by Reading C.

This additional step toward assuming responsibility for our own
interpretation contributes to the critical understanding of the interpretive process involved in our own interpretation. Consequently,
we can now address some questions.

What is at stake when we choose, as the analytical frame
through which we ground our interpretations upon textual evidence, a critical method that combines a literary approach and
a comparative study of religious traditions to elucidate the symbolic message of the text (as in Reading C)? We have seen that

this analytical frame focuses the reading upon certain distinctive features of the text: symbolic organization inside the text and the relationship of the textual symbols and models with the other biblical texts and traditions they evoke. In order to have a sharp picture of the symbolic message, it is essential to maintain this focus, and thus provisionally to block out other textual dimensions — in the same way that in order to have a clear picture of the white design (the vase, the candlestick, the chalice) we need to focus on it, and thus to block out the black design. Doing so self-consciously helps us to sharpen the focus. At this stage of our study, we know that when reading the Sermon on the Mount for its symbolic message we should block out two other textual dimensions: the text as window and the text as story. Knowing what the text as window refers to (the situation of Matthew's church; the ethical concerns of Matthew as redactor; see Reading A) does not help us recognize its symbolic message; actually, it confuses the issues and makes it more difficult to see clearly what this symbolic message is. Similarly, paying attention to the unfolding of the story of Jesus and his disciples (see Reading B) hinders recognition of the way in which the symbolic message affects reader-believers.

What is at stake when we adopt, as the hermeneutical frame used to enter into dialogue with the text and make sense of it, a perfectionist view of discipleship and the moral life, which stresses that disciples need to have a faith-vision about the kingdom and God's love (Reading C), rather than a deontological view of discipleship and the moral life (Reading A) or a consequentialist view (Reading B)? As we saw, these three hermeneutical frames help make sense of the text. The question is: Does this view of discipleship and the moral life, which certainly was meaningful in the Hellenistic culture, still make sense in modern Western cultures? In other contemporary cultural situations? In Reading C, imitating Christ is understood in terms of the implied symbolic pattern of conforming — conforming one's behavior to the model provided by Christ, but also conforming to the vision of life of the community, and thus being totally shaped (resocialized) by life in this community. But does this pattern truly make sense in the cultural situation in which we are today? Are we conceiving of ourselves from the perspective of a community? Or, are we choosing a community because it conforms to our views?

Finally, what is at stake when we choose as the problem addressed by this text, lack of hope and vision for life (Reading C), rather than lack of knowledge of God's will (Reading A) or not wanting to do God's will (Reading B)? We have a genuine choice among three realistic contextual frames, since the text offers solutions for each of these problems. Therefore the choice depends upon one's analysis of the situation, regarding the primary needs of people around us, and also regarding our own primary needs. We noted that at least certain segments of North American societies lack hope and/or vision for life. But, in this specific context where people who lack such a vision are totally alienated from the church institution, which they view with suspicion, would a teaching that emphasizes the connection between faith-vision and church (liturgical praying of the Lord's Prayer; blessed ones as models of discipleship to be found within the church) truly address the needs of such people? Do they need to be freed from their suspicion of the church institution in order to share its faith-vision? Or is their suspicion of the church institution appropriate, and do they need a faith that allows them to find hope and meaning for life as disciples not only within the church but also (and primarily?) beyond its confines?

Comparing Your Reading with Reading D: Discipleship as Imitating Christ Requires Having the Eyes of Faith – Matthew 5:3–12 as Transformative Words

What Kind of Teaching Do the Beatitudes Offer to Believers Today According to Reading D?

If your interpretation is somewhat related to Reading D, you brought to the beatitudes your concern that, in your present situation (for me, in European and North American societies), people are constantly lured to follow and imitate false prophets — unworthy leaders, be it in the social, political, economic, cultural, or religious realms. With this contextual frame, you concluded that believers learn from the beatitudes how to discern those who are trustworthy leaders by imitating Jesus, who discerned those who are the truly blessed ones. As disciples, believers are then called to follow those whom they have identified as truly manifesting God's will in their lives.

Reading D and Reading C are related, because both emphasize discipleship as imitation. But, as we will see, the view of imitation is quite different, in part because the contextual frame is not the same. Reading C presupposes that people lack and need a vision of life — a symbolic world — primarily established and embodied by a community. In order to have meaning for their life, people need to be members of such a community and to conform to its vision of life. Thus, the problem is that in the present secular culture, too many people lack such a vision of life, because they do not belong to the community of disciples. By contrast, Reading D presupposes that people's lives are primarily shaped through personal relationship with other individuals who influence them in some aspect of their lives either through words or deeds. Since anyone is, for better or for worse, influenced by all kinds of persons, without proper discernment one is bound to fall under bad influences. Thus, for Reading D, the problem that forms the contextual frame is that too many people do not know how to discern between trustworthy people (true leaders or prophets) and untrustworthy people (false leaders or prophets) who mislead them. To what extent do the beatitudes offer a solution for this problem? By proclaiming that certain people are blessed, Jesus demonstrates how to discern people who are trustworthy, and thus teaches reader-believers how to discern for themselves those people whose influence they should welcome and whose example they should follow.

The use of such a contextual frame is potentially appropriate. This teaching is not projected onto the text. Indeed, it soon becomes clear that the discernment taught by the beatitudes is in tension with the kind of discernment practiced in contemporary Western societies (and possibly elsewhere).

How Do Believer-Readers Make Sense of the Beatitudes According to Reading D?

The Views of Discipleship Used to Make Sense of the Beatitudes: Discerning the Manifestations of God and of God's Will in Life

If your interpretation is most directly related to Reading D, you have brought to the text a view of discipleship as imitating Christ, as in Reading C. Yet in this case the focus is different. According to Reading C, reader-believers should imitate Jesus' behavior because Jesus has displayed through his ministry and passion the attitudes and behavior described in the beatitudes (poverty in spirit, meekness, etc.). Jesus offers his own behavior as a model to be imitated by all members of the community, an imitation that requires sharing with the rest of the community the vision of the kingdom and of God's love as expressed by the beatitudes. By contrast, here, in Reading D, it is the way Jesus recognized blessed ones in the poor in spirit, the meek, etc. that reader-believers should imitate. Through this hermeneutical frame, discipleship and imitation of Christ are a matter of having the eyes of faith by which one can wisely discern manifestations of the kingdom and of God's will in one's present.

People need to learn to have such discernment because, in any given situation, it is far from obvious who are the blessed ones. Who would have thought that blessed ones are to be found among those whom we readily despise? Among those who have no self-confidence (poor in spirit) and are alienated from their loved ones (mourning)? Among the weaklings, who do not resist evil (meek)? Among the marginals, who are invisible to us (those who hunger and thirst for justice)? Among those who neglect religious, family, and job duties because of excessive compassion for others (merciful)? Among the naive (pure in heart), including those who are always ready to compromise instead of asserting their rights (peacemakers), and those who are persecuted and mocked because of their idealistic commitments to justice and the gospel of the kingdom (5:3–12)? And possibly, among people whom we despise for many other reasons?

Reader-believers who identify such models are like the wise housebuilder: they are in a position to build their lives on a solid foundation (7:24–27). The problem is that they do not know how to discern in their midst those who are truly the blessed ones. They are not wise. In sum, they need to learn from Jesus the practical wisdom that he used in the Sermon on the Mount for discerning how to serve God faithfully.

From this perspective the beatitudes (and the entire Sermon on the Mount) neither teach reader-believers what they should do (Reading A), nor entice them to do it (Reading B), nor provide them with ideal (eschatological) models of behavior to imitate as they strive for the kingdom (Reading C). Rather, the beatitudes teach reader-believers to discern models in less than ideal situations such as poverty, depression, abusive contexts. Because these models are less than ideal (being poor or oppressed is never a virtue in itself!), the blessed ones and their situations are not to be emulated. As has often been noted, Matthew avoids glorifying poverty when, in the first beatitude, he speaks of the "poor in spirit" instead of the "poor" (as in Luke 6:20). It is despite their dire situations (and not because of them) that Jesus recognizes something good and solid in those who are depressed, alienated from their loved ones, weaklings, deprived of justice, excessively compassionate, naive, peacemakers, persecuted, and mocked. Nevertheless, when such people are considered through Jesus' eyes, it appears that the goodness they display is so good and solid that it can and should be the sound foundation upon which disciples build their lives and ministries (see 7:24–27).

Some brief illustrations from my own experience might help clarify this important characteristic of the teaching of the beatitudes according to Reading D. In the Philippines, I had the privilege of visiting people in squatter camps and in sweatshops — people who live "on the edge," struggling to survive in the midst of deep poverty. Obviously, their situation is far from ideal and their lives are far from being models that disciples should strive to duplicate in their entirety. But among them I met blessed ones. Blessed is the woman in a squatter camp whom we asked for directions and who welcomed us into her makeshift home, offering us a glass of Coca-Cola when she saw our hesitation to accept the lemonade she had prepared with polluted water — she had sent one of her children to buy a bottled drink, even though she often has to prostitute herself to feed her children. Blessed is the woman who rejoiced in her long-awaited pregnancy, even as she worried that her baby might be harmed by the chemical-laced air she breathes in the sweatshop that she has organized and manages in order to help her village survive. Blessed is the seminarian who "fasted" and studied, avoiding a potlatch dinner with his classmates because he was ashamed that he had nothing to contribute to it. Similarly, elsewhere in the world, blessed is the student who is totally confused and frustrated because he cannot make up his mind between the heartfelt teaching he perceives in the Sermon on the Mount and the interpretation that his analytical training requires from him. Blessed are the homeless persons I saw taking care of each other in the park as I walked to my office. Blessed are the colleagues and pastors who make themselves vulnerable by sharing the tragedies and weaknesses with which they struggle in their ministries. That they are blessed does not mean that disciples should strive to duplicate their experiences and their behavior. None of them is perfect. None of them is in a situation that is a blessing. Poverty in any form is always a curse that generates more oppression and self-destructive attitudes. But each of them exhibits a quality — a virtue, a practical behavior — that should be part of the foundation of our life as disciples. This is why they are blessed.

Yet, in order to recognize the blessedness manifested in their responses to their dire situations, I needed to imitate Christ; I needed
to learn from the beatitudes how to discern blessed ones.

The View of the Moral Life Presupposed by This Understanding of Discipleship

Reading D involves, therefore, bringing to the text a certain view
about discipleship, and together with it a specific view of the moral
life. As was the case with Reading C, these views are found in perfectionist ethical theories, even though instead of emphasizing the
resocialization into a symbolic world (Reading C), the stress is now
on moral discernment. As Ogletree explains,

> Perfectionist theories stress the remoteness of value concepts
> and moral principles from concrete experience. If we are to
> apprehend what is going on in concrete situations and re-
> spond appropriately to them, we need more than our abstract
> moral notions, no matter how clear and precise they may
> be. We need *a developed capacity for moral discernment;* we
> need prudence, "practical wisdom" (Aristotle).[24]

From this perspective, to be a moral agent is to have character
(*ēthos*), including moral discernment (a sound eye, 6:22–23), pru-
dence, practical wisdom (being "wise as serpents and innocent as
doves," we need to beware of false leaders; see 10:16; 7:15). It is
not simply a matter of intellectually learning this wisdom — that
would be learning about virtues as abstract moral notions instead
of learning to be virtuous by being trained how to do one's functions well (a rough definition of virtue) in the process of character
formation.[25] Learning to be virtuous — to be disciples — is a matter of discerning good ways of doing things in concrete situations.
Here, as above (in Reading C), the acquisition of practical wisdom
involves apprenticeship. But instead of learning how to practice
virtues,[26] apprentices here learn how to practice moral discernment
as they imitate their master.

How the Beatitudes Transform a Discernment-Perfectionist View of the Moral Life

Adopting Reading D involves making sense of the beatitudes
in terms of a perfectionist view of the moral life that emphasizes discernment and a view of discipleship as imitating Jesus'
discernment. This is appropriate, inasmuch as the beatitudes radically challenge the discernment and practical wisdom acquired

primarily, at least in Western cultures, through formal academic training that most often calls for a detached, scientific, objective, rational approach, even in matters concerning human interactions. There are of course notable exceptions, related to the postmodern reaction against the dehumanizing character of such objective approaches. Yet, even in cases where the "mystery of the other" is already emphasized — for instance, in such fields as religious studies, theology, women's studies, cultural studies, philosophy, and some of the social sciences — the beatitudes and their teaching about discernment provide a much needed focus on the mysterious blessedness to be found in the radical otherness of those whom we ignore because they are too different from us.

What Is the Textual Evidence on Which Reading D Is Grounded?

The Beatitudes as Transformative Words: Thematic Features That Challenge the Reader-Hearers' Perception of Life around Them

This teaching regarding the transformation of the hearer-readers (transformation from people without discernment to people with discernment) is readily grounded upon the beatitudes. When these verses are read as an integral part of the Sermon on the Mount, it is clear that they contribute to the transformative thrust of this text, that is, to the dimension of the text that aims at transforming characters within it (here, the crowds and disciples) as well as implied readers (readers as inscribed in the text) and actual readers (when they identify with the implied readers). From the perspective of this analytical frame, the thematic features of the text are the most significant ones, because they express how certain views that the hearer-implied readers had about a given theme at the beginning of the discourse are transformed by the end of it.

Elucidation of the thematic-transformative thrust dimension of the beatitudes involves: (1) identifying the thematic organization of the Sermon on the Mount, and (2) studying the thematic features of the beatitudes.

(1) The thematic organization of the Sermon on the Mount begins to appear when one compares 5:1–2, which describes Jesus as beginning to teach ("opening his mouth," 5:2 [literally translated]) with 7:28–29, which states that Jesus concluded his teaching ("when Jesus had finished saying these things," 7:28). This is a first thematic transformation (or "inverted parallelism"), which

delimits the Sermon on the Mount as a thematic unit. Another transformation underscores that there is a twofold audience for the Sermon on the Mount: in 5:1–2, the Sermon is addressed to the disciples, with the crowds as, at best, second-rank addressees; in 7:28–29, only the crowds are depicted as responding to Jesus' teaching.[27] Jesus' relation to his audience and the composition of this audience are significant thematic features.

Since the framework of the Sermon on the Mount underscores that it has two kinds of audience, we must account for the shift from impersonal style (5:3–10, addressed to the crowds) to personal style (5:11–7:20, addressed to "you," the intimate group of disciples) and then back to impersonal style (7:21–27). Thus, we need to ponder the transformation marked by the differences between the introduction, 5:3–10 (not 5:3–12), and the conclusion, 7:21–27.

Matthew 5:3–10 and 7:21–27 are parallel, in part through their impersonal style, and are set in inverted parallelisms (the transformation) through their respective forms: words of blessing (beatitudes, 5:3–10) and words of judgment that include both condemnation and blessing (the final judgment, 7:21–27). Condemnation is for those not doing Jesus' teaching ("everyone who hears these words of mine and does not act upon them," 7:26) and for "evildoers" (7:23). Blessing, which means entering the kingdom, is for those who are doing the will of Jesus' Father (7:21). Consequently, the features of the beatitudes (5:3–10) that set up the parallelism are the description of the blessing as entrance into the kingdom ("theirs is the kingdom of heaven," 5:3, 10) and the description of the proper acts (being poor in spirit, mourning, etc.) as Jesus' expression of God' will — thus, what one needs to do in order to enter the kingdom, namely, righteousness (5:6).

This preliminary identification of the theme of the Sermon on the Mount gives us a clue for identifying the thematic subunits. The thematic organization of the Sermon on the Mount (identified in my commentary) is summarized in the schema on p. 105.

(2) The beatitudes are the preliminary expression of a theme to be transformed by the Sermon on the Mount. A discourse transforms the intended readers' view of a theme by first presenting it in a way readers will welcome (e.g., the introduction might emphasize the familiar or enticing) and then leading them toward a different perception of this theme, most directly expressed in the conclusion.

Here, the Sermon on the Mount first invites its readers to share in the euphoric vision of the beatitudes (5:3–10) — something they

A1 — 5:3–10. Beatitudes. Characteristics of the Disciples
  B1 — 5:11–16. The Disciples' Vocation
    C1 — 5:17–19. Conditions for Implementing the Vocation
      D1 — 5:20. Introduction of Antitheses
        E1 — 5:21–47. Antitheses: Overabundant Righteousness
      D2 — 5:47–48. Conclusion of Antitheses
      D3 — 6:1. Introduction to Next Unit
        E2 — 6:2–18. Overabundant Righteousness
      D4 — 6:19–21. Conclusion of Preceding Unit
    C2 — 6:22–7:12. Conditions for Implementing the Vocation
  B2 — 7:13–20. The Disciples' Vocation
A2 — 7:21–27. Judgment Scene. Characteristics of the Disciples

readily do — in order to lead them to accept the transformation of their view of an essential issue embedded in the beatitudes. The conclusion, the judgment scene (7:21–27), identifies this essential issue by contrasting those who say "Lord, Lord" and do not do the will of Jesus' Father (7:21a; or those who hear Jesus' words and do not do them, 7:26) with those who say "Lord, Lord" and do the will of his Father (7:21b; or those who hear his words and do them, 7:24).[28]

What is the difference between false disciples (who merely say "Lord, Lord" and do not do his teaching) and true disciples (who do what he taught them)? What makes them behave in such radically different ways? The concluding parable of the houses built on rock and on sand (7:24–27) expresses it by contrasting a wise man (7:24), that is, a man with practical wisdom, because he has moral discernment, with a foolish man (7:26), who lacks such wisdom and discernment. The wise man discerned what would be a good foundation for the house: solid rock rather than unstable sand. Such discernment distinguishes people who are blessed and will withstand the flood of the last judgment from those who will be destroyed by it: the blessed identify the rock that can serve as a good foundation and build on it.

According to this thematic reading, acquiring and practicing here and now an appropriate moral discernment is the most significant feature of discipleship. One needs to use this discernment here and now, because at the time of the judgment-flood it will be too late to do anything to correct the situation. The Sermon on the Mount does affirm the eschatological context of discipleship and the blessing or condemnation that disciples will receive at the last judgment. But the primary goal of the Sermon is to teach its readers about the importance of moral discernment (practical wisdom), and more specifically, the importance of identifying the good foundation upon which one's life-house must be based.

Faithful disciples (who do Jesus' teaching, 7:24; and God's will, 7:21) are people who know how to discern the hidden good (the foundation of a person's life), before it is revealed at the judgment. They know how to recognize those words that one should do — Jesus' words and the expressions of God's will. They already, here and now, use the same discernment that the Judge will use at the end of time, and thus do not stop at appearances when they evaluate someone.

In this way, they know not only how to discern a good foundation (rock) from a bad one (sand), but also a good builder from a bad one. Similarly, they know how to identify people who are models of discipleship to be followed and imitated. Indeed, one who says "Lord, Lord," prophesies, casts out demons, and performs other miracles in the name of Jesus (7:21–23), might be a disciple whom one should take as a model. But not necessarily! It all depends on whether or not this person does God's will, that is, if this person truly uses moral discernment and finds a solid foundation for his or her life.

As one ponders the beatitudes (5:3–10) from the perspective of the judgment scene (7:21–27), it soon appears that, despite the beatitudes' euphoric character, they are directly related to moral discernment. By proclaiming the beatitudes, Jesus exemplifies true moral discernment. Thus, the beatitudes provide readers with the lenses they need in order to have the true discernment that characterizes faithful discipleship.

In each beatitude the description of the behavior or attitude (e.g., "poor in spirit," "peacemaker") is a description of doing Jesus' words and God's will, that is, an example of building upon a good foundation. The choice of such behavior does not appear, at first glance, to be wise (to say the least), just as the foundations of the houses remain hidden until the flood. Yet the description of the eschatological blessing (e.g., "theirs is the kingdom," "they will be called children of God") reveals that the choice of this kind of behavior was wise indeed, in the same way that the flood reveals which house is actually built on the sound foundation, the rock. In the present, when there is no flood, the blessed ones choose a certain kind of behavior, because already now they discern that it is the will of God and thus that it is the kind of behavior that will withstand the judgment.

Thus, among those who have no self-confidence ("poor in spirit," 5:3), disciples with true discernment should recognize blessed ones who do not assert their own will, because inwardly they have made God's will their own will (cf. 7:21).[29] They belong to the kingdom of heaven, since they submit to the yoke of heaven. Similarly, among those who are persecuted, disciples can recognize blessed ones who are "persecuted for righteousness' sake" (5:10), that is, those who have made God's will (righteousness and justice) their own will, no matter what the consequences — "theirs is the kingdom." Similarly, for all the beatitudes. Disciples with true discernment should recognize that

- Among people who "mourn" (5:4) because they are alienated from their loved ones who demanded their allegiance there are blessed ones who are in such a situation because of their total commitment to the kingdom and God's justice, and because of their confidence that true comfort (from God) will be given to them: "they will be comforted."

- Among people who are "meek" (5:5) and who do not assert their rights when others want to take advantage of them there are blessed ones who respond this way because they are confident that their rights will nevertheless be asserted: "they will inherit the earth."

- Among people who "hunger and thirst for righteousness or justice" (5:6) there are blessed ones who eagerly look at everything around them for signs of God's righteousness; these blessed ones are people who seek to discern manifestations of God's righteousness, because inwardly they are confident that they will find such manifestations: "they will be filled."

- Among people who neglect religious, family, and work duties because of excessive compassion for others ("the merciful," 5:7) there are blessed ones who do so because inwardly they are confident that "they will receive mercy" (from God).

- Among naive people ("the pure in heart," 5:8) there are blessed ones who have undivided devotion to God (cf. 6:2–6) because inwardly they are confident that "they will see God."

- Among people who are always ready to compromise instead of asserting their rights ("peacemakers," 5:9) there are blessed ones who seek reconciliation at all costs and love their enemies because inwardly they know that they are children of God (cf. 5:44–48) and thus are confident that "they will be called children of God" (by God and by others).

All these are blessed ones, models of discipleship, in the sense that the good the disciples perceive in the lives of these people is the solid ground upon which disciples should build their lives and ministry (see 7:24–27), or, to use another metaphor, these blessed ones are the light that the disciples should lift up so as to give light to all in the house (see 5:15).

One might wonder where one should expect to find such blessed ones. The impersonal form ("they") of the beatitudes suggests that one can expect to find such models of discipleship anywhere in society, and not only in the church.

A Step in the Process of Assuming Responsibility for Our Interpretations

I could repeat about Reading D most of what I said about Reading C and the way in which its study helped all of us progress in our quest to assume responsibility for our own faith-interpretations.

This analysis helped the proponents of Reading D to gain a critical perspective on their faith-interpretations by making explicit the three kinds of interpretive frames they used: their contextual frame (the problem of the bad influences upon our lives when we do not know how to discern between good and bad leaders or prophets), their hermeneutical frame (imitating Christ's discernment as a way to be disciples with true practical wisdom), and their analytical frame (focusing on the transformative thrust of the thematic features of the text). Then it becomes clear that the distinctive feature of this kind of teaching is that believers today should learn from this text how to discern manifestations of the kingdom and of God's will anywhere in their present situations (and not only in the church) and that they should make these manifestations the foundation of their own lives as disciples and the center of their ministry (the light they should lift up to illuminate the whole house).

For proponents of other readings, this study of Reading D is another step toward assuming responsibility for their own faith-interpretations, because it demands that they recognize that by choosing another interpretation they have rejected Reading D, among others. This raises some questions to be addressed.

What is at stake when we choose, as an analytical frame, a structural method aimed at elucidating the transformative thrust of the text? Addressing this question involves recognizing that in order to have a sharp picture of the transformative thrust of the text, we should block out the other textual dimensions: the text as window, the text as story, and the text as symbolic message.

What is at stake when we adopt as the hermeneutical frame used to enter into dialogue with the text and make sense of it, a view of discipleship emphasizing the need to have eyes of faith through which one discerns manifestations of the kingdom and of God's will in the midst of the ambivalence of daily life? Is it more or less plausible than the other hermeneutical frames we discussed? Does this view of discipleship and of the moral life make sense in the cultural situations in which we find ourselves? Or is there another one that is more plausible?

Finally, what is at stake when we choose as a contextual frame the situations of people — including believers — who are lured to follow and imitate unworthy leaders ("false prophets") in the social, political, economic, cultural, or religious realms? Is this a major problem in our life-contexts? Or is the most pressing problem one of the others we discussed above? Or still another one?

Assuming responsibility for our faith-interpretations, whatever they might be, requires addressing such questions.

Comparing Your Reading with Reading E: Discipleship as Struggling for the Kingdom and God's Justice – Matthew 5:3–12 as Subversive Message

What Kind of Teaching Do the Beatitudes Offer to Believers Today According to Reading E?

Lastly, if your interpretation is most directly related to Reading E, you have brought to the beatitudes concerns arising from concrete situations in which people, including Christian believers, are powerless, in the sense that they have no control over their own lives; that they are deprived (of justice and the bare necessities of life); that they are oppressed; that they suffer (mourn) and thirst for justice. Even if we personally feel very much in control of our lives, none of us, unfortunately, can say that this contextual frame is un-realistic; the powerless, the deprived, the oppressed, the poor are always with us (Matt. 26:11), whether near or far, whether we acknowledge them or not.

The question then is: Do the beatitudes offer an actual solution for such a problem? Do they truly address the needs of actual poor people? Are they not exclusively dealing with the poor in spirit, that is, with people who have chosen a humble attitude, and are therefore very much in control of their lives? Is it not the case that the beatitudes present people with a good ethical attitude when they speak of the meek, those who mourn, those who thirst and hunger for righteousness (or perhaps, justice)? This is a plausible reading (look back at Readings A and B). Yet, as we will see be-low, the beatitudes can also be read as referring to the situations of people who are concretely poor and who as a consequence are also poor in spirit (that is, depressed) and of people who are struggling for justice (rather than righteousness). Thus, it is also plausible to read this text as a call for solidarity with the poor that is addressed to believers who are not themselves poor.

How Do Believer-Readers Make Sense of the Beatitudes According to Reading E?

Discipleship as Empowerment to Struggle for the Kingdom and God's Justice

If your interpretation is related to Reading E, you have brought to the text a view of discipleship as struggling for the kingdom and God's justice; through the ministry of the disciples, people who are powerless are empowered by God to participate in this struggle. In so doing, you have brought to the text a view of the moral life emphasizing that, in many contexts, people are totally powerless (unable) to do God's will, because they are deprived of the bare ne-cessities of life and are the victims of injustice, oppression, and/or discrimination of one kind or another.

Though they might know God's will (Reading A), might want to do it, because it involves devotion to a just cause (Reading B), might have faith in God's loving care and in the coming king-dom (Reading C), and might discern with the eyes of faith models of righteousness to be lifted up so that they might illuminate the whole house (Reading D), nevertheless, people who have no con-trol over their own lives and are powerless to care for their loved ones cannot envision a practice of discipleship divorced from their daily struggle for survival and justice. Any conception of discipleship that fails to have as its primary agenda the empowerment of the powerless would be a scandalous escapism that accepts the status quo and thus implicitly condones injustice and oppression. Conversely, for other members of the church, as long as the poor are with us — and are they not always with us (Matt. 26:11)? — discipleship must involve solidarity with the poor, the oppressed, and the marginalized. Otherwise, discipleship and the church become a parody of themselves and mock the gospel.[30]

From the perspective of this hermeneutical frame, the beatitudes empower the powerless to become agents of the kingdom and of God's justice, by revealing that for them God reigns, by promising that God will console them and give them justice and the land in possession, by affirming their identity as children of God, and by confirming that they suffer for the sake of justice. These powerful and liberating words help them to recognize that their oppression is neither a fate nor a punishment, but an injustice that contradicts God's justice and kingdom. Similarly, the beatitudes call and empower other members of the community of disciples to live in solidarity with the powerless.[31]

The View of the Moral Life Presupposed by This View of Discipleship

If you have chosen such a reading, you implicitly made sense of this text and of its teaching for believers by understanding discipleship in terms of a liberation and/or political view of the moral life, such as the one formulated in Latin America by Enrique Dussel[32] and in India by George Soares-Prabhu.[33]

This view of the moral life acknowledges human frailty. The primary human predicament is powerlessness, or inability, because we are again and again under the power of entities beyond our control.[34] The basic pattern of this ethical perspective is the same whether the entity putting human beings in bondage is primarily spiritual (e.g., demonic forces), political (e.g., martial law), economic (e.g., multinational economic systems), cultural (e.g., neocolonialism, sexism), or a combination of these.[35] In all cases, individuals and communities are coopted by what oppresses them, so much so that they often become accomplices of their oppressors. Even though they struggle against the powers that subjugate them, without outside help — from a biblical perspective, without help from God — they are unable to escape the bondage in which they find themselves.

From this perspective, the poor to whom the beatitudes refer are "poor in spirit" — depressed (5:3) and discouraged (5:4) because they are dispossessed of their land (which will be given back to them, 5:5), of their inheritance, and thus of their identity (so they are promised a new identity, 5:9). Such persons are neither the cause of their own misfortunes (e.g., as if they were lazy, as in Prov. 6:6–11; 10:4) nor the victims of unavoidable disasters. Rather they are victims of injustice — economically exploited and thus afflicted, destitute, and alienated. Yet, they are not passive victims. They aspire to justice. They are hungry and thirsty for justice (5:6); that is, they seek God's justice, or better yet, struggle for it (6:33). Thus, from a Marxist perspective, one can say that they belong to the class of people who are victims of avoidable injustice and violent oppression by the strong, like the injustice denounced by the prophets (e.g., Amos 4:1, 8:4–6; Isa. 3:14ff., 10:2; Hab. 3:14).[36] With Soares-Prabhu, we can conclude that a Marxist interpretation is appropriate to help us recognize that the beatitudes are not speaking of spiritual poverty, but rather of avoidable poverty that results from political, social, and economic injustices, rooted in ideological (and thus cultural) factors. From this perspective the beatitudes challenge the ideology that empowers the oppressors. No, it is not the rich, the secure, the self-confident who belong to the kingdom of heaven; rather it is the poor, the exploited, the destitute. Through this challenge of the dominant ideology, the beatitudes empower the poor and call them to continue their struggle for justice, knowing that God is on their side.

Other socioeconomic structures are emphasized by Michael Crosby.[37] The very fact that the Sermon on the Mount uses as one of its key metaphors the house (the two housebuilders in 7:24–27; the entire house lit by the light put on a lampstand, 5:15) and the patriarchal household (through ongoing references to father and children and their relationships) helps us recognize that the beatitudes and the rest of the Sermon on the Mount challenge traditional social structures by proposing the household of God, the kingdom of heaven, as an alternative to these structures.

Similarly, the political dimension of the beatitudes and of the rest of the Sermon on the Mount is apparent from the use of the political terminology of the kingdom (*basileia*), which offers an alternative to the Roman empire and its political structures: the kingdom of heaven as a different order according to God's will.

In sum, read from the perspective of a sociopolitical view of the moral life, the beatitudes challenge the existing oppressive order in its economic, socioeconomic, and political dimensions, empowering the poor to become agents of transformation as they struggle for justice, and calling other disciples to solidarity with the poor.

How the Beatitudes Transform the Sociopolitical Views of the Moral Life

Is there any need to emphasize that the beatitudes challenge the sociopolitical views of the moral life that we bring to them? It is clear that, while Marxist class analysis is most helpful in identifying the sociopolitical reality reflected by the beatitudes, the beatitudes' solution to this problem directly challenges Marxism, since God and God's justice play the decisive role in the subversive program of solidarity. Similarly, the socioeconomic models used by Crosby are most helpful for recognizing the economic dimensions of the beatitudes and of the Sermon on the Mount, but the exclusively materialist character of these models is put into question. As is already clear (and will become clearer as we pursue this reading of the Sermon), the beatitudes directly challenge the ideologies and value systems embodied in the secular political, economic, and social structures of societies today, as is also the case with the other readings.

What Is the Textual Evidence on Which Reading E Is Grounded?

The Significant Dimension of the Beatitudes: Subversive Thrust and Voices from the Margin

The textual basis for the preceding interpretation of the beatitudes is readily recognizable as soon as one reads them for their subversive thrust and voices from the margin. The legitimacy of this evidence involves paying close attention to the social, economic, political, and religious structures of authority presupposed, advocated, or rejected by the beatitudes, to the traces of struggles for justice behind and within the text, as well as to the voices in the text that reflect a different social and cultural construction of reality. Here it is enough to review Crosby's main conclusions concerning these features of the text in his book *House of Disciples: Church, Economics, and Justice in Matthew.*[38]

First, the word "blessed" is appropriately translated "helped" (as proposed by Alice Walker, although Crosby does not use this translation),[39] because Matthew underscores the empowering authority (*exousia*) of Jesus' teaching. "Because the members of the house church are blessed (with *exousia*), they can live the beatitudes."

Regarding the first beatitude, one first needs to recognize in the poor in spirit voices from the margin who are commonly silenced in other interpretations. The term "poor in spirit" need not be read as referring to an ethical attitude (although it can be); it can also be read as referring to the condition of actual poor people. As Luise Schottroff says, "It is not only hunger, lament, and disease but also the inability to praise God that crushes the poor to the ground, so that they are poor to the core, 'in spirit' (Matt. 5:3)."[40] Thus, Crosby can conclude, "Since the reign [of God] represents participation in the authority of the heavenly Father, those who are poor in spirit already share in the reality." From the perspective of the household economics of the Gospel according to Matthew (and according to Isa. 61:1–3, to which Matthew alludes), those who are thus empowered — the poor in spirit — are those who recognize their powerlessness and thus "their own need for God" and "dependence on God," and those "who dedicate their lives to work for a reordering of God's creation." From the same perspective, those who mourn are those who protest evil and injustice and recognize "the need to work for a reversal of some present form of status which oppresses." The economic dimension of the third beatitude, "Blessed are the meek, for they will inherit the *land*" (5:5), is clear as soon as one translates the promise as referring to the inheritance of the land (rather than the earth). The subversive thrust of this beatitude makes it clear that "land in its forms of power, possessions, and prestige can be approached in one of two ways: meekness, which grounds all life in God, or violence, which bases all life in greed and obsession for more power." The fourth beatitude, regarding "satisfaction from hungering and thirsting for justice" (5:6), refers to economic reality not only in its mention of justice, but also in its metaphor of hunger and thirst, which points to the basic human needs for daily bread (or rice!) and water. Those who order their justice, that is, their relationships with God and other people, according to God's plan are blessed.

While for Crosby this first set of beatitudes primarily empowers hearers for solidarity with the poor and oppressed (because Matthew addressed a wealthy church), these verses also apply to and empower the poor and oppressed themselves, because for them God reigns, as Bravo Gallardo emphasizes.[41] This becomes apparent as soon as one pays attention to the subversive thrust expressed in the very center of Jesus' message. As Wainwright says (with a caution aimed at signaling that this is one plausible reading among others), "Jesus' mission to call God's people back to God's purpose symbolized as *basileia* [kingdom] would probably be met with resistance, would create tension," because it is the prophetic proclamation of God's alternative (social, economic, political) order for life.[42]

Crosby continues: "Like the first four beatitudes, each *makarism* [beatitude] in the second group reveals dimensions of justice." These dimensions of justice call for solidarity with the poor and oppressed and "a new reciprocity in mercy" (5:7), with "a vision of God grounded in purity of heart" (5:8) — which, I add, includes not being ashamed of one's association with the poor and oppressed. This solidarity with the poor also entails peacemaking (5:9) and being persecuted for justice's sake (5:10). "In summary, we can say that those who justly reorder their relationships and resources are those whose households will be blessed."

In sum, once again, these brief remarks (which should be complemented by consulting Crosby's work) show that your interpretation is well grounded in textual evidence if it is comparable to Reading E.

A Step in the Process of Assuming Responsibility for Our Interpretations

This study helped the proponents of Reading E to gain a critical perspective on their faith-interpretations by making explicit the three kinds of interpretive frames they used: a contextual frame (the problem of powerlessness), a hermeneutical frame (discipleship as being empowered to struggle for the kingdom and God's justice, either as a socially and economically powerless person or as a person adopting a life of solidarity with the poor, with a liberation view of the moral life), and an analytical frame (focusing on the subversive thrust of the text and its voices from the margin). Then it becomes clear that the distinctive feature of this kind of teaching for believers today is that they are people who have been empowered by God, because by oneself one is unable to carry on one's vocation as disciple — struggling for the kingdom and God's justice.

For the proponents of other readings, this study of Reading E is another step toward assuming responsibility for their own faith-interpretations, because it demands that they recognize that by choosing another interpretation they have rejected Reading E, among others. This raises questions to be addressed.

What is at stake when we choose, as an analytical frame, a sociopolitical method aimed at elucidating the subversive thrust of the text and its voices from the margin? Addressing this question involves recognizing that in order to form a sharp picture of this subversive thrust of the text and to hear clearly its voices from the margin, we should block out the other textual dimensions: the text as window, story, symbolic message, and transformative word.

What is at stake when we adopt, as the hermeneutical frame used to enter into dialogue with the text and make sense of it, a view of discipleship emphasizing the need for empowerment? Is this choice more or less plausible than the other hermeneutical frames we discussed?

Finally, what is at stake when we choose, as a contextual frame, our own powerlessness and/or the presence of the poor, the oppressed, the powerless among us? Can we in good conscience ignore this problem? Is this truly the most basic problem in our life-contexts? Or is poverty, oppression, and powerlessness the consequence of a more basic problem?

Assuming responsibility for our faith-interpretations, whatever they might be, involves addressing such questions about each faith-interpretation we encounter. There is a high probability that, as was the case with the five faith-interpretations discussed in the preceding pages, these other faith-interpretations can also be shown to be appropriately grounded upon one or another dimension of the text, making sense of the beatitudes in terms of one or another view of discipleship and one or another view of the moral life.[43] Yet, recognition of the legitimacy of a multiplicity of faith-interpretations appears only when one notices that formulations of these interpretations often confuse the three interpretive frames. Believers, especially when they feel threatened in their faith, do not hesitate to justify the contextual teaching of the text for them today by claiming it is a "literal" rendering of "what the author meant to say," as if they had not interpreted it in an effort to address contextual problems and had not entered into dialogue with it through a hermeneutical frame. But believers should not feel threatened by a critical study such as the one presented in this book. Its goal is to help them assume responsibility for their faith-interpretations, so that they might indeed claim, "I believe this teaching of the text is the Word of God for us."

Such a confession of faith about our faith-interpretations presupposes that we read the text *as Scripture.* As can be expected, we are using differing views of Scripture in our interpretations. In the following chapters, our examination of faith-interpretations of Matt. 5: 17–48 will give us the opportunity to consider the diversity of roles that Scripture plays in any faith-interpretation of a biblical text.

Part 2

Assuming Responsibility for Our Views of Scripture and Their Roles in Our Interpretations of Matthew 5:17–48 and 7:12

Chapter Five

Discipleship as Fulfilling Scripture
Matthew 5:17–48 and 7:12

What Is the Teaching of Matthew 5:17–48 and 7:12 about the Role of Scripture for Believers Today?

A Different Focus for Our Readings

Once again, I begin by asking you to read from the Sermon on the Mount: Matt. 5:17–48 and 7:12. Yet, this time, I ask you to read this text for its teaching for believers today about the role of Scripture, rather than about discipleship. Once again, I will present the conclusions of five readings, as well as a preliminary analysis of these conclusions. You will be asked to conduct a parallel analysis of your own interpretation. Yet, this time, the procedures for the preliminary analysis will need to include new questions.

In order to formulate and analyze each interpretation of the teaching of a biblical text about discipleship, it was most helpful to identify the problem in the believer-readers' life-situation for which this teaching about discipleship provided a solution and thus transformed some aspect of the believer-readers' life. The contextual emphasis of this procedure was appropriate, because reading a text for its teaching about discipleship for believers today is primarily focused on a pragmatic, contextual issue.

This contextual procedure is also appropriate here, because we are once again dealing with the teaching of a text for believers today. Thus, as we read Matt. 5:17–48 and 7:12 and examine interpretations of these verses, it is appropriate to ask: What is the problem that this text's teaching about Scripture helps to address in the believer-readers' concrete situation? We can even ask more directly: How does this teaching help address the problem we previously identified (in chapter 3) as presupposed by each reading? In this way we will build upon what we have learned from our readings of the beatitudes.

But we need to ask additional questions, because this teaching about the role of Scripture also concerns hermeneutical issues. As we noted in chapter 2, when a text is considered as Scripture by believer-readers, a trusting relationship is established. A genuine dialogue between text and readers — a hermeneutical dialogue — can then take place concerning a specific subject matter. Consequently, as we formulate and analyze each interpretation of the teaching of a biblical text about Scripture, it will be most helpful to identify the characteristics of the relationship between text and reader-believers that is posited by this teaching. More specifically we can ask: According to this interpretation, what kind of trusting relationship does Matt. 5:17–48 and 7:12 establish between a scriptural text and believer-readers? How does the teaching of Matt. 5:17–48 and 7:12 define the way believers should enter into dialogue with a Scriptural text? How is the relationship, the *correspondence*, between scriptural text and believer-readers (and their experience) envisioned?[1] More concretely, I propose we address these questions in two ways:

- By proposing a metaphor for the way in which, according to each interpretation, the view of Scripture establishes a trusting relationship between text and believer-readers. I listed in chapter 2 some metaphors that are readily meaningful in Western cultures: lamp to my feet, canon, family album, good news, corrective glasses, empowering word, holy Scripture. Yet, let us remember that this list is neither normative nor complete.[2] Actually, we will find that the "holy Scripture" metaphor does not seem to apply to any of the teachings concerning Scripture in Matt. 5:17–48 and 7:12. In addition, you might need another metaphor for your own interpretation.

- By identifying the correspondence between text and the believer-readers' present experience reflected by the view of Scripture presented by each interpretation.

Assessing the Implications of These Different Views of Scripture: An Issue for Subsequent Chapters

Assuming responsibility for our interpretations will require from us to go beyond this preliminary analysis. As in preceding chapters, we will show that each interpretation is grounded on a specific textual dimension. But, in the present case, we also need to take stock of the fact that the very text offering believers diverse potential teachings about Scripture is itself Scripture for these same believers.

This situation will give us the opportunity to clarify the concrete implications of adopting one rather than another of the plausible teachings about Scripture. We will focus on two test cases, each dealing with a concrete and controversial issue: the passages about divorce (5:31–32) and about not resisting evil (5:38–42). We will repeatedly ask: For believers who read these passages in terms of any particular view of Scripture, what is the teaching about divorce? About not resisting evil? In this way we will prepare ourselves to assess the relative value of each of these teachings as a word to live by for believers in specific contexts.

Your Reading of Matthew 5:17–48 and 7:12 as Scripture: What Is Its Teaching about the Role of Scripture for Believers Today?

Please reread Matt. 5:17–48 and 7:12, keeping in mind the above question. Here is the text of the New Revised Standard Version, into which I introduce in brackets a few elements of alternative translations and some references to other biblical texts to which this passage refers.

5:17"**Do not think that I have come to abolish [abrogate, destroy] the law or the prophets; I have come not to abolish [abrogate, destroy] but to fulfill [do, perform, make complete, give true meaning].** 5:18**For truly I tell you, until heaven and earth pass away, not one letter, not one stroke of a letter, will pass from the law until all is accomplished [until all is accomplished by Jesus' death and resurrection? until the end of time? never?].** 5:19**Therefore, whoever breaks [does away with, transgresses] one of the least of these commandments, and teaches others to do the same, will be called least in the kingdom of heaven; but whoever does [practices] them and teaches them will be called great in the kingdom of heaven.** 5:20**For I tell you, unless your righteousness [justice] exceeds [is over and above, is more abundant, is superior to] that of the scribes and Pharisees, you will never enter the kingdom of heaven.**
    5:21"**You have heard that it was said to [by] those of ancient times [our ancestors], 'You shall not murder [kill]'; and 'whoever murders [kills] shall be liable to judgment' [Exod. 20:13; Deut. 16:18].** 5:22**But [And]**[3] **I say to you that if you are angry with a brother or sister [without cause],**[4] **you will be liable to judgment; and if you insult**

[say 'raca' to, say 'you stupid fool' to] a brother or sister, you will be liable to the council; and if you say, 'You fool,' you will be liable to the hell of fire. 5:23So when you are offering your gift at the altar, if you remember that your brother or sister has something against you, 5:24leave your gift there before the altar and go; first be reconciled to your brother or sister, and then come and offer your gift. 5:25Come to terms quickly with your accuser while you are on the way to court with him, or your accuser may hand you over [deliver you] to the judge, and the judge to the guard, and you will be thrown into prison. 5:26Truly I tell you, you will never get out until you have paid the last penny.

5:27"You have heard that it was said, 'You shall not commit adultery [cause a woman to become an adulteress]' [Exod. 20:14; Deut. 5:18]. 5:28But [And] I say to you that everyone who looks at a woman with lust [great desire, covetousness in his heart. 5:29If your right eye causes you to sin [makes you stumble, offends you], tear it out and throw it away; it is better for you to lose one of your members than for your whole body to be thrown into hell. 5:30And if your right hand causes you to sin [makes you stumble; offends you], cut it off and throw it away; it is better for you to lose one of your members than for your whole body to go into hell.

5:31"It was also said, 'Whoever divorces [sends away, dismisses] his wife, let him give her a certificate of divorce' [Deut. 24:1–4]. 5:32But [And] I say to you that anyone who divorces [sends away, dismisses] his wife, except on the ground of unchastity, causes her to commit adultery [to become an adulteress]; and whoever marries a divorced woman commits adultery [causes her to become an adulteress].

5:33"Again, you have heard that it was said to [by] those of ancient times [our ancestors], 'You shall not swear falsely, but carry out the vows you have made to the Lord' [Lev. 19:12; Num. 30:2; Deut. 23:21]. 5:34But [And] I say to you, Do not swear at all, either by heaven, for it is the throne of God, 5:35or by the earth, for it is his footstool, or by Jerusalem, for it is the city of the great King. 5:36And do not swear by your head, for you cannot make one hair white or black. 5:37Let your word be 'Yes, Yes' or 'No, No'; anything more than this comes from the evil one.

5:38"You have heard that it was said, 'An eye for an eye and a tooth for a tooth' [Exod. 21:23–24; Lev. 24:19–20; Deut. 19:21]. 5:39But [And] I say to you, Do not resist an evildoer [evil]. But if anyone strikes you on the right cheek, turn the other also; 5:40and if anyone wants to sue you and take your coat, give your cloak as well;

5:41and if anyone forces you to go one mile [one mile of compulsory service], go also the second mile. 5:42Give to everyone who begs from you, and do not refuse anyone who wants to borrow from you. 5:43"You have heard that it was said, 'You shall love your neighbor and hate your enemy.' 5:44But [And] I say to you, Love your enemies and pray for those who persecute you, 5:45so that you may be children of your Father in heaven; for he makes his sun rise on the evil and on the good, and sends rain on the righteous and on the unrighteous. 5:46For if you love those who love you, what reward do you have? Do not even the tax collectors do the same? 5:47And if you greet only your brothers and sisters, what more are you doing than others? Do not even the Gentiles do the same?

· ·

5:48"Be perfect, therefore, as your heavenly Father is perfect. 7:12"In everything do to others as you would have them do to you [Therefore all things whatsoever you would want others to do to you, do so to them];5 for this is the law and the prophets."

I suggest that you now take the time to write down in the space provided below a brief summary of your answer to the question: What do Christians learn from this text about the role of Scripture in their lives as disciples today? Beyond that, you might also want to ask: If believers allow Scripture to play a role for them, what will be the practical effects in their personal lives? In their community life? In their relations with others? What needs of Christian believers are addressed by the teaching of Matt. 5:17–48 and 7:12 about Scripture?

_____

_____

_____

_____

_____

_____

Comparing Your Conclusions with Those of Five Other Interpretations

To facilitate your recognition of the distinctiveness of your own interpretation, I invite you to compare your conclusions with those found in five other types of interpretations. As in the preceding chapters, my goal is to help you assume responsibility for your interpretation by becoming aware of the ways in which it differs from other interpretations and by verifying that its conclusions are properly grounded in the text.

To foster comparison of your interpretation with the five I present, I will make explicit in each case:

- *The Metaphor:* the view that best represents the trusting relationship established between text and believer-readers by a particular view of Scripture, and thus the function of Scripture for the believer-readers who accept this view.

- *The Problem:* the needs believers have in the situation we envisioned as we read Matt. 5:17–48 and 7:12.

- *The Solution:* the teaching of Matt. 5:17–48 and 7:12 about the role of Scripture that addresses these needs.

- *The Transformation:* the transforming effect that this teaching brings about in the believer-readers' lives — what is new for or about their lives in this teaching about the role of Scripture.

- *The Correspondence:* between text and the believer-readers' present experience reflected by this view of scripture.

Reading A1: Matthew 5:17–48 Offers Believers a Lamp to My Feet, the New Scripture-Law That They Should Implement in Their Individual Lives; Reading A2: Matthew 5:17–48 Offers Believers a Canon, a Rule for Community Life[6]

The Problem: In both the individual and communal versions of Reading A, one envisions people who live by the secular values of a Western capitalist culture or the (religious) values of a non-Christian culture — people who have lost any sense of the will of

God — and/or Christian believers who are confused by conflicting moral teachings. In sum, the problem is a lack of knowledge of God's will.

The Solution: Matt. 5:17–48 teaches the final revelation of God's will as the new law, which should function for individuals as lamp to my feet (Ps. 119:105); it shows the way of God's precepts, commandments, statutes, righteous ordinances (see Ps. 119:27, 32, 33, 106) that believers should follow as they walk with God. For the community of disciples this revelation of God's will is a *canon*, that is, a rule for the community, which, even though it must always be reinterpreted in terms of changing situations in life, defines the "better righteousness" that must characterize members of the church, and thus can serve as a rule (canon as measure) to reprove church members or even to decide who does and does not belong to the community.

The Transformation: For people who do not know God's will, the general transforming effect of the teaching of this text is that it reveals to them what they should do both as individuals and as a community. Yet, this teaching also transforms the view that these people and many church members commonly have about Scripture either as lamp to my feet or as canon. According to Matt. 5:17–48, though Scripture includes God's precepts, laws, ordinances, decrees, and rules for community life, it is not to be viewed as a rigid legalistic system. It must be fulfilled (5:17): as 5:21–48 shows, it must be constantly reinterpreted for new concrete situations (5:21–27: anger, worship service, on the way to court; 5:38–42: blow on the right cheek, court, forced labor on a road, money borrowing) in terms of love (5:44, 7:12), perfection (5:48), and judgment (5:29–30).

The Correspondence: Since Matt. 5:17–48 according to Reading A teaches believers that Scripture as revelation of God's eternal will by Jesus as Lord must be implemented in ways appropriate to the specific contexts, the correspondence between scriptural text and life can be formulated as follows:

> *As in biblical time*, the revelation of God's will made complete by Jesus was to be implemented in the circumstances of life in Jesus' or Matthew's contexts, *so in the believers' present*, the revelation of God's will made complete by Jesus is to be implemented in the circumstances of life in our present contexts.[7]

Reading B: Matthew 5:17–48 Teaches Believers That Scripture Is Good News, the Expression of the Will of a Loving Parent That They Should Make Their Own[8]

The Problem: In Reading B one envisions people who are totally devoted to worldly pursuits and/or Christian believers who are tempted to backslide, people who either want to do something other than God's will or do not want to do God's will. In sum, the problem is a lack of will to do God's will.

The Solution: Matt. 5:17–48 demonstrates the goodness of God's will, that is, the goodness of God's precepts, commandments, statutes, righteous ordinances. Following proclamation of the rewards and good consequences of doing God's will (5:3–16), the statement in 5:17 that nothing in the law and the prophets is to be abolished reaffirms their goodness (thus, following their teaching is good for believers and for others). The text teaches that, instead of viewing these commandments as external laws to which believers should reluctantly submit (by doing only what they "literally" say), one should internalize them so that they might inform one's entire behavior "from the heart." For instance, "you shall not murder," once it is internalized, also involves not being angry and making all efforts to be reconciled with other people (5:21–26). Loving others, forgiving them, reconciling ourselves to them, not resisting evil (5:21–26, 38–48; cf. 7:12) is not costly, but rather a gain (see 18:15–22). Not committing adultery and not divorcing (5:27–32) are not constraints but the preservation of the good gift from God that marriage is (see 19:3–9). The "best righteousness" (the behavior with the best consequences) should be that which disciples want to perform.

The Transformation: This teaching of the text transforms the view of Scripture that people who do not want to do God's will had, provided they are receptive to this teaching. Then the law and the prophets do not express a distant God's forbidding will that prevents believers from doing what they want (what they perceive as "really good for them," such as being like everyone else in society) and that they implement minimally to avoid punishment. Rather, Scripture is the expression of what is truly good for believers, because in his goodness God wants only good things for them. Thus, God's will is what they should want to implement in all aspects of their lives, because it is "the best" for them.

The Correspondence: Since according to Reading B, Matt. 5:17–48 teaches believers today as it taught believers in the past that

God's will is good news for them, the correspondence between the teaching of this text about Scripture for people in Jesus' and Matthew's time and for believers today can be formulated as follows:

> As *in biblical time*, the good news that God's will is good to do challenged the way of life offered by the world in Jesus' or Matthew's time, *so in the believers' present*, the good news that God's will is good to do challenges the way of life offered by the world in the believers' present situations.[9]

Reading C: *Matthew 5:17–48 Teaches Believers That Scripture Is a* Family Album *That Establishes Their Identity*[10]

The Problem: In Reading C one envisions people who are "harassed and helpless, like sheep without a shepherd" (Matt. 9:36), without hope and vision for their lives because traditional cultures have disintegrated, and/or Christian believers who are always in need of sharing in the hope and vision that gather them as a community of disciples. The problem is a lack of a sense of identity.

The Solution: Matt. 5:17–48 teaches that Scripture is a family album that gives believers a sense of identity as members of God's family, not only because Scripture was taught to their ancestors ("You have heard that it was said to those of ancient times," 5:21), but also because it concerns their own relationships with their heavenly Father (5:45, 48), brothers and sisters (5:22–24, 47), spouses (5:27–32), and all other members of God's extended family, which includes the evil and the good, the righteous and the unrighteous (5:45), and thus enemies (5:44) and other evildoers (5:39–42). Like any family album, this text gives believers an ideal vision of their relations with all the members of God's family, or, in eschatological terms, a vision of what these relations will be in the kingdom, a vision of "higher righteousness."

The Transformation: Matt. 5:17–48 conveys both a sense of identity as members of the family of God and basic convictions about Scripture as family album to people who formerly lacked or were in danger of losing their sense of identity. Even though such readers knew what was said to those of ancient times, they had failed to recognize that these were their ancestors and that the law and the prophets were meant to be the foundation of their individual and communal identities as members of the family of their heavenly Father. Matt. 5:17–48 conveys to such people these basic convictions about Scripture and identity by emphasizing that Jesus fulfills the law and the prophets (he allows his vocation and thus his identity to be defined by them) and by showing how the law fulfills its function as Scripture by providing an ideal vision of their relationship with God and with brothers and sisters in the community, as well as with other people beyond the community, including enemies.

The Correspondence: The correspondence between Scriptural text and life for people in Jesus' and Matthew's time and for believers today can be formulated as follows:

> *As in biblical time*, the renewed vision of human relations in terms of the kingdom and of the Father's present care as embodied by Jesus (and true disciples) challenged the common vision of human relations that failed to ground itself on past revelations, *so in the believers' present*, the renewed vision of human relations in terms of Jesus as a model of life in the kingdom and under the Father's present care challenges the disintegrating vision of human relations in modern societies. With this renewed vision, one can then identify in the present models of discipleship to follow.[11]

Reading D: Matthew 5:17–48 Teaches Believers That Scripture Is a Pair of Corrective Glasses Through Which They Can Discern the Expressions of God's Will That They Should Practice in an Overabundant Way[12]

The Problem: In Reading D, one envisions those, including Christian believers, who are constantly lured to follow and imitate false prophets, people whom they mistakenly take to be worthy leaders in the social, political, economic, cultural, or religious realms.

The Solution: Matt. 5:17–48 teaches believers how to identify and to fulfill in an overabundant practice of righteousness whatever expresses God's will in their context — be it the law and the prophets (5:17, 7:12), or what was said to (by) those of ancient times (5:21), or the righteousness practiced by the scribes and Pharisees (5:20), or the love practiced by tax collectors and Gentiles (5:46–47), or what they want others to do to them (7:12) — as it was in Jesus' and Matthew's time — or something else in the modern context. Fulfilling in an overabundant way the (partial) righteousness discerned in the behavior of people in their context involves affirming the value of the expressions of this righteousness — for instance, not murdering, as the scribes and Pharisees taught and practiced (5:20–21; 23:2), loving, as the tax collectors and Gentiles manifested their love for their friends and families (5:46–47) — and practicing this righteousness in all aspects of one's life (beyond the practice of these people; see 23:3), by preventing the destruction of one's relation with others not only by not killing them but also by not being angry and by striving for reconciliation (5:22–26), and by loving not only one's friends but everyone, including one's enemies. By this overabundant fulfillment of the present expressions of God's will, believers also fulfill the law and the prophets (the Bible as Scripture) used as corrective glasses, that is, as means for identifying the present expressions of God's will that believers should imitate.

The Transformation: By teaching them how to discern contemporary expressions of God's will, Matt. 5:17–48 transforms people who did not know how to recognize expressions of God's will and who should be identified as models of righteousness, possibly because of their convictions that Scripture is the complete revelation of God's will (a closed canon).

The Correspondence: Instead of revealing the once-and-for-all expression of God's will to be applied to the new situations in our time as they were applied in the diverse situations of Jesus' or Matthew's time (as Scripture does in Reading A), in Reading D Scripture functions as corrective glasses through which believers can recognize contemporary expressions of God's will. Therefore the correspondence between scriptural text and life can be formulated as follows:

> *As in biblical time,* expressions of God's will in Jesus' or Matthew's situation were to be implemented in all the circumstances of life in Jesus' or Matthew's situations, *so in the believers' present,* expressions of God's will in their situations are to be implemented in all the circumstances of life in our present contexts.[13]

Past expressions of God's will in Scripture remain essential and unique pointers that allow believer-readers to discover contemporary expressions or manifestations of God's will in the lives and values of the people around them, and therefore in the culture that, directly or indirectly, provides the necessary framework for this kind of behavior.

Reading E: Matthew 5:17–48 Teaches Believers That Scripture Is an Empowering Word That Enables Them to Discern That for Them God Reigns and to Struggle for God's Justice[14]

The Problem: In Reading E, one envisions, on the one hand, people (including Christian believers) who have no control over their own lives, who are deprived of justice and of the bare necessities of life, who are oppressed and powerless, who suffer (mourn) and thirst for justice, and on the other hand, all other Christian believers who are aware that, as disciples, they "always have the poor with (them)" (Matt. 26:11).

The Solution: Matt. 5:17–48 teaches such poor believers that Scripture empowers them to struggle for the kingdom and God's justice (6:33) and also functions as empowering word, conjuring the new reality of the kingdom for believers.[15] Its promise, "for them God reigns," is fulfilled not only in Jesus' ministry but also in the present, and it empowers them to contribute to the construction of "a new world of social relationships through *a new praxis of justice:* a praxis that consists in the reordering of relationships with God, with men and women, with the world, and with oneself." This teaching of Scripture "regrounds hope and the ability to resist" in the situation of powerlessness in which these believers are; it is "the foundation of a spirituality of resistance for the poor and the oppressed," which involves "living the new justice."[16] This new praxis of justice is marked by new relationships: (1) with God, now viewed as the one in control of life being the heavenly Father who reigns for those who are powerless to control their own lives (5:44–47); (2) with oneself, when Scripture and its new praxis of justice become intrinsic parts of one's being (see 5:22, 28) as a spirituality that shapes one's life; (3) with others and the world, through an active reordering of relationships according to God's justice, by working at being reconciled with others (5:21–26), by preserving and strengthening good relationships (marriage, 5:27–32), and by challenging and resisting evil in the world as one refuses to live according to a distorted and oppressive value system (5:33–48).

The Transformation: Matt. 15:17–48 transforms those who feel totally powerless before the social, economic, cultural, and religious forces that oppress and marginalize so many; it not only shows them how Scripture empowers believers, it actually functions as Scripture to empower them.[17]

The Correspondence: From the perspective of this reading of Matt. 5:17–48, the transforming power of Scripture is underscored. Consequently, the correspondence between Scriptural text and life can be formulated as follows:

> *As in biblical time*, Scripture conjured the manifestations of the kingdom and of God's justice in Jesus' ministry in favor of the powerless (God reigned for them) and empowered powerless people to struggle for the kingdom and God's justice, *so in the believers' present*, Scripture conjures the manifestations of the kingdom and of God's justice in their present situation (God reigns for the powerless) and empowers powerless people to struggle here and now for the kingdom and God's justice.

Your Reading: The Teaching of Matthew 5:17–48 about Scripture for Believers Today

How does your interpretation of the teaching of Matt. 5:17–48 for believers today compare with the five I presented? Please take the time to reflect on your own interpretation and to write down what is, for you:

The metaphor that best expresses the teaching of Matt. 5:17–48 about Scripture for believers today:

_____

_____

The problem addressed by this teaching in the believers' context:

_____

_____

The solution provided by this teaching of the text:

_____

_____

The transformation accomplished by the effect of this teaching upon the believers' life:

_____

_____

The correspondence between scriptural text and life:

_____

_____

As you take note of the distinctiveness of your conclusions, you should keep in mind that the six roles of Scripture mentioned above (and in chapter 2) are neither exclusive of each other nor a complete list of all possible roles. In any religious tradition, Scripture (whatever it might be) plays several roles in the life of believers. One of these roles becomes predominant as a result of the believers' particular circumstances and convictions. Yet, the other roles are never completely absent. Therefore, as you describe your own conclusions about the teaching of Matt. 5:17–48 about Scripture for believers today, you might need to find another metaphor to express the predominant role of Scripture according to your interpretation.

It remains that, at any given moment for a believer, Scripture plays one primary role. In each of our interpretations, we cannot help but give priority to one of the functions of Scripture and one of the correspondences between Scriptural text and believers' experience.

Assuming responsibility for our interpretation (whatever it might be) requires that we be aware of its characteristics. This involves, as in the preceding chapters, acknowledging the interpretive choices we made among plausible and legitimate options — choices of a contextual problem to be addressed by the teaching of the text (contextual frame), of a specific view of Scripture (hermeneutical frame), and of a specific dimension of the text as ground for our interpretation (analytical frame). Yet, assuming responsibility for our interpretation also involves elucidating the pragmatic implications of each of these options, because saying "I believe this is the Word of God for us today" — or, in secular terms, "This is the best teaching by which believers should live" — is a declaration concerning the effects of a teaching upon the lives of believers and the people around them. For this reason, in the following chapters, we will consider how, through the interpretive process, what the text says about divorce (based on Matt. 5:31–32) and about not resisting evil (based on Matt. 5:38–42) becomes a series of different teachings with powerful effects upon the lives of believers and those around them.

Chapter Six

Teachings about Divorce and Not Resisting Evil (Part 1)

Matthew 5:31–32, 38–42 as Lamp to My Feet, Canon, Good News, and Family Album

What Is the Teaching of Matthew 5:31–32 and 38–42 about Divorce and about Not Resisting Evil for Believers Today?

To clarify your conclusions regarding the teaching of Matt. 5:17–48; 7:12 about the role of Scripture for believers today, I ask you to reread the passages about divorce (5:31–32) and about not resisting evil (5:38–42) from the perspective of the teaching about Scripture that, in the preceding chapter, you discovered through your reading of Matt. 5:17–48. This reading exercise will help us better understand the characteristics and implications of our respective conclusions about the role Scripture should have for disciples.

I will present the various teachings about divorce and not resisting evil found by interpreting Matt. 5:31–32 and 5:38–42 from the five perspectives identified in the preceding chapters. In each case my comments will be introduced by a review of the conclusion regarding the teaching of Scripture and the textual dimension on which that conclusion is based.

We might be surprised by the diversity of teachings arising from Matt. 5:31–32 and 38–42 when these texts are framed by different views of Scripture. Our knee-jerk reaction might be to reject as irresponsible betrayals of the text those interpretations that clash with our own. Yet, my hope is that you will want to join me in taking the time to understand how these other interpreters have reached their conclusions. In the process, we will discover that our own interpretation is no less based upon the selection of one textual dimension as particularly significant (by reading through a specific analytical frame) and one plausible view of Scripture as particularly convincing (by reading through a specific hermeneutical frame). In this way we will be in a position to assume responsibility for our interpretation of the teaching of this text for believers, because each of us will have to ask: Why did I choose this interpretation rather than another one?

Your Reading of Matthew 5:31–32, 38–42 as Scripture

Here is the text of the passage about divorce (New Revised Standard Version, with some alternative translations and biblical references in brackets). What is its teaching for believers today about divorce from the perspective of the teaching about Scripture that you found by reading Matt. 5:17–48; 7:12?

5:31"It was also said, 'Whoever divorces [sends away, dismisses] his wife, let him give her a certificate of divorce' [Deut. 24:1–4]. 5:32But I say to you that anyone who divorces [sends away, dismisses] his wife, except on the ground of unchastity, causes her to commit adultery [to become an adulteress]; and whoever marries a divorced woman commits adultery [causes her to become an adulteress]."

_____

_____

_____

Here is the text of the passage about not resisting evil. What is its teaching for believers today from the perspective of the teaching about Scripture that you found by reading Matt. 5:17–48; 7:12?

5:38"You have heard that it was said, 'An eye for an eye and a tooth for a tooth' [Exod. 21:23–24; Lev. 24:19–20; Deut. 19:21]. 5:39But I say to you, Do not resist an evildoer [evil]. But if anyone strikes you on the right cheek, turn the other also; 5:40and if anyone wants to sue you and take your coat, give your cloak as well; 5:41and if anyone forces you to go one mile, go also the second mile. 5:42Give to everyone who begs from you, and do not refuse anyone who wants to borrow from you."

___

Reading A: Matthew 5:31–32, 38–42 as a Prohibition of Divorce and an Admonition Not to Resist Evil

Scripture as Lamp to My Feet and Canon: Analytical Frame — Matthew 5:17–48; 7:12 as a Window upon Matthew's Community

The evidence for the conclusion that Matt. 5:17–48, 7:12 teaches the final revelation of God's will as the new law — a lamp to my feet for individuals and a canon for the community — is the textual dimension that offers a window upon Matthew's church and its use of these verses as rule for community life. It is significant here that Matt 5:17–20 takes the form of a statement of "holy law" on the basis of which people in Matthew's church were ranked ("will be called least...will be called great in the kingdom of heaven," 5:19) or rejected ("will never enter the kingdom of heaven," 5:20) according to their performance or lack of performance of the law as revealed in its fullness by Jesus.[1]

As the authoritative Lord, Jesus fulfilled the law (Torah) by revealing how God's eternal will is to be implemented in specific situations as one evaluates one's own behavior and that of others.

Being great in the kingdom and the church, rather than least or excluded, is not a matter of simply doing what each commandment mandates (e.g., not committing murder), but of finding out how this commandment applies in all aspects of life (e.g., not being angry). According to this deontological understanding of discipleship and Scripture, Jesus' primary teaching is a set of basic principles in terms of which one needs to reinterpret and implement the commandments in each new situation: the principles of (1) love (the love commandment radicalized to include love for one's enemies, 5:44; and generalized by the Golden Rule, 7:12), of (2) perfection (the commandments apply to the whole person; to both outward and inward behavior), and of (3) judgment (keeping in mind the coming judgment).[2] Thus, "you shall not murder" means, according to the circumstances, do not be angry with others, or do not insult them, or be reconciled with someone who is angry with you even if it means abandoning your worship activities (5:21–26), or more generally, do whatever it takes to restore broken relationships in your specific situation.

Scripture as Lamp to My Feet and Canon: A Plausible Hermeneutical Frame for Believers Today

This interpretation of the teaching of Matt. 5:17–48 regarding Scripture is a plausible teaching for believers today, because it is an actual teaching that, for many Christian believers in Europe and North America (as well as in other parts of the world), challenges the legalistic understanding of Scripture and of the will of God often found in conservative Christian communities, especially in fundamentalist groups and movements. According to this interpretation, legalism becomes impossible, since the way to implement a commandment has to change so as to be the truly loving response to each situation, a response that demands a total commitment ("perfection") as one keeps in mind the coming judgment.[3] Yet, each of the teachings in 5:21–7:12 remains a law that disciples must use to evaluate their own behavior and the behavior of others in the community. In Matthew's time, these rules for community life, including the rules expressed by 5:31–32 and 38–42, defined the boundaries of the communities of disciples who lived in the sphere of God's eschatological Rule. So should these rules do today, according to this reading.

Matthew 5:31–32 as Lamp to My Feet and Canon: A Prohibition of Divorce, Except in Case of Adultery

When one reads Matt. 5:31–32 as a window upon Matthew's church — using historical approaches, including form criticism and redaction criticism — one notes the legal form of this teaching about divorce. It accounts for special cases and situations, as a community rule must do. Instead of the absolute but idealistic (eschatological) prohibition of divorce in Mark 10:2–9, Matthew introduces an exception ("except on the ground of unchastity," 5:32) that makes it "a practical instruction, with whose help the current problems of order can be resolved" in Matthew's church.

Matthew "adapts [this instruction] to the necessities of the community situation."[4] Practically, one cannot completely forbid members of the church to divorce, because some people might not be responsible for their divorce — for instance, in the case of the unchastity of one's spouse. But in such a case remarriage is prohibited; it would amount to adultery, because for a Christian the marriage is still considered valid despite the separation.

Since as lamp to my feet or canon these verses present a teaching about what believers should and should not do, it is essential to understand exactly which actions are prohibited or commanded. This includes having a clear understanding of how divorce and adultery are interrelated in the teaching of these verses *for Matthew's church*. As in the preceding verses prohibiting adultery and lust (5:27–30), adultery and thus divorce were defined in terms of a patriarchal structure. Committing adultery literally meant causing a woman to become an adulteress. Accordingly, a man committed adultery when he seduced a married woman, because he defiled her marriage. But there was no adultery (and no unchastity) when the woman was not married; a man was "fundamentally entitled to have more than one wife (Deut. 21:15ff.)."[5] Thus, the prohibition of divorce in 5:31–32 was aimed at preventing men from causing women to become adulteresses, as this alternate translation makes clear: "But I say to you that anyone who sends away his wife, except on the ground of unchastity, causes her to become an adulteress; and whoever marries a divorced woman causes her to become an adulteress" (5:32). Then it becomes clear that the exception did not weaken the prohibition of divorce; if unchastity and thus adultery had already taken place, it was too late to prevent it, as the prohibition aimed to do.

Matthew 5:31–32 as Lamp to My Feet and Canon for Believers Today: The Prohibition of Divorce in the Modern Western Context

Before being applied to believers today, the injunction prohibiting divorce needs to be adapted to the modern situation of the church. A legalistic interpretation (doing exactly what is written without taking into account the new context) would betray Jesus' teaching about fulfilling the law in a "better righteousness." In the modern context in Western cultures (and elsewhere, I suspect), the principles of love and of perfection require that the spouses be viewed as having equal status in the marriage.

Thus, not being faithful to one's spouse is unchastity and adultery, whether one is a man or a woman. This means that the exception to the prohibition of divorce is broader; divorce is now also permitted in the case of the husband's unfaithfulness to his wife. But the prohibition of the remarriage of divorced people is actually strengthened; now it also applies to divorced men.

This teaching is quite plausible today. At least in the Western world, many would-be believers, and indeed many church members — at least outside the Roman Catholic church — seem completely oblivious of God's will on this topic. Thus, it is not impossible that they might have a real need to know that for Christians divorce is prohibited, except in case of unchastity; that when divorce occurs, a life of chastity without remarriage is required; and that church members who do not follow this rule should be reproved (and not allowed in any position of leadership — they are least in the church/kingdom, 5:19) and eventually excluded (5:20). If would-be believers and Christians do not know that this prohibition of divorce exists, this teaching might be plausible.

But this teaching is not plausible (is not an actual teaching) for those who are already aware of this prohibition. Such people (and I suspect there are many, especially in the Roman Catholic church) would not learn anything from this teaching. They might not want to obey God's will and thus might need a teaching that would convince them to do it (see Reading B). More radically, they might have doubts that such a prohibition is truly God's will for Christian believers today. In such cases, they might need a teaching that will convince them either to believe (see Reading C) or to discern anew God's will for today regarding sexuality (see Readings D and E), as discussed below. In such cases, conveying the knowledge of the rule for personal and community life that divorce and remarriage are prohibited would fail to address the actual needs of such people. It would not be an actual teaching for such believers.

Matthew 5:38–42 as Lamp to My Feet and Canon: An Admonition Not to Resist Evil

When one reads Matt. 5:38–42 as a window upon Matthew's church, one notes — using form criticism and redaction criticism — that Matthew uses traditions about Jesus' teaching (also found in Luke 6:29–30, regarding how Christians are to respond to evil deeds in their daily life) as illustrations of the admonition not to resist evil. Matthew presents this in the form of antithesis ("You have heard.... But I say to you..."). As a result, Matt. 5:38–42 becomes a practical teaching regarding the behavior that members of the community should exercise toward outsiders, as is shown by the "anticlimactic" way in which the illustrations are listed: "from the greater evil to the lesser one: violent encounter [being struck on the right cheek], court trial [for one's coat], coercion [to go one mile], request [of money]."[6] Consequently, the radical injunction not to resist evil becomes an instruction to be practiced by the community through an attitude of self-denial in the most common situations of the Christians' personal lives.[7]

Matthew 5:38–42 as Lamp to My Feet and Canon for Believers Today: The Admonition Not to Resist Evil in the Modern Context

This admonition is, once again, a rule for the community of disciples to be practiced by Christian believers in all kinds of situations. As Strecker emphasizes, it is an error to think that this could be a rule of life in society; this is "not a maxim for governing the world — such a misunderstanding would lead to a reign of violence."[8] Rather this admonition expresses the distinctive way in which believers as disciples are to behave toward outsiders, so as to be "light of the world," with the hope that outsiders will want to join the community of disciples to live a life of "better righteousness" characterized by compliance, humility, and self-denial, as the beatitudes already express.

Is it plausible to say in the Western world that teaching this rule for personal and community life — that is, communicating the knowledge that self-denial is God's will for Christian believers — actually meets the needs of believers and would-be believers today? For those who are already practicing nonresistance to evil, there is nothing new in this rule; this is not a teaching for them, unless they were in danger of forgetting it. (But how can one forget that Christianity entails taking up one's cross, and thus self-denial?) At any rate, for the vast majority of Christians and would-be believers this rule seems to be an appropriate teaching; in most instances, they act as if they did not know it. Rather than practicing self-denial and not resisting evil, they often seek revenge, respond to violence with violence (and applaud when others do the same), and demand excessive retaliation — two eyes for one! For instance, when their possessions are threatened in any way (by a burglar, by corrupt persons or systems, by debtors, by creditors) Christians do not hesitate to defend themselves by wielding weapons (be they physical, legal, economic, political weapons) against those who threaten them. And all the more so when lives (their own or those of others) are in danger. They act as if they did not know that, in view of the coming judgment (principle of judgment), self-denial as a rule for personal and community life should apply in all circumstances (principle of perfection) to all relationships with others, including those who hurt us (principle of love).

But is it really the case that Christians (or would-be believers) do not know that self-denial is a central part of the gospel? Who in Western cultures would not know that Christians are to take up their crosses, following the example of Jesus during the passion (Matt. 16:24)? Who would not know — even if it is to mock this teaching — that such self-denial should be a trademark of Christian behavior? In sum, I doubt that such a rule would really be new for people in Western societies; I doubt that it is a plausible teaching that would meet actual needs of would-be Christian believers — without speaking of the Christians themselves who cannot but know that they should deny themselves and take up their cross.

The widespread noncompliance with this rule might result from a lack of will — it is perceived as too costly, because one is not convinced that it is a good thing to do (as these verses teach in Reading B) — and more radically, from basic doubt that such a rule is truly God's will for Christian believers today. In the latter case, believers and would-be believers need a teaching that will convince them either to have a faith according to which not resisting evil makes sense (as these verses teach in Reading C) or to discern anew God's will for today regarding our response to evil (as these verses teach in Readings D and E).

One of these other teachings might also be appropriate for Christian believers who already truly practice self-denial by not resisting evil; these other teachings would truly be new for them, and, at minimum, would lead them to reassess the value of adopting Matt. 5:38–42 as a rule for their lives each time they are victimized.

Reading B: Matthew 5:31–32, 38–42 as a Denunciation of Divorce and Adultery and as a Call Not to Resist Evil

Scripture as Good News: Analytical Frame – Matthew 5:17–48 as the Presentation of a Part of the Story of the Disciples

Textual evidence for the conclusion that the teaching of Matt. 5:17–48 is good news—the expression of the will of a loving parent that Christian believers should want to make their own — is readily provided by reading 5:17–48 as a part of Matthew's story about Jesus and his disciples. In such an interpretation, the most significant feature of these verses becomes the role they play in the story of Jesus making disciples out of the four fishers (4:18–22) and out of members of the crowds (4:23–5:2).

The preaching of the Sermon is a significant part of this process. Like many other sermons, it seeks to convince its hearers to want to do God's will. Following the call to discipleship (with promises and a description of the disciples' vocation, 5:3–16), 5:17–48 further explains what is expected from disciples. The question is: How does this description of the disciples' duties affects the hearers of the Sermon?

First, because 5:17–20 expresses conditions for entering the kingdom (5:20) and for being great in it (5:19), this passage continues to entice its hearers to become disciples. If they want these rewards, they should also want to fulfill all the commandments — that is, to perform them, to act according to them — following Jesus' example. Far from being above the law and the prophets by fulfilling them in the sense of revealing their complete meaning (as in Reading A), in this dimension of the text, Jesus fulfills them (5:17) by submitting to them. "I have come not to abolish but to fulfill" is read here as an explanation of what Jesus has already done since his baptism (3:15 underscores Jesus' determination "to fulfill [perform] all righteousness") and during the temptation (4:3–11, when he shows his total submission to God's will and what "is written" and his need to be nourished "by every word that comes from the mouth of God"). By his own actions, Jesus demonstrates that submission to God's will is "the best" one can do: the "best righteousness."

From this perspective, the antitheses ("You have heard....But I say to you...") are not so much an expression of Jesus' authority — although Jesus' teaching is authoritative — as a demonstration of the way in which he submits to the law by internalizing it, even as he calls disciples to do the same. True fulfillment of the law must come from the heart, that is, from making God's will one's own will (as is particularly emphasized by the first two antitheses, 5:21–30). Internalizing God's will as expressed in the law requires being convinced that it is truly good to do — the best for oneself and for others, bringing about the best consequences.

Through these verses (5:17–48), Jesus conveys to his hearers the conviction that God's will is the best for them and therefore something they should want to fulfill (perform). Indeed, like Jesus, they should want to fulfill "all righteousness," not just "minimum righteousness" (cf. Matt. 3:15; 5:20).[9]

Scripture as Good News: A Plausible Hermeneutical Frame for Believers Today

This interpretation of the teaching of Matt. 5:17–48 regarding Scripture is a plausible teaching for believers today, because its call directly challenges the many Christian believers in Europe, North America, and other cultural settings who fail to comply with God's will as expressed in Scripture. Obviously, this failure to do God's will is a common phenomenon in the secular societies of the West (which, from the perspective of other cultures, are viewed as "Christian" societies). Yet, this is also the case with many individual Christian believers today who are lax in their performance of God's will because they are not convinced it is the best for them. After having been taught (that is, convinced) by the Sermon on the Mount that God's will is good for them, believers will no longer want to do the minimum of what the law (or any other expression of God's will) prescribes. This is also a teaching for conservative and fundamentalist Christian believers who urge compliance with God's will. Indeed, this teaching challenges the legalistic view of God's will that demands performance of what is prescribed exactly as expressed in the text in order to ward off the coming judgment and other divine punishments. Because of the good news that God's will is truly the best for them, true believers will want to apply God's will to all possible situations in their lives in order to benefit as much as possible. "You shall not murder" is a good commandment, so as to prevent the radical and definitive separation from others that results from such acts of violence. This commandment affirms the value of avoiding or overcoming anything that could disrupt or threaten one's relationship with others. Thus, one should want to apply God's will on this issue in all aspects of one's relations with others, because "as with anger and contempt, the one who is hurt the most by a disagreeable disposition is the one who has it."[10] Thus, one should want to be reconciled with others, eventually by forgiving them (5:21–26). Even if at first it appears to be costly, reestablishing broken relationships is good for people, because in this way they avoid various kinds of punishments now and in the future (as noted in 5:22–26). More fundamentally, disciples should want to be reconciled with others and to forgive them, because of the positive benefits of this attitude. These benefits are spelled out in Matt. 18:15–22. Being reconciled with others is important not only because in seeking reconciliation one gains brothers and sisters ("If that one listens to you, you have gained a brother or a sister," 18:15 [my translation]), but also because having brothers and sisters is a necessary condition for having one's prayers answered (18:19) and for being in Jesus' presence (18:20). When one understands this, one does not want to put any limit to forgiving — unlike Peter, who did not understand (18:21–22). Why ever would one deprive oneself of such blessings?

Matthew 5:31–32 as Good News: A Denunciation of Divorce and Adultery as Destroying Good Marriage Relationships

Following the same pattern, 5:31–32 teaches the hearers (the former fishers and the crowds) that divorce and adultery are against God's will, and thus are bad for them. The preceding verses, 5:27–30, have shown that lust as well as adultery must be avoided at all costs, because they will have devastating consequences at the coming judgment. In the same way, one must avoid divorce, because it will ultimately have the same consequences, since it generates adultery; divorce causes the woman and anyone whom she might remarry to commit adultery (5:32). But, as the stipulation, "except on the ground of unchastity" (5:32), shows, there is no reason to restrain from divorce when adultery or any other form of unchastity has already betrayed and broken up the good marriage.

It is noteworthy that the exception signals that God's commandments regarding adultery and divorce are ultimately aimed at preserving a good relationship, marriage. This is even clearer in Matt. 19:3–9, where the teaching against divorce is based upon the good institution of marriage as a part of the good creating act (19:4–6; see Gen. 1:27; cf. 1:31, "God saw everything that he had made, and indeed, it was very good").[11] By recognizing the goodness of the marriage relationship as a precious gift from God, disciples should perceive the goodness of God's commandments against divorce and adultery; it is good to preserve this good relationship — provided, of course, that it exists.

Matthew 5:31–32 as Good News for Believers Today: A Call to Denounce Anything That Damages Good Marriage Relationships

The teaching for the hearers of the Sermon (the disciples and crowds in the Gospel of Matthew) can be directly applied to the believers' situation today. It is a matter of finding the best way of implementing it. This maximum implementation involves recognizing the goodness of the marriage relationship and striving to preserve it. Thus, as they internalize God's will, believers today should affirm and strive to preserve the goodness of all aspects of the marriage relationship, and not merely its sexual component. This means that they should denounce as bad for us everything that damages or destroys the goodness of marriage relationships. This includes denouncing adultery and any form of unchastity (and not merely a narrow definition of adultery, see 5:27–30), because they spoil the intimacy of the relationship of marriage (cf. Matt. 19:6, "no longer two, but one flesh"), and denouncing divorce, insofar as it breaks a good relationship, because it is the deplorable squandering of a precious gift from God. Yet, it also involves denouncing all physical and/or psychological abuse of one spouse by the other as a denial of marriage as a nurturing and supportive relationship.

In this spirit, believers today should approve of divorce, insofar as the good relationship of marriage has already been destroyed — be it by adultery, unchastity, or physical and/or psychological abuses. This means that divorce might be admissible in many cases where there is no adultery or unchastity. But far from being a devaluation of marriage, this broadening of the possibilities of divorce signals a greater appreciation for and a stronger affirmation of the goodness of the marriage relationship as a precious gift from God.

The plausibility of this teaching in contemporary European and North American societies is clear. Whether they are believers or not, many people have a general knowledge that adultery and divorce are against the will of God as expressed in the Bible. Yet adultery and divorce are common occurrences. A possible reason for this general devaluation of marriage is that these people do not implement God's will about marriage because they do not perceive it as good for them. Consequently, though they know God's will, they do not want to do it. When such people hear and receive the above teaching, they readily perceive it as most appropriate, since it entices them to want to do God's will, by underscoring that it is not the will of a capricious God, but the loving word of a parent who wants what is good for us. By (re)discovering the marriage relationship as a precious gift from God, they will want to preserve it and sustain it, even as they denounce any abusive relationship and approve of divorce in all the cases in which marriage has become a travesty of the good, constructive, nurturing relationship it is meant to be.

Matthew 5:38–42 as Good News: An Affirmation That Not Resisting Evildoers Is Good for Believers

For the hearers of the Sermon (the former fishers and the crowds), these verses are another expression of God's will regarding their relationships with other people — this time, evildoers, that is, people who harm them (5:39), attack them in court (5:40), force them into hard labor and oppress them in one way or another (5:41), and covet their money and other possessions (5:42).

Once again, the hearers of the Sermon are invited by the preacher on the mount to internalize a commandment, this time, "an eye for an eye and a tooth for a tooth" (Exod. 21:24; Lev. 24:20; Deut. 19:21). For this, they need to recognize the good news in this commandment, so as to understand why fulfilling it (implementing it in a maximum way) requires them not to resist evildoers. The good intent of this commandment, the *lex talionis*, is readily apparent as soon as one considers its context in Torah. Its goal is to put strict limitations on revenge, in order to stop the cycle of violence. In Torah, "the aim of retribution is to establish a proper community, to convict and overcome evil and eradicate it from the body politic of the people of God."[12] From this perspective, not resisting evil is offered by Jesus as the best way of overcoming evil and eradicating violence. As Bonhoeffer writes in an early work (before World War II),

> The only way to overcome evil is to let it run itself to a standstill because it does not find the resistance it is looking for. Resistance merely creates further evil and adds fuel to the flames. But when evil meets no opposition and encounters no

obstacle but only patient endurance, its sting is drawn, and at last it meets an opponent which is more than its match. Of course this can only happen when the last ounce of resistance is abandoned.... By preferring to suffer without resistance, the Christian exhibits [exposes] the sinfulness of contumely and insult. Violence stands condemned by its failure to evoke counter-violence.[13]

That this new antithesis takes up the case of a commandment outside of the Ten Commandments underscores that all God's commandments must be heard as good news, as requiring from the hearers something that is good for them. Similarly, the hearers should then be convinced that not resisting evildoers, despite its apparent cost, is good for them, because it is indeed the best way to stop the cycle of violence.

Matthew 5:38–42 as Good News for Believers Today: A Call Not to Resist Evildoers

Not resisting evildoers is costly. It involves losing money and other possessions (5:42), being exploited and oppressed as well as losing outward control over one's life (5:41), giving up one's legal rights (5:40, referring to the provisions of Exod. 22:25–27 and Deut. 24:10–13 for protecting the poor against legal abuses by the rich), and accepting physical abuse (5:39). Nevertheless, by now the readers of the Sermon on the Mount as Scripture — believers and would-be believers — are expected to understand that not resisting evildoers is good for them, since it is God's will, and that they should maximize (rather than minimize) the application of this teaching in their lives. But how could nonresistance to evildoers be good for them?

The answer is given throughout the rest of the Sermon on the Mount. Discipleship, with all its benefits for the disciples themselves and for others, requires a profound "decentering." Nonresistance to evildoers, with all its cost, "must be preceded by something deeper: the killing of selfishness, self-love, self-will, and self-importance," as Arnold says, commenting on 5:38–42.[14] One's self is no longer understood by itself, as if it were self-centered. It is now defined through one's relationship with God and with others, including evildoers and enemies (5:44). Like God (5:45), disciples have "a commitment of life to life and for life."[15]

As a refusal to enter the destructive cycle of violence, which feeds upon itself as long as it is resisted, not resisting evildoers is the only option that will not perpetuate evil. Yet, for this purpose, it is essential that the very act of not resisting evildoers clearly signals that one does not condone evil. As in the beatitudes about the meek, the text does not call believers to a passive submission to evil; it calls them to adopt an attitude that will break the cycle of violence and evil. Arnold offers an excellent example of the way to practice this teaching. After an incident in which two brothers had been robbed at gunpoint of the weekly wages of the workers at the Bruderhof community, he wrote,

> We could have reacted in either of two ways, both of which would have been a betrayal of the cause. One extreme would have been to use force, which would have happened if the brothers had defended themselves with a stick, or if afterwards we had called the police or the civil authorities and given the power into their hands. The other extreme would have been to think we must protect the culprits from the clutches of the authorities, which would have meant that we supported the crime. Instead, we called a public meeting.... We have to raise a strong protest against this armed robbery. The Church of God is bound to protest publicly against any injustice.[16]

Is this a realistic teaching? While the difficult balancing act advocated by Arnold is possible in the case of a nonviolent community, where one can benefit form the collective wisdom of the group, it is virtually impossible for individuals seeking to resist evildoers. Actually, an individualistic implementation would be incompatible with the context of this teaching, which, as Arnold emphasizes, presupposes renouncing an individualistic perspective ("the killing of selfishness, self-love, self-will, and self-importance"), and thus conceiving of oneself in terms of one's relationships with others, and thus with a community.

Concretely, this means that it is not plausible to implement nonresistance to evildoers in individualistic situations, that is, in situations in which an individual in isolation from a community is confronted with evildoers. For instance, from the perspective of this reading, nonresistance to evildoers does not apply in the cases of battered spouses and of conjugal (and date) rapes, because in most given cases public protest (a necessity, as Arnold insists) against such private forms of injustice is psychologically impossible. In fact, in this case the teaching of 5:31–32 is to be implemented: calling believers to divorce so as to make public the evil that has betrayed and broken the good relationship of marriage. Furthermore, Arnold's reading of 5:38–42 calls for a more general public protest against domestic violence and date rapes, and against the lethargy of the societies and the churches that by their silence condone such violence.

Yet, even in a community setting, nonresistance to evildoers seems to be quite impractical, as Jordan concedes:

> The truth might be that in its initial stages unlimited love is very impractical. Folks who are determined enough to hold on to it usually wind up on a cross, like Jesus.... Surely nobody would be inclined to call this practical. Yet, in its final stages, unlimited love seems to be the only thing that can possibly make any sense. Crucifixions have a way of being followed by resurrections.[17]

In other words, as Bonhoeffer emphasizes with Jordan and Arnold, all this makes sense only insofar as one keeps in mind that this is not a secular teaching, and, therefore, not a moral principle for secular life, a life in a world without God. Actually, according to this reading, envisioning a secular life would amount to denying God! Without God, this teaching does not make any sense, and there is no hope that evil can be overcome. But, as Bonhoeffer writes, with God, "the cross is the only power in the world which proves that suffering love can avenge and vanquish evil.... [The disciples] are called blessed because of their visible participation in the cross" — and this in all aspects of their lives.[18]

Reading C: Matthew 5:31–32, 38–42 as a Vision of Relationships in Gods' Family Now and in the Coming Kingdom

Scripture as Family Album: Analytical Frame – Matthew 5:17–48 as a Symbolic Message

The textual evidence for the conclusion that Matt. 5:17–48 teaches that Scripture as a family album gives believers a sense of identity as members of God's family is the symbolic message of the text, because this textual dimension presents a network of family relationships with Jesus.

The conclusion that Matt. 5:17–48 teaches that Scripture is a family album does not deny that this text can provide instructions for individual or community life (as a lamp to my feet or canon) or that it can persuade its hearers to internalize its good news. This conclusion simply affirms that the primary teaching of this text is to communicate to readers the faith that establishes their identity as children of God. Without this identity and without this faith in God and the coming kingdom as a framework, discipleship as a vocation to be actualized in deeds would not make sense. This teaching of the text is perceived when one views as particularly significant the symbolic framework of the instructions.

Matthew 5:17–48 sets reader-disciples in a network of family relationships with Jesus (who has a particular vocation, 5:17–20), with ancestors (5:21, 27, 31, 33, 38, 43), with brothers (and sisters, 5:22, 23, 47), with spouses (5:31–32), with evildoers and enemies (5:38–44), with their Father in heaven (5:45–48). This is why the teaching of 5:17–48 according to Reading C can be summarized by saying that it teaches that Scripture is a family album. Before focusing on relationships with spouses and evildoers, let us briefly review the other relationships as expressed in 5:17–20, 5:21–30, and 5:43–48.

As always, we ask about the proposed teaching: What is new for readers? First, what was new for the intended readers in Matthew's time? Then, what is new for believer-readers today?

Matthew 5:17–20. This passage opens with the words, "Do not think that I have come to abolish the law or the prophets; I have come not to abolish but to fulfill" (5:17). This verse can be read as an affirmation that Jesus fulfills the laws and the prophets by his teaching in 5:21–48 (as Reading A does). But it can also be read as a statement about Jesus' vocation: it is by his actions, and more specifically, by his obedience, that Jesus fulfills the law and the prophets. In this way, Jesus' praxis during his ministry is the model that disciples are to imitate. Then 5:21–48 (and indeed, 5:21 — 7:12) should be interpreted as the description of the righteousness that Jesus practices in his ministry — a praxis that disciples are called to imitate as they acknowledge and affirm their relationship to Jesus in the present in light of the eschatological future (the coming kingdom, 5:18–20).[19]

Matthew 5:21–26 and 5:27–30. The antitheses by their very form represent an important characteristic of both Jesus' and the disciples' relationship with ancestors: they are like them (they belong to the same family of God and have a similar vocation) and also unlike them (now, since Jesus' ministry, they have to envision this vocation in light of the coming kingdom). Thus, the antitheses "demonstrate how the Son of God fulfills in complete sovereignty God's word of law and prophets in putting his word over against Moses." As such they prolong and specify the symbolic figure of "Jesus preaching on the mount as the new Moses"[20] (Jesus is like Moses) by emphasizing in what ways he is unlike Moses. The antitheses make a similar point about disciples. As Jesus is unlike Moses, so disciples are unlike the ancestors who received the law. As Jesus is like Moses by proclaiming God's word as establishing an "order of law," so disciples as religious leaders are like their ancestors who were called to envision a new community implementing a new order of law. What is kept of the old order? What is really new?

Regarding the first and second antitheses, 5:21–26 and 5:27–30, Luz underscores that the teaching of Jesus ("But I say to you that if you are angry with a brother or sister, you will be liable to judgment," 5:22; "...that every one who looks at a woman with lust has already committed adultery with her in his heart," 5:28) is *"nothing new"* within contemporary Jewish [teaching]."[21] These antitheses contrast two aspects of the commandments of Torah already distinguished in Judaism: (1) Torah as a legal system that provides civic order in society (or in the community) and is implemented by courts of law; and (2) Torah as the will of God, which claims the whole person through its moral requirements (the more demanding aspect for the individual). In Jewish civic order of law, punishment for murder and adultery is necessary; in Jewish ethics, being wrathful and being lustful (having lustful intention) must be recognized as sinful.

In sum, in and of itself, the content of Jesus' teaching in 5:21–30 is not new. It is the antithesis form that creates newness.

By opposing the two aspects of the commandments as two "sentences of law," the antithesis gives to the moral demands of God's will the very status that the order of law has.[22] Of course, this teaching is unrealistic in present society; the commands not to be wrathful or lustful cannot be enforced by courts so as to provide the basis for an actual civic order. The only court that can enforce them is that of the eschatological judgment, as the descriptions of the punishment in Gehenna (5:22, 29–30) make clear. What the antitheses envision is the fulfillment of the law in the kingdom.

In sum, the first and second antitheses set up a contrast between the fulfillment of Torah in the present evil society (where the law alone can be implemented as a civic order) and its fulfillment in the kingdom (where the moral teaching becomes the law of civic order).[23] Disciples are to abide by the law of the kingdom, that is, by Jesus' "demands [which] surpass those of the Torah, without contradicting the Torah."[24] These antitheses are, in Luz's words, "a ray of hope for a new, better human being in the coming of the kingdom of God,"[25] which contrasts with the present situation in which hatred and lust (and related sexist attitudes) are omnipresent. Furthermore, when in the midst of the present (evil) society one recognizes people who live according to this teaching of Jesus, these people are seen as signs of the coming kingdom, models of discipleship for the believers' imitation.

Matthew 5:43–48. In the last antithesis with its extreme demand to love your enemies with an unconditional love, the symbolic interpretation of the preceding antitheses finds its ultimate justification. Here again Jesus' teaching fulfills (surpasses without invalidating) the Torah; the love of enemies is the "more" that the higher righteousness involves (5:46–47; cf. 5:20). One should not love one's enemies with the hope of making friends of them — "love with the hope of... " is not love![26]

Clearly, the injunction to love one's enemies is impractical and unrealistic.[27] Thus, one could say that it is the order of law of the kingdom, which is contrasted with the order of law of the world (as in 5:21–30), and that those who live this way are children of God in an eschatological sense (as in 5:9). One could say that they manifest in the present the better human being of the coming kingdom, who will be perfect.[28] But there is no eschatological reference (for instance, about the kingdom) in this concluding antithesis. Actually, there are none after 5:21–30. Rather, a strong emphasis is put on behaving like one's Father in heaven (5:45) — being "perfect as your Father in heaven is perfect" (5:48). This, of course, does not mean that one should literally do what God does! These verses emphasize that one should envision one's relationships with others by keeping in mind the Father's present care for all human beings, including evil ones.

In sum, the new order of law is not merely future (in the eschatological kingdom), as a utopian vision would be; it also is a present reality. This presence of the new order of law is manifested in natural phenomena (sunshine, rain) governed by the heavenly Father. This presence of the perfect new order of law is also manifested by people who behave like their Father in heaven. This new order of law — God's family — is a present reality manifested by Jesus and others, who reflect and represent God's love for evil people as well as for good people. True discipleship requires recognizing this present reality and thus striving to bring about the community that lives according to this (eschatological) order of law as the family of God the Father.

Scripture as Family Album: A Plausible Hermeneutical Frame for Believers Today

This interpretation of the teaching of Matt. 5:17–48 regarding Scripture is a plausible teaching for believers today, because we are in a similar situation. We are still in a far-from-perfect world. The kingdom is not yet here. Thus this teaching of 5:17–48 is an actual teaching for many Christian believers in Europe and North America and especially for secular people, who have lost all sense of Christian identity as members of God's family and as citizens of the kingdom. For believers and would-be believers today, this renewed vision of human relations — the new order of law — is not conveyed only by these verses, but also by the embodiment of this vision in Jesus as a model for the disciples.

Matthew 5:31–32 as a Part of Our Family Album: Marriage, Divorce, and Adultery, Now and in the Kingdom

The third antithesis, Matt. 5:31–32, must be interpreted as the first and second ones have been, even though it clearly alludes to a practical regulation used in Matthew's community (cf. the exception to the prohibition of divorce, 5:32).[29] It contrasts the order of law in the present evil society with the order of law in the kingdom. Matthew 5:31–32 is interpreted in terms of the parallel passage, 19:3–9, which underscores that Moses' teaching about divorce (5:31; 19:7; cf. Deut. 24:1–4) was a concession given because of "your hardness of heart" (19:8). Thus the antithesis form contrasts the present evil society in which, because of the hardness of heart of its members, divorce and remarriage of divorced people may legally take place, with the order of law in the kingdom, which prohibits divorce and remarriage (marrying a divorced woman is committing adultery). Once again, those who abide by this teaching are, in Luz's words, "a ray of hope for a new, better human being in the coming of the kingdom of God."

Yet, these verses also need to be read in terms of the concluding antithesis, 5:43–48, as an expression of what constitutes proper, "perfect" relationships in God's family. The divorce prohibition and its exception are conceived of "in cultic-ritual terms, as in Judaism: adultery and unchastity are a contamination which destroys marriage. Through adultery, the marriage *is* already destroyed."[30] In the same way that cultic-ritual contamination destroys one's relationship with God, so the contamination of adultery and unchastity destroys the marriage relationship. Since for Matthew love relationships are now the true ritual relationships (as emphasized in Matt. 9:10–13 through a reference to Hos. 6:6, "I desire mercy, not sacrifice"), betrayal of the love relationship of marriage is also a betrayal of the (ritual) sanctity of marriage, as not loving one's enemies is a betrayal of one's relationship with God — not being perfect as one's Father in heaven.

In sum, the injunction against divorce, except in the case of unchastity, and against remarriage of divorced persons is an "order of 'law of the kingdom,' and not of the world,"[31] and part of the perfection exemplified by the present care of the heavenly Father.

Matthew 5:31–32 as a Part of the Family Album of Believers Today: The Sanctity of Marriage, a Teaching for Modern Western People

The teaching of this antithesis for believers is that marriage, divorce, adultery, and remarriage need to be perceived from the perspective of this twofold vision of relationships in God's family now and in the coming kingdom, a vision that includes the recognition of God's present loving care for the righteous and the unrighteous. This teaching is quite plausible in the Western world today. In this cultural context, most would-be believers and many believers lack this vision and therefore do not conceive of the marriage relationship in terms of sanctity or in terms of the disciples' vocation to manifest in all aspects of life the loving and merciful perfection of their heavenly Father.

According to this teaching, believers as disciples should view marriage as one of the areas of human experience where the order of law of the kingdom is manifested in the present world. In marriages that manifest the sanctity of the love relationship, believers are invited to recognize blessed ones who benefit from and live by a gracious gift of God. These preliminary manifestations of the kingdom are to be imitated by believers as they themselves strive to manifest the kingdom in the present world. Recognizing such manifestations of the kingdom establishes and/or reinforces the believers' faith — their vision of the kingdom and of God's present loving care.

Yet, one should not expect these blessed ones to be perfect. As the negative form of this teaching (against divorce and remarriage) expresses, in the present situation people (including believers) cannot help but live in the tension between the kingdom and the present world. Thus the disciples' faith-vision is further reinforced each time they take note of the absence of the kingdom. From this perspective, divorce, unchastity, remarriage of divorced people — the believers' own failures as well those of others — become constant reminders that the order of law of the kingdom to which they are called and for which they hope is radically different from the order of law of the world in which they live.[32]

Matthew 5:38–42 as a Part of Our Family Album: Violence and Nonviolence, Now and in the Kingdom

The fifth antithesis, Matt. 5:38–42, once again contrasts the order of law of the kingdom with the order of law of the present world. Since "the general admonition to suffer injustice is widespread in all antiquity,"[33] here also, the content of the teaching is not new in and of itself. The newness is created by the antithesis form and by the lack of any mention of motivation (e.g., resignation to one's powerlessness or hope to make friends of one's enemies) for the renunciation of revenge.[34] The parodic illustrations — and not practical injunctions — (5:39b–42) of the general command, "do not resist an evildoer," bring to the fore its shocking character; they include overlooking vehement insults (5:39b), giving up one's legal rights (5:40; according to Exod. 22:26–27 and Deut. 24:12–13, the law prohibited taking the cloak of a poor man),[35] and not resisting the demands of foreign powers (5:41). The last illustration (5:42), which reflects the situation of Matthew's community, does not weaken the shocking character of the antithesis; giving up one's possessions, rather than lending them, is impractical in the world.[36] Thus, once again, the order of law of the kingdom is in tension with the way of life in the present world, in which revenge, the use of force, and the exploitation and oppression of the powerless are the rules. Thus, those who do not resist evil (e.g., Jesus during the Passion) are models of discipleship as they represent the better human being of the coming kingdom, whom disciples should imitate now in various situations.

Similarly, from the perspective of the loving care of the heavenly

Father, evildoers are like the evil and the unrighteous upon whom God makes the sun shine and the rain fall just as upon the good and the righteous (5:45). God still views himself as their Father and considers them as children of his family. Despite everything, evildoers should be viewed by disciples as brothers and sisters in the family of God.

Matthew 5:38–42 as a Part of the Family Album of Believers Today: Recognizing Evildoers as Brothers and Sisters in God's Family

This teaching is quite plausible in the Western world today, where most would-be believers and many believers lack this vision and can imagine only revenge and violence when they are confronted by evildoers.[37] According to this teaching, believers as disciples should view people who are meek, unresisting of evil in all kinds of situations as manifestations of the order of law of the kingdom in the present world. Yet, as in the preceding case, one should not expect that the meek who do not resist evil are perfect. They cannot help but live in the tension between kingdom and present world. Thus, interpretations that affirm this teaching simultaneously underscore the limitations and flaws of those identified as contemporary saints who manifest the order of law of the kingdom in the present.

For instance, in her comments on "blessed are the meek" (a beatitude directly related to 5:38–42), Evelyn Mattern proposes Mahatma Gandhi, Martin Luther King Jr., and Dorothy Day as models of nonviolent and meek responses to structural violence in the twentieth-century world.[38] (Of course, Gandhi, King, and Day would not necessarily have identified themselves with Reading C; they might also have interpreted the text in accordance with Readings B, D, or E.) The three can be viewed as manifestations of the order of the kingdom, when, like Jesus, they did not resist evil (though without being servile or passive); they were humble, "not arrogant or a know-it-all," and thus the opposite of "the never-apologize, must-be-number-one syndrome" so frequent in Western cultures (and possibly elsewhere). In sum, Gandhi, King, and Day were models of discipleship when they expressed and embodied "a healthy assertiveness" in response to violent situations and evildoers, while avoiding the extremes of "arrogance" and "passive aggression."[39] Gandhi contributed to freeing his people from colonial rule, King contributed to freeing "all Americans from the bondage of legalized segregation," and Day stood up "against the state by doing civil disobedience on behalf of peace [and] farm-workers" with others from the Catholic Workers while living in "community with the poor."

Yet, it is noteworthy that, for Mattern, the fact that Gandhi, King, and Day were not perfect is an intrinsic part of their value as manifestations of the order of the kingdom in the present. She stresses that, because of their flaws, "it is more unsettling but ultimately more fruitful to ponder the graces of contemporary [saints]," rather than those of third-century saints. Thus, for Mattern, because Gandhi was such a manifestation of the order of the kingdom in the present, he also embodied the flaws of the present by his "lifelong harshness toward women." Similarly, as a present manifestation of the kingdom, King embodied the flaws of the present by his use of "women as sexual objects" and his less-than-perfect intellectual honesty in his graduate school papers. And in the same way, as a present manifestation of the kingdom, Day embodied the flaws and limitations of the present world by her "hard edges and intellectual inconsistencies."[40]

The believers' faith-vision is neither contradicted nor challenged by the limitations of these and many other contemporary saints. Rather, the ambivalence of present-day saints reinforces the faith-vision, as a constant reminder that the kingdom is still to come. When believers see not only the flaws of contemporary saints, but also manifestations of violence and their perpetuation through the revenge cycles in which victims are caught, they are reminded of the promised kingdom with its "higher righteousness." With this vision of the kingdom as a radically different order of law, believers have to view evildoers — despite all their flaws — as members of God's family. Then the cycle of violence is broken. Believers can no longer demonize evildoers. Actually, with this faith-vision believers must recognize evildoers as brothers and sisters in God's family, even when they are not members of the community of disciples in which these kinship relations are made explicit. The relationship with evildoers is necessarily deeply transformed. Therefore, believers can no longer simply react to violence. As Gandhi "was waiting on the truth" so as to be guided "by *satyagraha* (or truth force),"[41] so believers have to wait on the truth so as to be guided by the faith-vision of the kingdom and God's present loving care.

A Step in the Process of Assuming Responsibility for Our Interpretations

How does your interpretation compare with those discussed above? Did you find that your conclusions about the teaching of Matt. 5:31–32, 38–42 are similar to those of Readings A, B, or C?

We might be tempted to brush aside as irresponsible those interpretations that are unlike our own. Yet let me emphasize once again that each of them is properly grounded in the text, though it might have selected as most significant a textual dimension that we have not considered in our own interpretation. Furthermore, each is framed by a plausible view of Scripture. Thus, the study of these Readings helps us take a step in our quest to assume responsibility for our own faith-interpretation. Now we can see more clearly the role that the view of Scripture played in interpretation, whether or not we read these verses as a lamp to my feet, canon, good news, or family album. At least we now recognize that we read Matt. 5:31–32, 38–42 from the perspective of a specific view of Scripture that we used as a hermeneutical frame, whether or not it is one of these four. In the following chapter we will consider how these same verses are interpreted when they are read through the hermeneutical frames of two other views of Scripture: corrective glasses and empowering word.

Chapter Seven

Teachings about Divorce and Not Resisting Evil (Part 2)

Matthew 5:31–32, 38–42
as Corrective Glasses
and Empowering Word

In this chapter we will review the conclusions of the last two Readings (D and E) regarding the teaching about Scripture of Matt. 5:17–48 and 7:12 by exploring the specific teaching they perceive in the passages about divorce (5:31–32) and not resisting evil (5:38–42). For each of us it will offer the opportunity to compare our interpretation of the teaching of these passages with two readings that might be unfamiliar if we live in mainstream societies in North America or Europe. Thus, I take the time to provide illustrations, many of which are interpretations "from the margins" of the First World, including from the Two-Thirds World. Whether or not our own interpretation is similar, this comparison will help us progress in our quest to assume responsibility for our faith-interpretation by reminding us that we used a particular view of Scripture to frame our interpretation. In addition it will help us to sharpen our understanding of the characteristics of the view of Scripture that we chose as a hermeneutical frame for our interpretation. Following this comparison, we will be better able to ask — and answer — the question: Why did I choose this interpretation rather than another one?

Reading D: Matthew 5:31–32, 38–42 as Lessons in Discernment – How to Identify Present Expressions of God's Will to Be Practiced in an Overabundant Righteousness

Scripture as Corrective Glasses: Analytical Frame – the Transformative Thrust of Matthew 5:17–48 and 7:12

The conclusion that Matt. 5:17–48 and 7:12 teach readers that Scripture is a pair of corrective glasses is readily grounded in the text. It simply requires us to consider as the most significant dimension of these verses the transformative thrust of the text, that is, the thematic structure through which the discourse most directly transforms the views of the intended receivers (characters and implied readers). This transformative thrust concerns the way in which Jesus fulfills expressions of God's will, rather than any aspect of the content of these expressions of God's will as in the preceding readings.[1]

The phrase, "the way in which Jesus fulfills expressions of God's will," emphasizes that the most significant textual dimension of Matt. 5:17–48 and 7:12 is the presentation of Jesus as one who identifies expressions of God's will in different contexts and who fulfills them. This textual feature teaches the implied readers: (1) how to recognize expressions of God's will that fulfill Scripture; and (2) how to fulfill (perform overabundantly) these expressions of God's will. This teaching concerns therefore two kinds of fulfillment: one to be observed, one to be performed.

(1) *The implied readers learn how to recognize the expressions of God's will that are to be fulfilled.*[2] This is signaled by the fact that the text challenges the readers' view of what Scripture is, as shown by the transformations that occur between 5:17 and 7:12 and between 5:17–20 and 5:45–48.[3]

As is commonly recognized, Matt. 5:17 and 7:12 bracket the central unit of the Sermon on the Mount, because both refer to "the law and the prophets." Beyond this parallelism, note the transformation. At the beginning of the unit, 5:17, "Do not think that I have come to abolish the law or the prophets; I have come not to abolish but to fulfill," expresses the theme from the perspective of the implied readers. The theme of fulfilling Scripture is presented in terms of what the implied readers readily recognize as Scripture: the law and the prophets, that is, the Scripture of the Jewish people, among whom are Jesus and his disciples as well as the scribes and Pharisees (5:20). By the end of the unit, the implied readers' view of Scripture is totally transformed. Now Scripture includes everything you wish others would do to you: "In everything do to others as you would have them do to you [Therefore all things whatsoever you would want others to do to you, do so to them]; for this is the law and the prophets" (7:12).

The text anticipates that the implied readers will be surprised. Should they truly consider their wishes, "what you want others to do to you," as Scripture! We find it difficult to equate "all things whatsoever you would want others to do to you"[4] with God's will. What we want from others is not always good! The text supports this caution with its opening word, "therefore," which qualifies the statement; it is a matter of doing to others the truly good things one wants from others, as parents "know how to give good gifts to [their] children" (7:11). Matthew 7:12 concludes a passage in which Jesus emphasizes the discernment (of earthly parents).

It appears, therefore, that Matt. 5:17–48 and 7:12 teach readers not so much what God's will is, but rather, how to identify expressions of God's will in the present. One of these expressions of God's will is, of course, the law and the prophets, the scriptures taught and used by the religious authorities of the time, the scribes and Pharisees (5:20; see also "The scribes and the Pharisees sit on Moses' seat; therefore, do whatever they teach you and follow it," 23:2–3a). This expression of God's will is designated in 5:21 as what "was said to [by] those of ancient times" (5:21). Yet, beyond this, one should also be ready to recognize an expression of God's will in what one wants from others (7:12).

Still another kind of expression of God's will, namely, practices of righteousness, appears when we compare the beginning and end of the subunit 5:17–48. In 5:17–20 and 5:45–48, respectively, Jesus and God are to be imitated (5:17–18 and 5:45, 48) by performing in an overabundant way God's will as manifested in the practices of the scribes and Pharisees (5:20) and in the practices of tax collectors and Gentiles (5:46–47). As the implied readers expected, it is the law and the prophets that the scribes and Pharisees put into practice; their righteousness, limited as it is, manifests God's will. As long as the implied readers take 5:20 by itself, they are not especially challenged by it, because this verse also seems to include a condemnation of the scribes and Pharisees. But they are surprised when, in 5:46–47, the behavior of the tax collectors and Gentiles is cited as an example, indeed, as an expression of God's will that disciples should fulfill. From this perspective, it ap-

pears that, in 5:20, the behavior of the scribes and Pharisees —
their (limited) righteousness — is also given as an example to the
disciples.

In sum, the teaching for the implied readers is that they should
identify expressions of God's will in their experience, as Jesus did
in his own. For Jesus, expressions of God's will are primarily found
in the law and the prophets (also identified as what "was said to
[by] those of ancient times" and as what the scribes and Pharisees
practiced in their righteousness), but also in the love practiced by
tax collectors and Gentiles and in what they want others to do
to them.

(2) *The implied readers learn how to fulfill these expressions of
God's will.* As stated in both 5:20 and 5:47, for disciples, fulfilling
God's will involves "doing more than" (exceeding) the good things
that the scribes and Pharisees do as they practice righteousness
(carry out "what was said to those of ancient times" — not murdering, etc.; see 5:21, 27, 31, 33, 38, 43), as well as doing more than
the good things that the tax collectors and Gentiles do (5:46–47),
and doing more than what they want others to do to them by doing
so to others (7:12). This is an "overabundant righteousness," that
is, the performance of a righteous deed that overflows its original
limitations. For example, the prohibition of murder now applies to
one's entire life, including to one's anger; the tax collectors' love of
those who love them now applies to one's enemies; the Gentiles'
welcoming greetings of brothers and sisters now apply to one's enemies; one's desire to be well treated by others now applies to all
behavior toward others.

In effect this overabundant righteousness involves identifying in
one's context expressions of God's will actually being practiced
by people, though only in a limited way, then lifting up this hidden lamp so that it might give light to all in the house (5:15) by
applying it to all aspects of life, and thus to all one's relationships.

The implied readers as disciples also learn from 5:17–48 how
to fulfill these expressions of God's will in an overabundant righteousness by reinterpreting them in terms of love and perfection,
somewhat as in Reading A.[5] The most significant difference is that
this overabundant practice is not limited to lifting up the good
things in the law and the prophets (or more specifically, to lifting
up the righteousness of religious people). It involves lifting up all
kinds of expressions of God's will, including those embodied in the
way of life of people considered sinners (such as the tax collectors)
or nonbelievers (such as the Gentiles). The loving aspects of their

behavior are to be imitated and extended into all aspects of the disciples' lives.

Scripture as Corrective Glasses: A Plausible Hermeneutical Frame for the Disciples' Present Life

We are surprised. Should believers truly consider their wishes, "what they want others to do to them," to be expressions of God's will? Are they truly expected to consider the good behavior they see embodied by other people — including people they despise — to be an expression of God's will that they should treat as the Bible itself? Then, would it not be right to interpret traditions found in their own cultures as "what was said to [by] those of ancient times," that is, as teachings that have the same status as the law and the prophets? If these possibilities are indeed potential teachings of 5:17–48 and 7:12, what is distinctive about biblical revelation? About Jesus and his teaching?

These questions and the puzzlement they reflect result from the fact that, in the contemporary European-American situation (and in other cultural settings as well), Christian believers commonly define Scripture exclusively by its function of providing a knowledge of God's will, with the presupposition that God's will is expressed in the form of "eternal principles" that are then to be applied to each situation (as in Reading A). From this perspective, expressions of God's will are exclusively found in the Bible as Scripture and in behavior that implements these eternal principles. For the many Christian believers who interpret in this way the *sola scriptura* ("solely by Scripture") of the Reformers,[6] a teaching of 5:17–48 that emphasizes expressions of God's will outside of Scripture (as Reading D does) cannot be an actual or plausible teaching, since it challenges their basic presuppositions about Scripture.

The teaching of Matt. 5:17–48 and 7:12 as interpreted in Reading D does not in any way diminish the authority of the biblical text. It simply demands that believers take seriously 5:46–47 and, especially, 7:12: "Therefore all things whatsoever you would want others to do to you, do so to them, for this is the law and the prophets." Jesus' teaching and the Bible as a whole do contain expressions of God's will, showing what believers should do. Yet, in Matt. 5:17–48 and 7:12 Jesus demonstrates how disciple-believers should identify God's will for themselves in their specific situations; thus, the expressions of God's will to which he points to are simply specific instances related to the period and time of his ministry (or

of Matthew's church), not eternal and universal principles to implement in one's life.[7] At any rate, such principles are not the primary
need of believers and would-be believers, who, rather, need to identify manifestations of God's will, because from these they will learn
not only what to do, but also how to do it. These manifestations
of God's will — people seen to be doing God's will — are models
to imitate. Yet, imitating these models does not mean merely duplicating what they do (they are far from perfect), but doing more
than they do.

Here, learning a new way of life is a matter of practice — of
learning how to do it — and not simply a matter of implementing
ideas or abstract teachings. Therefore, the unique role of the Sermon on the Mount as Scripture is to help disciple-believers identify
God's will for them in their specific situations. For this purpose,
Scripture is like a pair of corrective glasses that allows believers to
recognize expressions of God's will that they should imitate and
perform in an overabundant way as a witness to the kingdom.

Where are these expressions of God's will to be found? As we
have shown, they are found in Scripture, in the presentation of
Jesus' ministry in the Gospels, and in Jesus' teaching. But the same
teaching also accentuates that God's will for believers today is,
more often than not, manifested by the views and behavior of
their contemporaries, both the evil and the good, the righteous
and the unrighteous (5:45–47). Believers need to practice in an
overabundant way all these expressions of God's will that they discover around them, whether they are found in the Bible, rooted in
some ancient past, or simply manifested in the common behavior
of people around them.

Does the Bible have a special status? Of course. It is a col-
lection of past expressions of God's will. But in addition, it is
Scripture as essential and unique corrective glasses without which
believer-readers could not discover, in their present, expressions
(or manifestations) of God's will in the way of life and values of
the people around them and therefore in the culture that, directly
or indirectly, provides the necessary framework for this kind of
behavior.

Who needs to be challenged by such a teaching? All those, including Christian believers, who have difficulty identifying truly
worthy leaders to follow in the social, political, economic, cultural,
or religious realms. It is precisely because they have such difficulties
that this teaching addresses their needs.

I include myself among those who constantly need to learn

anew from others how to do God's will and thus again and again need to learn how to read the Sermon on the Mount as corrective glasses. This learning takes place through the intermediary of others, whether we learn from those who in our midst are "scribes and Pharisees," or "tax collectors," or "Gentiles," or whether we learn by reflecting on what we would like others to do to us.

Illustration: The Filipino Sense of Indebtedness as an Expression of God's Will

As should be expected, many aspects of this teaching became apparent to me in dialogue with Christian believers who are quite different from me, particularly, Christian believers whose non-Western cultures and traditional ways of life have commonly been dismissed as inferior or even as immoral because they are "pagan" or "Gentile." They taught me to recognize some of the traditions that, in their cultures, are expressions of God's will. In turn, this recognition led me to pay closer attention to the many Western cultural features that we, European and North American Christians, are spontaneously identifying as expressions of God's will.

Thus, I have learned much from colleagues and students in the Philippines. During a recent visit, Dr. Mariano Apilado suggested that Filipino traditions and their embodiments in history function for him as Scripture, that is, as what "was said to [by] those of ancient times."[8] This general comment becomes understandable as soon as one considers a specific example: the relationship between Scripture and a traditional Filipino value as presented by Revelation Velunta in his essay "*Ek Pisteōs eis Pistin* and the Filipinos' Sense of Indebtedness."[9] In this article Velunta lifts up a traditional Filipino value, *utang na loob* (literally, "debt of the heart"), by affirming it as an expression of God's will for Philippine society, despite the limited way in which it is properly practiced. In his words,

> *Utang na loob* is not really a value in itself; it is a response to *kagandahang loob.... Kagandahang loob* is goodwill or beneficence. It is absolute unselfishness, or self-forgetfulness; it is acting purely for the sake of others. It never imposes, never forces, is completely free. *Kagandahang loob* is compassion.... [It] is, in one word, grace.... *Utang na loob* [is] a response to grace.

This Filipino value can be lifted up, as Velunta does, by equating it with Paul's view of faith. This is appropriate, not only because it is a response to grace, but also because of its beneficial role in Filipino society, where it is the glue that holds together families and communities. Because of this deep sense of indebtedness, for instance, one cannot but honor, respect, and thus help one's parents, teachers, neighbors, and all others who contributed to one's education and growth as a child and adolescent.

> *Utang na loob* is a unique kind of debt. However it may have been incurred, no matter how insignificant the debt, there is no way by which one is absolved of the debt except perhaps by having the "lender" him/herself incur a similar *utang na loob*. . . . It creates an extra-legal but even more binding debt because it involves a personal debt, *one that can only be paid back not only in person but with one's person.* Utang na loob as a debt of gratitude is not absolved legally but through a personal involvement which acknowledges the unmerited and unsolicited graciousness. . . . *Utang na loob* between familiar persons is usually not recognized as *utang na loob* precisely because it is so spontaneous.

As such, *utang na loob* can be viewed as a special kind of love that involves the acknowledgment that one is indebted in some deep sense to the person one loves. This is in sharp contrast to the kind of "love" that, as a compassionate or gracious attitude toward undeserving people, ends up being patronizing, condescending, and thus humiliating for those to whom it is imparted. A love governed by *utang na loob* affirms and confirms the worth and identity of the person who is loved. In this case, *utang na loob* has a covenantal sense, according to which "the reigning attitudes are complete trust and fiduciariness; the exchange is one of gift and gratuity."

Yet, the actual practices of *utang na loob* in Filipino society today have many limitations (just as the tax collectors' and the Gentiles' ways of loving had their limitations, Matt. 5:46–47). This is because they take on a contractual sense, according to which "symmetry, a mutuality of duties and obligations or expectations" and "reciprocity" between strangers or non-intimates become social norms. Such a contractual sense of *utang na loob* becomes burdensome and oppressive because "Filipinos do not want to be considered, even unjustifiably, as *walang* [lacking] *utang na loob.* That would be equivalent to being viewed as a person with no sense of personal honor." Thus, persons use *utang na loob* as a means to demand services from others and ultimately as a means to abuse and oppress others.

Nevertheless, *utang na loob* remains a positive value and a basic condition for life in community because it calls each to acknowledge with gratitude his or her dependence upon the other members of the community and to act accordingly. Thus, *utang na loob* can be lifted up as an expression of God's will.

When this is recognized, disciples in a Filipino cultural context are called to manifest *utang na loob* as it will be manifested in the kingdom, by practicing it in an overabundant way. They should express *utang na loob* in words and deeds, not only toward the persons to whom they feel directly indebted ("those who love you," the people who are particularly close to you, 5:46–47), but also toward everyone they encounter, including enemies and persecutors (5:44). Therefore, lifting up *utang na loob* to let it overflow involves for disciples affirming and confirming the worth and identity of everyone around them by acknowledging their indebtedness to each. The disciples' attitude toward others is transformed by their anticipation that they are indebted to others around them, even though at first the debt might be far from obvious. At a minimum, they have to take notice for the first time of many things they receive from others, although they were not aware of this before.

According to the view of Scripture as corrective glasses as expressed in Matt. 5:17–48 and 7:12, disciples in any cultural and social context should follow this pattern, that is, identify expressions of God's will around them — loving and constructive attitudes and deeds, truly good behavior — and then fulfill these expressions of God's will by practicing them beyond their original settings.

Matthew 5:31–32 as Corrective Glasses: Good Intimate Relationships Such As Marriage Are Expressions of God's Will to Be Lifted Up

As corrective glasses, Matt. 5:31–32 allows disciples to identify good intimate relationships, such as marriage, as manifestations of God's will that they should affirm and lift up so as to preserve these gifts from God, even as they reject anything that threatens these relationships. In 5:27–31, the Scriptural prohibition of adultery ("You shall not commit adultery," Matt. 5:27; Exod. 20:14; Deut. 5:18) is presented as an expression of God's will that provides corrective glasses allowing disciples to identify and avoid any kind of wrong intimate relationship, including any form of sexual desire directed toward a person who is married (Matt. 5:28 refers to a woman who is married to someone else, otherwise there would be no adultery "in the heart"). By contrast, scriptural permission for divorce, "Whoever divorces [sends away, dismisses] his wife, let him give her a certificate of divorce" (Matt. 5:31; cf. Deut. 24:1–4), is not to be viewed as a norm that believers should implement. Divorce is evil insofar as it creates a situation through which one might cause other people to become adulterers (that is, to become involved in wrong unions, including remarriages): "Anyone who divorces his wife, except on the ground of unchastity, causes her to commit adultery; and whoever marries a divorced woman commits adultery" (Matt. 5:32). Yet, the exception (as well as Deut. 5:18) shows that this prohibition of divorce is actually aimed at preserving existing good unions in marriage — a good gift from God, as Matt. 19:3–9 makes explicit. When this good union does not exist any longer (in the case of "unchastity"), divorce is possible.

In sum, the primary teaching of 5:31–32 for the implied readers is: identify the good intimate relationships (in marriage) that exist between people around you, affirm them, and preserve them by avoiding anything destructive to them. Disciples are responsible both for their own adulteries (understood here as the direct or indirect — "in the heart" — destruction of someone else's marriage) according to 5:27–30, and for any adultery committed by other people that their own deeds or attitudes might have directly or indirectly promoted.[10]

Matthew 5:31–32 as Corrective Glasses for Believers Today: Identifying Good Intimate Relationships in Present Societies, Affirming Them as Expressions of God's Will, and Preserving Them

In the same way that, in Matt. 5:27–28 and 31–32, Jesus broadened the application of the scriptural commandment beyond its original scope (e.g., from adulterous acts to lustful inner attitudes to the procedures of divorce) by taking as most significant the pattern of relationships (what destroys good intimate relationship is evil) rather than the actual nature of these relationships (adulterous acts, sexual desire, separated spouses who enter new intimate relationships), so believers today should use 5:31–32 as corrective glasses allowing them to assess all kinds of situations in which existing intimate relationships are threatened, protected, nurtured, and affirmed.

Using these corrective glasses it does not take long to recognize that, among others, pastoral counselors (whether ordained or lay, ministers of congregations or pastoral psychotherapists) are people who, in today's European-American cultures, affirm, nurture, and protect existing intimate relationships. Blessed are those pastoral counselors. They are models of discipleship who fulfill this Scripture and from whom we, believers, have much to learn as we seek to emulate them.[11]

For pastoral counselors, as for Matt. 5:27–32, the premise is that intimate relationships, including their sexual dimensions, are good things, good gifts from God. Pastoral counselors emphasize the important role of intimate relationships in establishing and sustaining each person's identity as a fundamentally relational being. Thus, James Nelson and Sandra Longfellow write,

> Theologically, we believe that human sexuality, while including God's gift of the procreative capacity, is most fundamentally the divine invitation to find our destinies not in loneliness but in deep connection. To the degree that it is free from the distortions of unjust and abusive power relations, we experience our sexuality as the basic eros of our humanness that urges, invites, and lures us out of our loneliness into intimate communication and communion with God and the world.[12]

Sexuality and intimate relationships are gifts of God in the sense that they are "the divine invitation to find our destinies not in loneliness but in deep connection." This deep connectedness of true human identity can be called covenantal, that is, a relationship based on faith and trust. Paul F. Palmer explains:

> Covenant (*foedus*) is as expansive and as all-embracing as contract is restrictive and limiting. From the root *fidus* and the verb form *fidere*, which means to trust, to have faith in, to entrust oneself to another, a covenant is seen as a relationship of mutual trust and fidelity (*fides*).... Covenants are not broken, they are violated when there is a breach of faith on the part of either or both of the covenanters.[13]

Thus, in order to function as "the divine invitation to find our destinies not in loneliness but in deep connection," intimate relationships and their covenantal character must be respected and faithfully maintained. Adultery and any other violation of the covenantal character of these intimate relationships must be avoided at all cost, as is emphasized by Matt. 5:27–32. Yet, beyond what these verses express, in European-American cultures we have progressively learned to recognize that the divine gift associated with intimate relationships (entrusting oneself to another, finding one's identity in deep connectedness with others and God) cannot exist as long as these intimate relationships are not "free from the distortions of unjust and abusive power relations." More specifically, we learn from pastoral counselors that affirming, nurturing, and protecting authentic intimate relationships involves making sure that they are and remain characterized by love, justice, and mutuality. Love, as a mysterious bond through which the lovers are more united than separated even as they respect each other as a mysterious Other, justice, as "the right relations between persons and the various components of their worlds,"[14] and mutuality, as that which defines the boundaries of the reciprocal and faithful relationship, are three conditions for experiencing intimate relationships as divine gifts. Thus, beyond and besides a concern to overcome the threats to intimate relations specifically identified in Matt. 5:27–32, namely, adultery, lust in the heart, and divorce, believers today can fulfill this Scripture by their concern to overcome anything that would hinder or prevent loving, just, and mutual relations.

Looking through the corrective glasses of Matt. 5:27–32 at pastoral counselors and what they teach about intimate relationships, we can indeed say, "Blessed are such pastoral counselors." They, who teach us so much about the divine mystery of intimate human relationships, are indeed models of discipleship whom we should emulate.

Still looking through the corrective glasses of Matt. 5:27–32 we can also say, "Blessed are those who find in their intimate relationships the divine invitation to find their destinies not in loneliness but in deep connection, and ultimately in intimate communication and communion with God and the world." People in such relationships manifest the kingdom and are models we are called to emulate. If we look around us through the corrective glasses of Matt. 5:27–32, we can be confident of finding such people. Such manifestations of the kingdom are seen among people who were duly married before the church — even though, unfortunately, no married couple is perfect and many cannot be viewed as models, because of unfaithful, unjust, or abusive power relations. Yet, we also need to look beyond married couples for models of intimate relationships. There are such manifestations of the kingdom that we should emulate among people who live together without being married and yet share a covenantal relationship (a common situation especially in Europe following the cultural revolution of May 1968); even though, unfortunately, no nonmarried couple is perfect and many cannot be viewed as models, because of unfaithful, unjust, or abusive power relations. There are also manifestations of the kingdom among lesbian and gay couples, who are often models of intimate relationships from whom heterosexuals have much to learn; even though, unfortunately, no homosexual couple is perfect and many cannot be viewed as models, because of unfaithful, unjust, or abusive power relations.

You may be surprised by this last comment. Imagine the surprise of the first disciples when Jesus pointed to tax collectors and Gentiles as people among whom they should expect to find models of discipleship! Let me simply add that all the authors quoted above regarding the divine character of intimate relationships, covenantal relationship, love, justice, and mutuality are quoted by Joretta L. Marshall in her remarkable book *Counseling Lesbian Partners*, in which she calls all of us — homosexuals and heterosexuals — to authentic intimate relationship in the form of "a dynamic covenantal partnership of love, justice, and mutuality."[15]

Matthew 5:38–42 as Corrective Glasses: Blessed Are the Meek Who Value Relationship with Others above Everything Else

As in Matt. 5:31–32, in these verses too, Jesus rejects a view of Scripture that would see in the law (the *lex talionis*), "an eye for an eye and a tooth for a tooth" (Exod. 21:23–24; Lev. 24:19–20; Deut. 19:21), a commandment or norm that disciples should implement in their dealings with others. They should not use this law about legal tort claims to protect themselves from people who have hurt or abused them in some way, because if they did that, Scripture would actually be contributing to the estrangement of the disciples from those around them. As in each of the preceding antitheses, the disciples are invited to interpret Scripture in such a way that it might help them to maintain and/or (re)establish good relationships with others. Looking at specific situations of their lives through the corrective glasses of scriptural texts (about murder, adultery, divorce, swearing, and now about legal tort claims against an evildoer), disciples discern ways Scripture is fulfilled when, in keeping with God's will, good relationships with others are maintained, protected, and/or (re)established. Here the focus is on relationships within the public realm (not intimate relationships, as above), which are governed by legal regulations (see the *lex talionis*, 5:38; the reference to being sued, 5:40), or by the undue use of force (see the reference to beating, 5:39; to forced labor, 5:41), or by financial transactions (see 5:42).

From this perspective, the teaching of "an eye for an eye and a tooth for a tooth" is not that the restitution or revenge should be proportional to the damage done by the evildoers, but rather that disciples (blessed ones) are those who not only do not resist evildoers, but also lift up their relationship to evildoers as a valued relationship. "Note that the four illustrations of the principle of nonresistance show that this is not a matter of passive submission to evil people. It is an active participation in the relationship as set by the evil people."[16]

The teaching for the implied readers is to recognize as blessed those who value relationship with others more than their own well-being and possessions and who manifest this conviction by actively participating in the relationship even when the terms are set by evildoers. Blessed are those who turn the other cheek, give their cloak as well, go also the second mile, give to everyone who begs from them. Blessed are the meek.

Matthew 5:38–42 as Corrective Glasses for Believers Today: Discerning Manifestations of God's Will in the Midst of the Evil of the World

We believers who look through Matt. 5:38–42 as corrective glasses have our sight focused upon two features of the situation around us: patterns of relationships governing life in society, and blessed ones who lift up these patterns by living them in an overabundant way.

The laws, customs, and traditions setting the patterns of relations for life in our society are the equivalent of the *lex talionis*, "an eye for an eye and a tooth for a tooth" (Exod. 21:23–24; Lev. 24:19–20; Deut. 19:21). Of course, these laws, customs, and traditions are not perfect. In most instances, they are shaped as a reaction to evildoers; they propose a pattern of life that reflects the particular evil troubling that society, and in the process often generate other evils — as the *lex talionis* prevents an endless, vendetta-like cycle of revenge by introducing strictly limited but legalized revenge. Laws and other patterns of social life are dictated by people who have power, wealth, and authority, in most instances directly or indirectly acquired and used at the expense of others (see 5:39–41), but also at times by needy people who importunately demand help (see 5:42); thus, the mixed character of these laws and traditions. But seen through the corrective glasses of this text these laws and patterns of social life, despite their imperfections, are viewed as expression of God's will, because they nevertheless make possible good relations in society. This is demonstrated by people — models of discipleship — who live by these laws and social customs by practicing them in an overabundant way.

This teaching made sense for me when I heard the teaching for believers today that the Reverend Blesvilla Ambrosio Yap recently formulated in her context in the Philippines, as she pondered how to instruct members of her church who were police officers and were confronted with corruption and irregularities in the police force. She proclaimed that Christian believers should fulfill not only the law and the prophets, but also the Filipino civil laws and constitution. Of course, these civil laws are not perfect. Many were promulgated in order to support a dictatorship and (including more recent laws) neocolonialist exploitation (for instance, depriving the indigenous farmers of land by leasing it indefinitely to foreign companies). Yet, like the law and the prophets, these civil laws as expressions of God's will need to be fulfilled. Christian police officers should not only enforce the law, but also go the extra mile by making sure that the goal of the civil laws and the oath they took as police officers to promote a just society for all be fully implemented. Thus, Christian police officers should be totally at the service of the people in their districts, strive to make sure that all the laws are enforced and applied equally to everyone, avoid anything in their conduct that might give the impression of corruption or irregularities, and denounce the corruption and irregularities that they see in the police force. Carrying out these responsibilities involves taking advantage of the contradictions inherent in different laws and implementing to the fullest those laws that prevent the implementation of the unjust laws. Of course, this behavior is not without danger. Blessed are such police officers, who promote the just implementation of the laws and might be persecuted for righteousness' sake (5:10).

The same point could be further illustrated by evoking the United States civil rights movement and its so-called civil disobedi-

ence. Even though sit-ins in segregated restaurants and stores broke
local laws and ordinances, they were simply overabundant (going
the extra mile) implementations of federal laws and of their intent
as expressed in the U.S. Constitution.

Considering the present situation in the United States through
the corrective glasses of Matt. 5:38–42, we can note that an important part of the legal system is dominated and shaped by the effort
to overcome the tragedy of drug addictions and related crimes.
Yet, this legal system is not perfect; it has also engendered a huge
jailed population, disproportionally composed of young African-
Americans and other minorities. There is something wrong and
unjust when one finds more young male African-Americans in jails
than in colleges! Yet, imperfect as they are, these laws, customs,
and traditions should be affirmed and uplifted by going the extra
mile and promoting a full implementation of the laws and their
ultimate goals. Some churches, for instance, work to promote a
healthy society free from addictions not only by having a strong
drug-free policy for their members, but also by developing educa-
tional, religious, and sports programs that take aim at the causes
of addiction among youth, and by denouncing policies and implementations of laws by police, administration, courts, and jails
that betray their original good intention. Blessed are the churches
and their members who hunger and thirst for justice, the just
implementation of the law.

These and many other blessed ones, whom we recognize when
looking around us through the corrective glasses of the Sermon
on the Mount as Scripture, demonstrate that the daily life of our
imperfect secular societies includes, despite the often dominant
role of evildoers, many expressions of God's will. But in order
to see these manifestations of God's will, believers must refrain
from a knee-jerk reaction against evil. Not resisting evil is a condition for discerning these manifestations of God's will in the midst
of the evil of the world, as we affirm and emulate the blessed
ones who already live by these manifestations of God's will in an
overabundant way.

Reading E: Matthew 5:31–32, 38–42 as Empowering Word – Bringing about the Reality of the Kingdom for the Powerless

Scripture as Empowering Word: Analytical Frame – the Subversive Thrust of Matthew 5:17–48 and Its Voices from the Margin

The conclusion that Matt. 5:17–48 teaches that Scriptures are an empowering word for the poor and oppressed can easily be grounded on the text by reading it for its subversive thrust and for its voices from the margin. It is a matter of paying close attention to the structures of authority presupposed, advocated, or rejected by the text,[17] to the traces of struggles for justice behind and within the text, and to the voices that reflect in the text a different social and cultural construction of reality. Since all these features are clearly marked in 5:31–32 and 38–42, a few general remarks about 5:17–48 are sufficient.

The subversive dimension of the text can be recognized as soon as one reads Matt. 5:17. By taking Jesus at his word, we note that he denies that he has authority over Scripture, contrary to interpretations that emphasize his extraordinary authority, an authority greater than the law (especially in Readings A and C, which are, of course, grounded on other aspects of the text).

One might think (with Reading B) that the structure of authority is simply put upside down. Is not Jesus submitting to Scripture and its authority when he says, "Do not think that I have come to abolish the law or the prophets; I have come not to abolish but to fulfill" (5:17, when "fulfill" is understood as "do or perform")? Does not Jesus emphasize that Scripture will remain authoritative until the end of the world (5:18)? Is he not teaching disciples that they should accept the authority of Scripture rather than pretend to master it, that is, to claim the authority of discarding certain commandments (5:19)?

Yet, as is shown by the so-called antitheses (5:21–48),[18] fulfilling Scripture does not involve simply doing what it demands from believers, nor simply submitting to an authoritative Scripture.[19] Rather, fulfilling Scripture requires internalizing it (see 5:22, 28). It then becomes clear that the presentation of Scripture in 5:17 denies the hierarchical structure of authority — of Jesus over Scripture or of Scripture over Jesus, and of Scripture over believers (who are also called to fulfill the Scriptures).

From the perspectives of Readings A, B, and C, this does not make sense. If Scripture does not have authority over believers, how can it function as Scripture? How can it be Scripture? For Reading E — that is, for people who read the Gospel with an awareness of the plight of oppressed and powerless people — the question is reversed. How can one conceive of Scripture as having hierarchical authority over believers? That authoritative text could not truly be Scripture for the persecuted poor!

For such readers, Matthew fundamentally challenges all conceptions of Scripture's hierarchical authority over believers, because such conceptions of Scripture duplicate, and thus condone and even promote, the oppressive forms of authority that the proclamation of the kingdom denounces as contrary to God's justice. This concern is why, in the preceding chapter, Matthew emphasizes a function of Scripture that does not involve a structure of authority over believers: Scripture provides nourishment for believers. In response to the first temptation, Jesus replies, "It is written, 'One does not live by bread alone, but by every word that comes from the mouth of God' " (4:4). Scripture is bread,[20] nourishment, empowering word. Scripture does not exercise authority or power over believers in the sense of commanding them to adopt a certain vision of their vocation as disciples. Yet, in a very different sense, Scripture is authoritative and powerful, because it empowers believers when they nourish themselves with it.

Scripture is an empowering and liberating nourishment for the powerless and the oppressed precisely because it does not claim for itself authority over believers. Thus, it is in a position to promote an alternative order of life, the kingdom, which truly embodies God's justice, rather than oppressing as hierarchical orders of life do. The following verses begin to make this broader subversive point. In them, the hierarchical structure of authority disappears from the concept of teaching: practicing and teaching Scripture cannot be separated ("whoever does them [commandments] and teaches them," 5:19). Greatness in the kingdom, the alternative order of life characterized by God's justice (5:19), and even inclusion in it (5:20) depend upon renouncing this hierarchical structure of authority as a hermeneutical frame for understanding one's relationship to Scripture (as well as to other people). Praxis and teaching of Scripture are integrated (5:19); thus, teaching cannot be viewed as superior to praxis, as is the case when praxis is viewed as the submissive concrete application of an abstract teaching. Yet, as long as one does not internalize Scripture and nourish oneself with it, praxis and teaching of Scripture cannot be truly integrated (5:19) and Scripture cannot be fulfilled with an over-abundant righteousness-justice (5:20) that encompasses all of life (e.g., the commandments about murder and adultery apply to all relationships with others, 5:21–31).

The hierarchical structure of authority and power is dismantled throughout the alternative order of the kingdom, and not merely in the conception of Scripture. Note that in 5:21–26 fulfilling Scripture involves giving up any sense of superiority, including moral superiority. Even when disciples have nothing for which to re-proach themselves (that is, when they are not angry with someone else), they cannot self-righteously wait for those who have some-thing against them (who are angry with them, 5:23–24) to take the first steps toward reconciliation. From the perspective of the king-dom, they are as responsible as the offending party for the health of the relationship. Giving up any pretense of moral superiority, disciples should go to any length to reestablish good relations with angry neighbors (5:23). After all they are siblings, brothers and sisters, and thus have equal status.

Fulfilling Scripture also involves ceasing to give more impor-tance to certain relationships than to others; one's relationship to neighbor is as important as one's relationship to God (5:23–24). In the kingdom, issues of hierarchical authority and power do not govern one's behavior; otherwise, one remains in the oppressive order of the world, where justice is synonymous with judgment (before court or council, or at the last judgment, 5:22), with pun-ishment, abuse, bondage, and torture (in jail, 5:25–26, or in the hell of fire, 5:22). This justice is authoritatively meted down fol-lowing a hierarchy of power (from accuser to judge, from judge to guard, from guard to prisoner, 5:25). As long as the pattern of hi-erarchical authority is not broken, there is no escape from the cycle of oppression and bondage (5:26).

The disciples are freed from this cycle because, like Jesus, they nourish themselves with the bread of Scripture, fulfilling it (rather than submitting to it or mastering it). In this way, Scrip-ture empowers them to sustain, maintain, and reestablish good relationships with others through reconciliation (5:24), a type of behavior that involves exchange (e.g., of gifts), reciprocity, and mutuality.[21]

In sum, the teaching of the Sermon on the Mount regarding Scripture empowers disciples for a new praxis of justice, because they are drawn into a new pattern of relationship with Scripture itself. Then they can duplicate this nonhierarchical, nonoppressive pattern in new relationships with God and with others. The reality of their world is changed. They recognize that God is the one who is in control of life as the heavenly Father who reigns for those who are powerless to control their lives (5:44–47; 6:25–31), and also as the heavenly Father who showers blessings (sunshine and rain, 5:45; the things needed for life, 6:8, 25–31, 7:7–11) on both the evil and the good, on both the righteous and the unrighteous (contrary to the judgmental and hierarchical view of God's authority). Consequently, the disciples' relationship with God does not need to be marked by unconditional submission; one's relationship with a brother or sister might have precedence over one's relationship with God (5:23–24). Similarly, the disciples' relationships with others are transformed through an active reordering according to God's justice, which dismantles any oppressive hierarchical structure of authority.

Such are some of the subversive features of Matt. 5:17–26. As is clear after our discussion of the four preceding Readings, there are other dimensions to this text, including hierarchical features, upon which other interpretations can be grounded. For instance, judgment can easily be read as a feature of the justice of the kingdom rather than as a feature of the oppressive world that the kingdom challenges, as appears when one pays attention to the subversive thrust of the text. Yet, in this Reading E, these tensions between subversive and hierarchical features should not be dismissed or ignored, because they allow the believer-readers to hear voices from the margin, which further reveal the role of Scripture as empowering word.[22] It is by reading in terms of these tensions (as analytical frame) that I can hear the voices of victims of the judicial process, revealing the gap between traditional human justice (with its judgments, courts, and jails and other punishments) and the justice of the kingdom. Yet, these voices from the margin are more directly heard by reader-believers who listen to the text from a marginalized context.

Scripture as Empowering Word: A Plausible Hermeneutical Frame for the Persecuted Poor, for African-Americans, for Two-Thirds World Women, and for Those Who Accept the Call to Solidarity with the Poor and the Oppressed

These conclusions regarding the teaching of Matt. 5:17–48 about Scripture as empowering word provide a hermeneutical frame that makes sense for believers who read the Bible out of a situation of oppression, particularly when it is perceived as a situation of powerlessness. To illustrate this point, I will refer to the work of four biblical scholars: Carlos Bravo Gallardo, Elsa Tamez, Kwok Pui-lan, and Brian Blount.[23] Each envisions Scripture as empowering, although they do so in different ways appropriate for the particular situations from which they as Christians read the Bible.

As we saw, a teaching of the Sermon on the Mount regarding Scripture as empowering word makes sense for Carlos Bravo Gallardo, the Mexican Jesuit priest, and for the persecuted poor among whom he lives. As Bravo Gallardo says, Scripture "regrounds hope and the ability to resist" in the situation of powerlessness in which the persecuted poor exist; it is "the foundation of a spirituality of resistance for the poor and the oppressed," which involves "living the new justice."[24]

For Elsa Tamez and Latin American women, the central issue concerns the way in which Scripture becomes truly empowering. Tamez emphasizes that for the persecuted poor, and especially women in the Two-Thirds World who are victims of multiple oppressions, Scripture become liberating and empowering only when one "gain[s] distance from the text" and "ignore[s] the interpretations that almost automatically come to mind even before reading the actual text."[25] This includes ignoring the traditional view of (hierarchical) authority of the Scriptural text. Tamez explains,

> To distance oneself means to be new to the text (to be a stranger, a first-time visitor to the text), to be amazed by everything, especially by those details that repeated readings have made seem so logical and natural. It is necessary to take up the Bible as a new book, a book that has never been heard or read before. This demands a conscious effort that implies reading the texts a thousand times and very carefully.
>
> This way of reading is going to be conditioned by or embedded in the life experience of the Latin American reader.

...This is the process of coming closer to daily life, which implies the experiences of pain, joy, hope, hunger, celebration, and struggle. The Bible is not read as an intellectual or academic exercise; it is read with the goal of giving meaning to our lives today. In the confusing situation we find ourselves, we want to discern God's will and how it is present in our history. We think that the written word offers us criteria for discerning. Already this is a way of reformulating the principle of biblical authority.[26]

As Tamez emphasizes, for Latin American women this new understanding of biblical authority is to be contrasted with the view of authority embedded in the "macho" cultures and readings (hierarchical views of authority). Thus, Scripture becomes empowering word for life in a context of death, a liberating word for Latin American women, "the gospel of life."

Every liberation reading from the perspective of Latin American women must be understood within the framework that arises from the situation of the poor. In a context of misery, malnutrition, repression, torture, Indian genocide, and war — in other words, in a context of death — there is no greater priority than framing and articulating the readings according to these situations.... Therefore a reading from a woman's perspective has to go through this world of the poor. This will be a guarantee that it has a core theme of liberation, and it will shed light on other faces of the poor, such as blacks and native peoples.[27]

In her Chinese context, Kwok Pui-lan's view of the authority of Scripture has its own distinctive features, as compared with Tamez's "gospel of life." Yet the two perspectives are quite compatible, as is shown in Kwok Pui-lan's presentation of "examples of oral hermeneutics by Asian women" framed by a dialogical view of Scripture as "talking book" — a view that dismantles the understanding of Scripture as "external authoritative discourse" (hierarchical authority).[28] Note how readily her comments on a Bible study (on Gospel texts about women) that she presented in 1989 at an Asian mission conference in Indonesia tie in with many features of the teaching of Matt. 5:17–48 according to Reading E (Scripture as empowering word):

The Bible study tries to capture and express my double consciousness of my Chinese background and of the biblical tradition. It shows the "internal dialogization" that weaves the two stories together. The contemporary story of Chinese students is not subordinated to the biblical story, nor is the Bible the text and the Chinese situation the context.... On the other hand, the Chinese experience is not treated as the text, with the Bible and church tradition as the context for understanding.... By framing the story in a new way, by playing with the borders, and by creating stylizing variants, this example shows that meaning is not fixed, but negotiated in the discourse. Oral representation retells the story in *one's own words*, transforming an external authoritative discourse into an internally persuasive discourse.... The Bible is understood to be a talking book, constantly eliciting further conversation and dialogue, instead of an external, privileged text handed down from a distant past.[29]

Views of Scripture as empowering word, as gospel of life, and as talking book are also closely related to certain African-American views of Scripture, especially the view presented by Brian Blount,[30] who emphasizes that Scripture engenders a "performance spirituality" that fundamentally transforms the reality of oppression (rather than duplicating it and condoning it, in an unfortunately common reaction to abuse) by "conjuring" the reality of the kingdom.[31] Speaking about the "performance spirituality" of African-American hermeneutics (which Theophus Smith calls "conjurational spirituality"), Blount concludes his study of the Sermon on the Mount as follows:

I would argue that, given this hermeneutical perspective, actions of righteousness like meekness, purity of heart, love, forgiveness, prayer, motivated from the interior by a spirituality that makes them a better righteousness, can be understood to be actions that "conjure" God.... Acts of righteousness remain unimportant in and of themselves. One does not do the imperatives because they are law, but because the actions create something powerfully unique, a "blessed" reality, a transformed community, which stands apart from all others because, through its fulfillment of the sermon imperatives, it mimics the transforming reality of the kingdom. In this contemporary, "sectarian" world, the community would therefore be seen to be a unique community that provides access to (conjures) the kingdom of God.[32]

These four biblical scholars use alternative, contextualized metaphors to speak of the authority of Scripture: good news for the persecuted poor (Gallardo), gospel of life (Tamez), talking book (Kwok Pui-lan), "conjure sacred book" (Blount, following Smith). They might or might not find the metaphor I proposed, empowering word, helpful in their respective contexts — metaphors are highly contextual. Yet, I believe that all these metaphors point to different functions of Scripture and its authority for believers in situations where social, economic, political, or cultural oppression renders people powerless, and/or for other believers who are in solidarity with the powerless.[33]

Matthew 5:31–32 as Empowering Word for Believers Today: Conjuring a New Relationship between Women and Men

When we read Matt. 5:31–32 as empowering word, our attention is focused upon shifts in the structure of authority embedded in the text. To begin, the formula "It was said.... And I say to you... " challenges a view of Deut. 24:1–4 as "external authoritative discourse" (Kwok Pui-lan) or as "law" (as something that dictates what we must do; cf. Blount). The hierarchical view of the authority of Scripture is dismantled.

The patriarchal structure of authority, which feminist scholars have helped us to recognize, is also clear.[34] Throughout Matt. 5:31–32, the active subject — the one who divorces and who gives a certificate, causes to commit adultery, marries — is the man. The woman has no active positive role: she is either the object of the man's action (she is dismissed) or the passive receiver of the certificate. Her only potentially active role is negative: committing adultery. The phrase "causes her to commit adultery" (5:32) presupposes that the husband cannot break his own marriage.[35] Yet, this patriarchal structure of authority is undermined by the tension resulting from 5:32, which casts in a negative light an action (divorcing) of the man in 5:31 that would be considered positive according to Deut. 24:1–4. Furthermore, the exception shows that divorce is not, in and of itself, the problem. The real problem is the pattern of relationship between man and woman, which is questioned and therefore transformed through this teaching.

Because of this tension, we hear voices from the margin: those of women who are silenced by the patriarchal structure of authority and reduced to the status of (sex) objects taken or dismissed by men. The empowering word for women can also be heard, provided that we distance ourselves from interpretations that read this text as a law: a prohibition of divorce (except in extraordinary cases). Here, it is no longer a matter of knowing whether a prohibition of divorce is or is not to the economic and emotional advantage of women. The teaching of this text concerns the entire relationship between woman and man (to be understood in terms of the creation story, as Matt. 19:2–12 makes explicit).[36] Men are taught not to treat women as objects. But, even more important, women are offered empowering nourishment: they are invited to recognize the relation between woman and man as a partnership between equals. The specificity of this empowering word will vary with the context. Yet, it can be related to the empowering word that Chinese women of Shanghai found as they reread Gen. 2:18–24 (since this text is related to the teaching about the woman-man relationship, as suggested by Matt. 19:2–12). Kwok Pui-lan reports,

> In our discussion of the creation story of Genesis 2, the other Asian women theologians and I were conscious of the fact that the story was sometimes used against women because Eve was created second and she was to be Adam's helper (Gen. 2:18). But the Chinese Christian women in my group did not read the story in terms of male domination over female. One Chinese woman said that the term *helper* implied that Eve was a capable woman, that she could offer help to others. Living in a socialist country where equality between the sexes is emphasized in public discourse, these Chinese women focused on the complementarity of the two sexes in their interpretation.[37]

So it is with Matt. 5:31–32. This text was sometimes used against women, because of the patriarchal features it includes. Yet, when interpreted as gospel of life this text is no longer read in terms of male domination over female. Rather it conjures the transformative reality of the kingdom, where hierarchical, oppressive structures of authority are replaced by responsible relationships among persons who are in control of their own lives and, as capable women and men, do to others as they would want others to do to them (7:12).

Matthew 5:38–42 as Empowering Word for Believers Today: Gaining Control over One's Life by Not Resisting Evil in Solidarity with Others[38]

When we read this new passage, Matt. 5:38–42, as empowering word, we find, as above, a shift in structure of authority expressed by the formula, "It was said.... And I say to you...," which dismantles the hierarchical view of the authority of Scripture. Then, as we take seriously this shift, the text's voices from the margin catch our attention, and each of these voices evokes other voices from the margin in today's world.

An eye for an eye and a tooth for a tooth (Matt. 5:38; Exod. 21:23–24; Lev. 24:19–20; Deut. 19:21) evokes victims of violence, deeply marked in their flesh by accidental and deliberate violence, violence committed by justice systems, people seeking revenge, criminals, sadists, or torturers. Whatever the source of violence, one hears the victims' cries.

Being struck on the right cheek (5:39) evokes persons who are shamed, insulted — the victims of emotional violence, whether or not accompanied by physical violence. This verse evokes all the voices that are shamed into silence by the powerful emotional violence of racism, classism, and sexism (including domestic violence). It evokes the cries — often, silent cries — of victims of physical violence, whose bodies are so deeply violated by beatings, tortures, and rapes that they are held captive by terror and shame as much as by the brutal force of burglars, criminals, special police forces, gangs, and rapists.

Being sued for one's coat (5:40) evokes the legal violence that deprives a person of the necessities of life, even as it claims to strive to prevent this evil (as is suggested by the allusion to Exod. 22:26–27 and Deut. 24:12–13, regarding the illegality of taking permanently away from a poor man the cloak he uses to sleep in and that he has given as a collateral for a debt). From the perspective of people in Two-Thirds World nations (where I have recently been for brief visits), this is the economic violence perpetrated against them by multinational companies, First World countries, and the International Monetary Fund, which take possession of the most basic resources put up as collateral for debts.[39] This is the violence of poverty and hunger, so clearly visible in the homeless of the streets of First World cities and in the enormous crowded shantytowns and squatter camps of Two-Thirds World cities. This violence is insidious because, before the law, no one — no individual, no company, no industry, no country — can be denounced as responsible.

Being forced to carry something for a mile of compulsory service (5:41) evokes oppression by imperialist and colonialist powers, such as the Roman empire, and thus forced labor in periods of occupation and war, past and present. More generally this verse evokes the exploitation of certain persons by others, even if minimal wages are paid. This oppressive violence in the present becomes visible when one compares the minimum wages of part-time workers (without benefits) with the salaries of CEOs in any country, and even more clearly when one compares in any multi-national company the wages of workers in factories located in North America and Europe with those of workers in sweatshops in the Two-Thirds World (they receive a few cents for each dollar received by First World workers).

Though strangely linked with the preceding verses (since here the disciple is no longer the victim), 5:42 evokes the poor individual in desperate need of financial assistance who can only beg for help, and is turned down.

As we noted, other Readings (especially Readings B and C) find in Matt. 5:38–42 a vision of the kingdom and its radical legal, political, and economic reordering of life in society. This text does evoke such a vision. Thus, some scholars have concluded that "Jesus is not presenting a new program for human society; he is announcing the end of human society, the end of the world."[40] So it seems, when one contemplates the cosmic dimensions of an evil that engulfs millions of people. Thus, these verses promise once again the coming of the kingdom and of God's justice, for which the poor and the oppressed thirst and hunger. This promise and the hope of sharing in the coming kingdom even if one is personally crushed by present evil should not be seen as escapism, but as empowerment. Individual believers are reminded that they are not alone, but are part of this multitude of people, the children of God (5:45), for whom God reigns.

Beyond offering the empowerment of this eschatological hope, these verses, when read as empowering word, also transform the present life-reality of the powerless. From this perspective, "Do not resist evil" does not call powerless, oppressed people to submission. On the contrary, as the following verses confirm, it reveals that whatever the source of their powerlessness, the dreadful reality of their total lack of control over their lives can be transformed. This does not mean that each individual is empowered to overcome the massive evil that pervades life in human societies. Until the end of time they will have to pray, "Your kingdom come. Your will be done, on earth as it is in heaven." In the meantime, they will have to live with this evil in the midst of a world where poverty, exploitation, legalized oppression, racism, and all kinds of emotional and physical abuse are rampant and seem to dominate all human relations. But in the midst of such an evil world, Matt. 5:38–42 empowers the powerless. Those who have no control over their lives are given control over their lives. A new reality is conjured.

Not resisting evil means turning the other cheek and voluntarily making oneself the object of racist and other emotional abuse. This was, for instance, what African-Americans did in the sit-ins of the civil rights movement. As a result, even more racist abuse, both emotional and physical, was directed at them. But their reality was transformed: they had regained at least some control over their lives; the shame of racism was now upon the racists and could be replaced by black pride.

Not resisting evil means voluntarily refusing to use the law to defend oneself. In the text, it means refusing to use the law regarding the illegality of permanently taking away from a poor man the cloak he uses to sleep in and that he has given as a collateral for a debt (Exod. 22:26–27; Deut. 24:12–13). Thus, in this case not resisting evil is giving up on the legal system and therefore making oneself totally vulnerable to the law. But, in the process, a new reality is conjured. From this perspective, today's poor, legally deprived of land and housing, can respond by bypassing the legal system (which was supposed to protect them), by simply establishing squatter camps. A few squatters could be quickly evicted by authorities applying the law. But there are so many children of the kingdom that soon, squatter camps become a reality, a new community of the dispossessed, which is also a community in which the dispossessed regain some control over their lives as they organize themselves.

Not resisting evil means voluntarily going an extra mile of compulsory service. Imagine the scene represented by the text. Going an extra mile means continuing to carry the Roman soldiers' gear, even as the troops recruit other people for this compulsory service. Consequently, it involves not only gaining control over one's life but also helping the newly drafted people, sharing the load with them, lightening their load. Today, it might mean investing more time in the workplace where one is exploited in order to regain control over one's life by active solidarity with other workers. This might involve slowing down the work pace (dragging feet, taking time for camaraderie, humanizing the workplace) so that the hourly wage might better reflect the work done. It might involve staying longer at the workplace in order to organize a union. It might involve "participating in the masquerade of evil," as Dietrich Bonhoeffer did (after a radical change of perspective in response to the horrors committed by Nazi Germany during World War II) by becoming a member of the secret service of the German army in an attempt to undermine their grossly oppressive machinations and actively promote the dismantling of their destructive power, and ultimately by participating in a plot to kill Hitler.[41]

While exploitations and abuses of every kind might remain as strong as usual, nevertheless, through the empowering word of Matt. 5:38–41, the contextual reality of the powerless has changed. By entering the masquerade of the evil that oppresses them, as they are invited to do by the text, they are no longer victims without control over their lives. Indeed, they have taken control of their lives! The hierarchical structure of authority that reduced them to the rank of manipulated objects has been dismantled. They have been empowered to be full-fledged persons, subjects of their own actions. They have regained their dignity. Once again they are children of God, who are therefore in a position to struggle for the kingdom and God's justice (6:33).

But believer-readers cannot stop their reading at 5:41. Another verse remains: "Give to everyone who begs from you, and do not refuse anyone who wants to borrow from you" (5:42). The disciples are those who are importuned by the needy who beg from them. Are beggars now to be viewed as evildoers who should not be resisted? Of course not. With irony, the text has reversed the roles. Disciples should recognize that they also occupy the position of evildoers. Their success in overcoming evil, in avoiding dispossession and exploitation, has made (some of) them rich. They have possessions, which they feel they need to protect. Consequently, despite appearances, they have also lost control of their lives, which are now controlled by their "treasures on earth" (6:19–21). In this situation, as in the preceding, disciples are empowered to regain control over their lives by not resisting "evil," that is, by giving to everyone who begs from them. After all the teaching remains the same: solidarity with those who are shamed, oppressed, and deprived is the way to regain control over one's life and to participate in the kingdom, which gathers all the children of God.

Chapter Eight

Choosing an Interpretation

The Challenge of Discipleship,
Matthew 6:1–7:11

Why Did I Choose This Interpretation Rather Than One of the Others?

Each of us needs to address this question in order to assume responsibility for her or his interpretation. Yet soon this question sharpens: Which interpretation should I choose? It is both a matter of assessing an earlier choice and of self-consciously identifying oneself with one interpretation.

For us, Christian believers, the critical study of the Sermon on the Mount as Scripture culminates in the decision to confess, "*I* believe (*credo*) this given interpretation is the Word of God that the Sermon on the Mount has for us today" Choosing "the best" teaching of the Sermon is also a commitment to live by it. This choice confronts us with the challenge of discipleship that the Sermon has for us. We can no longer hide by pretending that we did not know that we chose one interpretation among several options. We must elucidate and assess the values and convictions on which we based this choice.

This assessment is no less important for you readers of the Sermon on the Mount who are not Christian believers. As you now realize, you also have chosen an interpretation. It is therefore appropriate to ask: Why did you make this choice? Which values and convictions played a role in your choice? Furthermore, now that you can see more clearly other options, you might want to discuss with Christian believers how you are affected by their choices. Indeed, you might want to prick their conscience by challenging them to choose a teaching of the Sermon that does not harm you and others.

As we ask, Why choose one interpretation rather than another? we need to recognize that the question "why?" raises much more unpredictable issues than the questions "how?" and "what?" I will not be in a position to help you as directly as I did in the preceding chapters. Helping you identify what choices you made was simply a matter of describing how several existing interpretations were framed and focused as all interpretations are. By contrast, probing the reasons (the "why") of these choices involves elucidating values and convictions that fluctuate along with the circumstances and convince us that such a teaching is or is not for us.

Why did I choose this interpretation? Is it really the best teaching of the Sermon on the Mount by which believers should live in my present context? Obviously, I cannot answer these questions for you. Yet, you cannot address them by yourself either. You can only address them in dialogue with other people.

I cannot tell why you chose an interpretation. Even if I knew which interpretation you adopted, I would know neither your convictions — the self-evident truths and values that you spontaneously use as you decide how to live your daily-life — nor your concrete life-situations.

You by yourself cannot tell why you chose an interpretation. This is so because convictions become apparent only when we are dialoguing with others who share them. Convictions are communal. I am not denying that we can have idiosyncratic convictions and live by them. But if we do so we are alienated from all people around us. Unless we have lost touch with reality — the reality as perceived by a community — we share the convictions that govern our lives and our interpretations with at least a group of people. Consequently, it is only in actual, live conversations with others around us — including people who made different choices — that we can hope to get a glimpse of our own convictions and to discern the relative value of different interpretations. It is only with other people that each of us can say, "*I* believe (*credo*) this is the best teaching of this text for *us* today," and thus, at the very least, the best teaching for a small group of people who share life and are dialogue partners in a specific context; yet, obviously, this group and this context can also be quite broad.

To help you initiate a dialogue with people around you regarding the choice of a teaching by which Christian believers should live in your context, I invite you to review the different kinds of choices we make when we adopt one interpretation rather than another (as discussed in the preceding chapters). Thus we will be in a position to reflect on our reasons (including the role of convictions and contexts) for making these choices. Then, we will reread Matt. 6:1–7:11. Yet, instead of reading this passage for its teaching for believers today (as in preceding chapters), we will selectively focus upon how the text challenges us to elucidate basic convictions governing our choice of interpretation.

Accounting for Our Emotional Responses to Different Interpretations of Scripture in Our Critical Study

Since it now is clear that our different conclusions regarding the teaching of the Sermon on the Mount for believers today are equally legitimate and plausible options, there is no objective reason (e.g., regarding what the text demands) to prefer one interpretation above another. Yet these choices are not inconsequential. The passionate debates among proponents of different interpretations show how emotional and ideological are these debates. These choices are based on deep seated convictions about religious and moral matters.

For instance, I suspect some of you feel that some of the conclusions of the five Readings I presented are scandalous. Your knee-jerk reaction is to dismiss them as irresponsible. Conversely, you might have been deeply moved and inspired by other interpretations, so much so that you are ready to abandon your original interpretation. I know. I have the same kind of positive and negative gut-feeling reactions. It is at this convictional level that there are disagreements and debates.

In this critical study we must stop and ask: Why? Why am I dismissing or embracing these interpretations? Why this emotional involvement with some interpretations and not with others? Why this feeling that an interpretation is either most appropriate or totally out of line? What kind of deep seated values and/or convictions are involved?

Could we just ignore these emotional and ideological debates in our critical study? By no means! These issues are clearly a part of the process of interpreting the Sermon on the Mount. Therefore, in order to be critical — that is, in order to make explicit the different aspects of the interpretive process that led us to our conclusions — we cannot but elucidate the role of convictions in our choice of an interpretation.

Different Roles in This Discussion for Readers Who Are Christian Believers and for Readers Who Are Not

What is the "best interpretation" of the teaching of the Sermon on the Mount for believers today? Here is the center of the debate. We disagree about the relative values of the diverse interpretations. What we mean by the "best interpretation" depends in part on where we stand in relationship to this New Testament text.

All of us, whether Christian believers or not, have formulated what we see as the teaching of this text as Scripture for believers today. Everyone can do this in a legitimate and plausible way. But readers for whom this text is Scripture and those for whom it is not have very different ways of assessing the relative value of these interpretations. Christian believers do so primarily in terms of their basic convictions. Other readers do it primarily in terms of the ways people are concretely affected in life by the choice of an interpretation by Christian believers. Yet, of course, each assessment of the relative value of an interpretation is based on both kinds of considerations.

For Christian Believers, Choosing an Interpretation Is a Challenge of Discipleship

For us, Christian believers, basic convictions play a significant role in the choice of an interpretation. We have a lot at stake. Our entire lives as disciples depend upon this choice. For us, the best interpretation of the teaching of the Sermon on the Mount for believers today is the teaching by which we should live. It is the Word of God for us today.

Because the Sermon on the Mount is Scripture for us (in whatever sense), we are very close to this text. Therefore, in the preceding exercises (even though they were not devotional readings), we were inclined to identify ourselves with the believers to whom the teaching of this text is addressed. More likely than not, we chose an interpretation with a teaching that is meaningful and helpful for our lives as believers. Our personal convictions were involved.

There is nothing wrong with this. But the question, Why did I choose this interpretation? challenges us to make explicit the convictions that led us to our choice. These are our convictions regarding our relationship with God and with Jesus Christ, of our identity and vocation as disciples, and of our relationships with others.

Our convictions influenced our interpretation; we spontaneously chose an interpretation that somehow fit them. Conversely, our reading of the Sermon on the Mount as Scripture challenges our convictions. Since this teaching involves something new for or about the believers' life, this newness necessarily challenges us and our convictions. In our dialogue with the text, the text, in effect, says to us, "You are attached to your convictions. Fine. You came to me with your convictions about God, Jesus Christ, authority, evil, sin, salvation. No problem. I can address the concerns raised by your convictions. Here is God's Word for you. Here is what you need to do. Now, put up or shut up! Apply this teaching to your life or give up your claim to these convictions!"

So far, by keeping a distance between the text and ourselves, by speaking of the teaching for an anonymous group we called "believers today," we did not directly feel the bite of this challenge. But as we ask the question "why?" we can no longer avoid this challenge, which is all the more direct now that we recognize we have a real choice. Our convictions are on the line. Part of the challenge of discipleship is assuming responsibility for our convictions.

In addition, other readers force us Christians to recognize that our convictions cannot be assessed in a vacuum, as if they were somehow unrelated to life. Our choice of an interpretation as Word of God for us has concrete implications, as non-Christian readers remind us.

Non-Christian Readers Challenging the Choices of Interpretation by Christians

As my experience with many groups tells me, those of you who read the Christian Scripture from the perspective of outside observers do not have any difficulty formulating the teaching of this text for Christian believers today. You now recognize that, reading as non-Christians, you chose an interpretation, as everyone else did. Yet your reasons are different from those of Christian believers.

You chose a particular interpretation in part because of the way you conceived of Christian believers, and because you are affected by them, as individuals or as communities, in your personal life as well as in public life. Your choices most directly reflect the concrete ways Christian teachings end up affecting you.

I cannot speculate on your reasons for choosing one interpretation rather than another. But I can say that the choice of interpretations by non-Christian readers is always very instructive for me because it challenges us, Christians, to recognize how our ways of life as disciples and our choices of interpretations affect other people. We are often surprised to discover how other people are hurt by these choices, both emotionally and physically. We did not mean for our interpretations of the Sermon on the Mount to condone (and even promote) anti-Semitism, apartheid, colonialism, cultural imperialism, battering of spouses, hypocritical marginalization and exclusion of so-called sinners. And yet, our interpretations sometimes (often?) do so. We can recognize it if we care enough to listen to those who are hurt.

In sum, you non-Christian readers remind Christian believers that their choices of interpretations are never simply matters of conviction. They are also contextual matters by which real people are deeply affected in their daily life.

The Threefold Ground for Choosing an Interpretation: Issues Open for Discussion

The ground for our choice of an interpretation is actually threefold, since we frame our interpretations in three different ways. Different convictions and values presided over the choices we made as we framed our interpretations in terms of certain theological-hermeneutical categories rather than others, in terms of certain contextual issues rather than others, and in terms of a certain kind of textual-analytical evidence rather than others. Let us briefly review each type of choice. This will help us assess the respective roles that these three choices played in each of our particular interpretations as we enter in dialogue with others.

Why Did We Frame Our Reading in Terms of Certain Contextual Issues Rather Than Others?

By now you are aware that we framed our reading of the text in terms of a specific contextual problem, and that there is no actual teaching — something new about or for life — for believers, if the text does not offer a solution for it. Since this text is held as Scripture by believers, they read it with the expectation that it has a teaching for them. Therefore, we framed our interpretations of its teaching in terms of our particular perceptions of the problems that believers encounter in a certain context. Each of us can now assume responsibility for the choice of a particular problem (as a contextual frame) falling in one of four general categories:

lack of knowledge (or wrong knowledge); lack of will (not wanting to do something); powerlessness (due to human limitations or oppression); lack of faith (or wrong faith), either communal or personal.

Questions for discussion with those who define the contextual problem in a different way include:

- *How do we delimit the context in which we locate the believers to whom this teaching is addressed?* In my personal experience, this is a most important question, especially for male European-American scholars, because we often do not realize that we interpret out of a limited context rather than out of a universal context.[1] This concerns convictions about the nature of the life-context in which we live and read.

- *On what do we ground our perception of the contextual problem?* Three more specific subquestions might be helpful: (1) what important personal experiences play a role in our perception of the contextual problem? (2) what is the evidence that this actually is a major problem in the chosen context? (3) what role did our convictions about the nature of evil and sin play in our perception of this problem?[2]

Conversely:

- *Which contextual problems in a given situation do we ignore?* Concrete life examples are most helpful for this discussion. For instance, it is very common for us, middle-class Europeans and North Americans to forget the plight of the homeless, the poor, the marginalized.

- *Who would be directly or indirectly hurt by this choice of interpretation?* Here also, concrete life examples are most helpful. Let us not forget that others might be hurt as a result of the actions that believers perform in accordance with a particular teaching (for instance, does this course of action condone or promote anti-Semitism?) or simply because a problem is not addressed (the wounded man died in the ditch because no Samaritan came to his aid).

Discussion of these questions should help us recognize that our choice of an interpretation presupposes certain convictions regarding the nature of the life-context in which we live and related convictions regarding evil, sin, and salvation (problem, need, transformation, solution); otherwise we could not discern a genuine teaching of the text for believers today.

Why Did We Frame Our Reading by Focusing It on One Aspect of the Text Rather Than Another?

By now you are aware that we focus each of our readings on one of several meaning-producing dimensions of the text. You know, at least in a general way, that any given biblical text has a number of textual dimensions, which I designated by a series of metaphors representing the ways a biblical text produces meaning: text as window, story, symbolic message, transformative thrust, subversive thrust, or voices from the margin. As we assumed responsibility for our respective interpretations, we identified the particular textual dimension upon which our interpretation is focused (and thus the often implicit *analytical frame* we use) because for various reasons we perceived this given textual dimension as particularly significant. It remains for us to clarify why we selected such a focus.

Questions for discussion with those who focus their readings upon different textual dimensions include:

- *Is the focus on a specific textual dimension a personal choice?* Were we personally attracted by this textual dimension rather than another? In such cases, it is a matter of personal sensibility and aesthetics. To assess the (more or less important) role this choice of a textual dimension played in our interpretation, it might be helpful to ask: Am I usually focusing my interpretation on this kind of textual dimension? Is this part of an interpretive pattern for me? Or is it exceptional? If it is part of a pattern, my aesthetic sensibility played an important role in my choice of an interpretation, but not if it is exceptional.

- *Is the focus on a specific textual dimension a cultural choice?* Does our choice of a textual dimension reflect clear tendencies in our culture? Did we follow a pattern that is recognizable in interpretations by people around us? In interpretations found in the media? In interpretations found in popular books (including commentaries)? In sermons?

Discussion of these questions should help us recognize that our choice of an interpretation presupposes some kind of convictions regarding what is significant, particularly meaningful, and thus authoritative, in the sense that we have to learn something from it.

Why Did We Frame Our Reading in Terms of Certain Theological Issues Rather Than Others?

Similarly, you now know that we make sense of a scriptural text by entering into dialogue with it about a specific subject matter, which frames our interpretation. When we are aware that this text is held as Scripture by certain believers (whether or not we are believers ourselves), we realize that we make sense of it in terms of theological issues closely related to the believers' convictions. The range of theological issues (used as hermeneutical frame for such readings) can include virtually any aspect of human relationships with the divine, with other people, and with the world.

In the preceding chapters, in order to facilitate meaningful comparison of our interpretations, I asked that all of us frame our readings in terms of theological issues related to discipleship and Scripture. We assumed responsibility for our choices of specific theological categories by acknowledging that we posited specific views of discipleship and of Scripture as the appropriate way to frame the teaching of the Sermon on the Mount for Christian believers today. This acknowledgment included recognizing that in each case we had a range of choices.

Thus, we noted that discipleship could be cast in terms of at least five different conceptions: (1) discipleship as doing God's will with an emphasis on (a) learning from Jesus what God's will is, or (b) being enticed and exhorted by Jesus to do God's will, or (c) being empowered by Jesus to do God's will; (2) discipleship as imitating Jesus with an emphasis on (a) learning from Jesus how to act as he did, or (b) learning from Jesus how to discern manifestations of the kingdom today as models.

Similarly, we noted that each interpretation emphasized a certain role of Scripture for disciples. I proposed a series of metaphors to represent the primary roles of Scripture I found in diverse interpretations: Scripture as lamp to my feet, canon, good news, family album, corrective glasses, empowering word, holy Bible.

It remains for us to clarify why we chose to frame our interpretation in terms of one view of discipleship and one view of Scripture — whether or not they are in the list I provided — rather than in terms of other views.

Questions for discussion with those who enter into dialogue with the text on different theological issues include:

• *How much does our choice of specific views of discipleship and of Scripture reflect our own convictions?* Since convictions are self-evident for us, we usually cannot acknowledge them until someone with different convictions points out our own to us.

Discussion of this question should help us recognize that our choice of an interpretation presupposes certain convictions regarding the relationship between God and human beings (otherwise we could not conceive of discipleship), or more generally, convictions about a structure of authority in terms of which we conceive of the relationship not only between God and human beings, but also between Scripture and believers, and between believers and other people.

Reading Matthew 6:1–7:11 to Elucidate Basic Convictions about God as Father and about Authority Presupposed by Our Choice of an Interpretation

To prepare yourself for your discussion with others regarding what is "the best" interpretation of the Sermon on the Mount for believers today in a given context, I invite you to reread Matt. 6:1–7:11. I do not ask you to reread Matt. 6:1–7:11 in order to identify its teaching for believers today. Rather, I ask you to identify what you learn from Matt. 6:1–7:11 about the conviction about authority you presupposed in your interpretation of 5:1–6:48 and 7:12–29. For this I ask you to allow your reading of this passage to question, confront, and challenge your previous interpretation of the other parts of the Sermon on the Mount. My hope is that the rereading of this text will help you become aware of the role that your conviction about authority played in your choice of an interpretation.

What Are Your Convictions about the Relationship between God and Human Beings and about Authority Did You Presuppose?

To help you elucidate the convictions about authority embedded in your previous interpretations of the Sermon on the Mount, I ask you to ponder Matt. 6:1–7:11 first regarding the relationship between God and human beings it posits according to your interpretation of these verses. As you reread this text you might want to keep in mind the following questions:

- *What kind of relationship between God and human beings, and thus what kind of structure of authority, do you see in Matt. 6:1–7:11?*

- *What convictions about God and authority did you presuppose in your interpretations of the rest of the Sermon on the Mount?* How did you conceive of the relationship between God and human beings? What structure of authority — authority of God, of Jesus, of Scripture, of religious leaders, of community, of traditions and other cultural values, of political and/or economic powers — did you presuppose? To what extent are your presuppositions and convictions challenged by Matt. 6:1–7:11.

Here is the text of Matt. 6:1–7:11 in the New Revised Standard Version, with some alternative translations in brackets. I give you space for your answers below.

6:1"Beware of practicing your piety [righteousness, justice] before others [human beings] in order to be seen by them; for then you have no reward from [beside, in the house of] your Father in heaven.
6:2"So whenever you give alms [do some act of charity], do not sound a trumpet before you [do not call attention to yourself], as the hypocrites do in the synagogues and in the streets, so that they may be praised by [win admiration from] others. Truly I tell you, they have received their reward. 6:3But when you give alms [do some act of charity], do not let your left hand know what your right hand is doing, 6:4so that your alms [act of charity] may be done in secret [in the hidden place]; and your Father who sees in secret [what is hidden] will reward you.
6:5"And whenever you pray, do not be like the hypocrites; for they love to stand and pray in the synagogues and at the street corners, so that they may be seen by others [human beings]. Truly I tell you, they have received their reward. 6:6But whenever you pray, go into your room and shut the door and pray to your Father who is in secret [in the hidden place]; and your Father who sees in secret [what is hidden] will reward you.
6:7"When you are praying, do not heap up empty phrases [go babbling on, repeat the same things again and again] as the Gentiles do; for they think that they will be heard because of their many words [that the more they say the more likely they are to be heard]. 6:8Do not be like them, for your Father knows what you need [what are your needs] before you ask him. 6:9Pray then in this way: Our

Father in heaven, hallowed be your name [may your name be made holy, honored as holy, sanctified]. 6:10Your kingdom [reign] come. Your will be done, on earth as it is in heaven. 6:11Give us this day our daily bread [our bread for the next day]. 6:12And forgive us our debts [the wrong we have done], as we also have forgiven our debtors [those who have wronged us]. 6:13And do not bring us to the time of trial [put us to the test], but rescue us from the evil one [evil].

6:14"For if you forgive others their trespasses [the wrong they have done], your heavenly Father will also forgive you; 6:15but if you do not forgive others, neither will your Father forgive your trespasses [the wrong you have done].

6:16"And whenever you fast, do not look dismal [gloomy], like the hypocrites, for they disfigure their faces so as to show others that they are fasting. Truly I tell you, they have received their reward. 6:17But when you fast, put oil on your head and wash your face, 6:18so that your fasting may be seen not by others but by your Father who is in secret [in the hidden place]; and your Father who sees in secret [what is hidden] will reward you.

6:19"Do not store up for yourselves treasures on earth, where moth and rust consume and where thieves break in and steal; 6:20but store up for yourselves treasures in heaven, where neither moth nor rust consumes and where thieves do not break in and steal. 6:21For where your treasure is, there your heart will be also.

6:22"The eye is the lamp of the body. So, if your eye is healthy [sound, undivided], your whole body will be full of light; 6:23but if your eye is unhealthy [bad], your whole body will be full of darkness. If then the light in you is darkness, how great is the darkness!

6:24"No one can serve two masters; for a slave will either hate the one and love the other, or be devoted to [cling to] the one and despise the other. You cannot serve God and wealth [mammon, money].

6:25"Therefore I tell you, do not worry [be anxious] about your life, what you will eat or what you will drink, or about your body, what you will wear. Is not life more than food, and the body more than clothing? 6:26Look at the birds of the air; they neither sow nor reap nor gather into barns, and yet your heavenly Father feeds them. Are you not of more value than they? 6:27And can any of you by worrying [being anxious] add a single hour to your span of life? 6:28And why do you worry [are you anxious] about clothing? Consider the lilies of the field, how they grow; they neither toil nor spin, 6:29yet I tell you, even Solomon in all his glory was not clothed like one of these. 6:30But if God so clothes the grass of the field, which is alive today and tomorrow is thrown into the oven, will he not much more clothe you — you of little faith? 6:31Therefore do not worry, saying [do not ask anxiously], 'What will we eat?' or 'What will we drink?' or 'What will we wear?' 6:32For it is the Gentiles who strive for [run after, struggle for] all these things; and indeed your heavenly Father knows that you need all these things. 6:33But strive first for [run first after, struggle first for] the kingdom [reign] of God and his righteousness [justice], and all these things will be given to you as well. 6:34So do not worry [be anxious] about tomorrow, for tomorrow will bring worries of its own. Today's trouble is enough for today.

7:1"Do not judge [condemn], so that you may not be judged [condemned]. 7:2For with the judgment you make you will be judged [for as you condemn others, so you will yourselves be condemned], and the measure you give will be the measure you get. 7:3Why do you see the speck in your neighbor's eye, but do not notice the log in your own eye? 7:4Or how can you say to your neighbor, 'Let me take the speck out of your eye,' while the log is in your own eye? 7:5You hypocrite, first take the log out of your own eye, and then you will see clearly to take the speck out of your neighbor's eye.

7:6"Do not give what is holy to dogs; and do not throw your pearls before swine [to the pigs], or they will trample them under foot and turn and maul you.

7:7"Ask, and it will be given you; search [run after, struggle for], and you will find [attain, reach]; knock, and the door will be opened for you. 7:8For everyone who asks receives, and everyone who searches [runs after, struggles for] finds [attains, reaches], and for everyone who knocks, the door will be opened. 7:9Is there anyone among you who, if your child asks for bread, will give a stone? 7:10Or if the child asks for a fish, will give a snake? 7:11If you then, who are evil, know how to give good gifts to your children, how much more will your Father in heaven give good things to those who ask him!"

Use the space provided below to write down what you learn from this text about your convictions about authority. What is the view of authority that is reflected in this text, according to your interpretation? How does it compare with the conception of God and of God's relationship to human beings you presupposed in your interpretations of the other parts of the Sermon on the Mount? It might be helpful for you to write down your answer before I suggest alternative ways in which convictions about authority can be envisioned.

_____

_____

_____

_____

_____

_____

_____

_____

Alternative Convictions about God as Father and about Authority

To help you prepare your discussion with others regarding what is the best teaching of the Sermon on the Mount for believers today, I invite you to compare your conclusions regarding the conviction about authority embedded in your interpretation with six common ways in which authority is construed. Of course, this list does not intend to be comprehensive. It simply aims at prompting you to elucidate the characteristics of your own convictions, so that you might be ready to assess the relative weight you want to give to your convictions and to your responsibility toward others (to the way your choice of an interpretation affects other people around you).

In the following paragraphs I invite you to rehearse the kind of discussion you need to have with other members of your community in order to elucidate the convictions you use as you choose an interpretation. Imagine that you are sitting around a table with six other readers of the Sermon on the Mount. You have presented your own conclusions regarding the view of authority presented by Matt. 6:1–7:11. Now, one after the other, your companions present their own conclusions. You are invited to listen. Yet, what is called for is an active listening: comparing your own view with the one presented, but also beginning to envision the implications for your assessment of the relative values of different interpretations.

In each case, I will first briefly describe the way in which God as Father is construed, then, express in a few words the structure of authority that functions as a conviction, and finally suggest to which view of Scripture this conception of God is related.

1. *God as Father teaches children what is good and bad, what they should or should not do.* God as a father figure is the one who rewards or does not reward his children on the basis of their deeds. The children cannot escape God's scrutiny; as their "Father who sees in secret" (6:4, 6, 17), God knows exactly what they are doing and, accordingly, will or will not reward them (6:1, 2, 4, 5, 6, 16, 18). Here, God as Father instructs his children how to give alms, pray, fast, not to judge others (6:1–17; 7:1–5, 7–11). From this perspective, by praying the Lord's Prayer disciples as God's children ask God's help to do his will, which includes (in reverse order) help in resisting temptation, in forgiving others, daily bread, as well as help in doing God's will, in their work to bring about the kingdom, and in respecting God's authority ("hallowed be your name").[3] Total allegiance (that cannot be divided between God and money, 6:24; see also 6:19–23) to God as Father and Master and complete submission to, trust in, and dependence on his absolute power and authority free disciples of any anxiety (6:25–34).

In this interpretation, *the structure of authority is vertical:* God is holy, powerful, transcendent, has the knowledge of good and evil that human beings do not have; the proper human attitude is respect, submission, obedience, and, whenever one fails to obey, guilt, because God always knows what his children do. This structure of authority is presupposed by the view of Scripture as "lamp to my feet" (Scripture reveals to believers the will of God that they should implement in their lives).

2. *God as Father is the householder, the paterfamilias who sets the rule for the household.* Here, God as a Father figure, a paterfamilias, is the center of the household. All activities of the children — members of the household — should be done for the sake of God, rather than for the sake of outsiders (6:1–6, 16–18). But because God, as paterfamilias, is in complete control of what happens in the household, one does not need to be anxious about anything. God knows what his children need and provides it (6:7–8; 6:25–34; 7:7–11). Conversely, God requires complete allegiance as a condition for belonging to God's household (having one's treasure in heaven rather than earth, 6:19–21; serving God rather than Mammon, 6:24), sharing in the benefits of his household. Without this complete allegiance one is excluded from God's household (one receives the rewards of the world, outside the household, 6:2, 5, 16; one's possessions are destroyed, 6:19;

one is in darkness, 6:23; one is judged with the criteria of the world one has used, 7:1–5; and/or one throws away pearls and is torn apart, 7:6).

In this interpretation, again *the structure of authority is vertical:* God is powerful, transcendent; God is the only one who can provide for the needs of the believers, who are therefore totally dependent upon him. The strict conditions for membership in the household of God — the community — include respect, submission, and obedience to the will of God, which is the rule of the community. Without this complete submission to God's will one is excluded from the community. This structure of authority is presupposed by the view of Scripture as "canon," the rule of the community that believers must implement in their lives.

3. *God as Father is the householder, the paterfamilias* **who cares** *for each member of the household under his authority.* God as a father figure is here also a paterfamilias, but primarily as a provider and as the one who unites and holds the family together. All activities of the children should reflect their relationship with God and the rest of the household (6:1–6, 16–18), and should be done in imitation of God as Father (5:45–48). Because God is a loving Father who not only can give to his children what they need, but wants to do so even before he is asked (6:8; 7:7–11), children-disciples do not need to convince him to give them what they need (6:7–8). Yet, believer-children need to acknowledge his authority to benefit from his loving care — they need to seek first the kingdom and God's righteousness (6:33); then, they will not need to worry about anything (6:25–34). Praying together as a family, "Our Father in heaven" (6:9), believers can recognize themselves as those children of God whom God cares for by providing all that they need (6:9–13), and thus submit to the authority of God as their Father in heaven with all their lives (6:19–24).

In this interpretation, once again *the structure of authority is vertical:* God is powerful, transcendent, even though, this time, the love and care of this father figure is emphasized. Yet, recognition of his authority remains a condition for membership in the household of God, which strives to imitate God's care and love for everyone. This structure of authority is presupposed by the view of Scripture as "family album," which establishes the believers' identity as children of God, the benevolent, loving patriarch.

4. *God as Father is the loving parent who reaches out to his wrongheaded children.* God as a father figure is here a loving parent who strives to establish and maintain an intimate, loving relationship with his children. Believer-disciples should not forget that they belong to the household of God, and that rewards await them in the house of their "Father in heaven" (6:1), which is any hidden, private place (6:4, 6, 18) where they can be in intimate relationship with God. As the believers' heavenly close friend, God is always well inclined toward his children. They do not need to convince him to take their side (as the Gentiles do, 6:7); he already wants to give them the good things that they need (7:7–11), and even anticipates their needs (6:8). Believers therefore should not be anxious, because their Father is constantly, though secretly, present with them, providing all that they need (6:25–34). As believers they can fully rely on their heavenly friend and Father. Therefore they do not need to gather treasures on earth (6:19–21) or seek to serve other masters (6:24); their loving Father invites them to trust him totally, so as to be free to devote themselves totally to the kingdom and to pursuing God's righteousness (6:33), manifesting in this way God's love to others, as they do by forgiving others (6:12, 14–15).

In this interpretation, *the structure of authority is horizontal:* God is a friend sharing the lives of believers, enticing them to participate in his kingdom and to manifest his love to others. Such an authority neither imposes, nor demands, nor commands. Rather, it offers itself by reaching out to others; it shares their lives with the hope of freewill cooperation; it shows the way toward the good life, the feast, of the kingdom. This structure of authority is presupposed by the view of Scripture as "good news" the loving word of a parent.

5. *God, the creator of all human beings, longs to become "our Father in heaven."* Fatherhood is a figure for a two-way, reciprocal relationship. To survive and to have meaningful lives, human beings need ongoing interventions of God as a fatherly provider of all the necessary things for life, as is underscored in 6:25–34 and 5:45. Indeed, human beings can count on God's loving care; like a good parent he gives to his children what is good for them (7:9–11) and anticipates our needs (6:8). Yet, without the reciprocal response of his creatures, he cannot be "our Father in heaven," as he longs to be. In other words, his authority as the holy, heavenly Father needs to be given to him by his children. All his children need to hallow

his name, that is, to sanctify his name, to honor him as holy; thus, the disciples pray "hallowed be your name" (6:9). Such a sanctification of the name occurs when people acknowledge God as their Father and thus praise him for all the good things he mysteriously provides for them, directly or indirectly through the good deeds of the disciples. This is what is expressed in 5:16: "Let your light shine before others, so that they may see your good works and give glory to your Father in heaven." Thus, in order to allow God to become their Father in heaven, people need to have a sound eye (6:22–23), to look around them, including at nature (6:26, 28), to recognize that God constantly takes care of them (6:25–34), is with them in the intimacy of their lives ("in secret places," 6:4, 6, 18). Thus, in order to make God their Father, disciples are constantly to seek God's kingdom and God's righteousness with the eyes of faith that allow them to discern the holy manifestations of the kingdom of God's righteousness, whereas without the eyes of faith they were ready to throw these pearls to the pigs (7:6). The problem is that they have a split vision (6:22–23) and therefore want to serve two masters (6:22–24); or again, they have a log in their eye, which prevents them from recognizing that the very person they are ready to condemn as unworthy actually manifests God's righteousness better than they do — that person's eye has only a speck rather than a log (7:1–5).

In this interpretation, again *the structure of authority is horizontal:* it is a reciprocal relationship. Indeed, human beings need God and God's gifts in their life. But conversely, in order to be their Father in heaven, God needs believers who recognize his role in their life, and thus acknowledge and establish his authority over them. This structure of authority is presupposed by the view of Scripture as "corrective glasses." Scripture as prophecy and promise does not have authority in and of itself. A prophecy or a promise becomes truly authoritative for believers — is truly trustworthy — only when, with the eyes of faith, they can recognize at least a partial fulfillment of it.

6. *God as Father, by sharing the suffering of helpless people — suffering with them, sympathizing — empowers them to share in the struggle for the kingdom and God's justice.* God as loving Father is always on the side of those of his children who are neglected or rejected (7:1–4), deprived of the necessities of life (lacking bread or clothing, 6:11, 25–32), struggling for justice (6:33). The sympathy of this loving Father involves his awareness of his children's

needs (6:8) and his willingness to address their cry for help and give them the good things they need (7:7–11), including rescuing them from the evil ones who crush them (6:13). But God does not do so by bringing about his kingdom and his justice through a powerful manifestation of a vertical authority that would crush evil and unrighteous people. This would simply perpetuate the violence of oppression that needs to be overcome. Rather, "your Father in heaven... makes his sun rise on the evil and on the good, and sends rain on the righteous and on the unrighteous" (5:45), and is fully "God with us" by sharing our lives, so much so that any one can find him in the private spaces of one's life (6:4, 6, 18), even as he is being rejected by people who ignore him while pretending to act in his name (6:1–6, 16–18), or who serve someone else while pretending to serve him (6:24; 6:19–21; cf. 7:21–23), or who throw him, the holy one, to the pigs (7:6). Our Father in heaven is "God with us," that is, a loving Father who shares his children's suffering when he becomes meek and helpless with them, so as to share their struggle for the kingdom and true justice, inviting, begging, all of his children to join him in this struggle.

In this interpretation, once again *the structure of authority is horizontal:* God does not "lord it" over his children (see Matt. 20:25–28). On the contrary, God's fatherly authority finds expression in meekness, in sharing our lives, in putting himself, his kingdom, and his justice in the hands of his children, and in the process empowering them to share in the struggle for the kingdom and for God's justice. This structure of authority is presupposed by the view of Scripture as "empowering word," which includes the promise to the powerless, the poor, the despised that for them God reigns, a reign of true justice that any recourse to oppressive, vertical authority would contradict.

What Are the Characteristics of the Conviction about Authority That Your Choice of an Interpretation Presupposes?

Now that you have a sample of convictions about authority that one can presuppose, can you say which of the six views of authority I presented is the closest to your view, and how the others differ? Thus, the discussion around the table can begin.

There is, of course, nothing wrong with using convictions in choosing one's interpretations. Yet, for us, Christian believers, the recognition of the role that convictions played in our interpretations, is another challenge of discipleship, because we might feel that we have to forsake some of our beloved convictions. Indeed, as we recognize other possibilities than the one we spontaneously adopted, we are in a position to assess its implications.

To begin with, does this given conviction fit the view of Scripture we used? Or is there a mismatch? Furthermore, keeping in mind that convictions about authority are structures that we use in all aspects of our lives and of our relationship with others, it might be time for us to apply the Golden Rule (7:12) by asking ourselves, "Under which kind of authority would I prefer to be? And why?" Here are other questions for discussion around the table with your companions: How in specific situations does the use of one kind of authority or another affect the persons involved? Could it be that the teaching of the Sermon on the Mount that corresponds to this kind of authority has the same effect upon people around us?

With such questions, and by elucidating other convictions involved in our respective choice of interpretations, the relative value of each teaching of the Sermon on the Mount for believers today can be progressively elucidated. Then, the real challenge of discipleship confronts each of us. As the best teaching of the Sermon on the Mount for believers today becomes apparent, it is, if we are Christian believers, the Word of God for us in this situation. We are called to live by it.

Why Did I Choose to Invite You to This Critical Study of the Sermon on the Mount as Scripture?

In conclusion, I still have to answer this question: Why did I choose to invite you to a critical study of the Sermon on the Mount as Scripture rather than another kind of practice of critical study? I will address this question at length in the appendix. Yet, to a large extent you can figure out the answer by yourself, provided you remember that throughout this book I have identified myself with Reading D, even though I was moved and inspired by other readings, especially Reading E. I believe that my emphases on the practical dimension of reading in concrete situations of believers today, on the multiplicity of legitimate and plausible interpretations, and on my expectation of learning (something new!) from each interpretation, including yours, are consistent with the teaching of the Sermon according to Reading D. I learned from the Sermon how to conduct a critical study of biblical texts as Scripture.

Of course, this choice is related to the contextual situation in which I learned, as a child and then as a young adult, to read

Scripture.[4] As a descendant of Huguenots who died or were tortured and jailed for their convictions that all believers have direct access to God's Word by reading Scripture on their own, it is not surprising that I would want my readers to have the privilege to read the Bible on their own. Furthermore, as a member of a very small Protestant minority in a Catholic and secularized context, it is essential for me to make it clear that *Scripture Matters*, as John Burgess accentuates in a recent book.[5] Yet, in this same context, I was soon confronted with faith-interpretations that condone the most flagrant injustice — including the Holocaust — and other faith-interpretations that call for struggle against such injustice, and thus led my parents to hide Jewish refugees during World War II. Scripture matters. But the choice of an interpretation of Scripture matters even more. Ultimately, we do not live by Scripture. We live by the Word of God, that is, by the teaching of Scripture that results from the choice of an interpretation. Thus, it is essential for each of us to assume responsibility for our interpretation, so as to be in a position to confess, "*Credo, I* believe, this interpretation is truly the Word of God for us today."

Appendix

Why a Critical Study of the New Testament as Scripture?

Because of the pedagogical goal of this book, I have not discussed in its body the didactic, ethical, hermeneutical, and pragmatic reasons I have for developing a practice of critical studies of the Bible as Scripture, or in brief, a practice of *scriptural criticism*. I will do so in this appendix, because I anticipate that teachers might want to discuss these matters with their more advanced classes in a religious studies department, a seminary, or a church setting.[1]

Didactic Reasons for Developing a Practice of Critical Studies of the Bible as Scripture

In view of the many pedagogical features of this book, it is clear that I have written it as a textbook, by presenting in a very different way the conclusions of my detailed study, *Discipleship According to the Sermon on the Mount*.[2] This writing process reminded me that critical biblical study always is, among other things, a didactic practice.

Acknowledging the Didactic Character of Critical Biblical Studies

This book is shaped by didactic concerns in part because I have developed it over several years first in the form of lecture notes, then as a textbook for my classes in the religious studies department at Vanderbilt University (Nashville, Tennessee, U.S.A.), in seminaries on three continents (la Faculté de Théologie, Université de Neuchâtel, Switzerland; the Divinity School at Vanderbilt University; and Union Theological Seminary, Philippine Christian University, Dasmariñas, Philippines), as well as in adult Bible study classes in several churches in Nashville. I mention the contexts in which I taught, because the didactic character of a book is necessarily shaped by the particular readers one envisions and their

211

needs. The participants in my classes in each of these very different settings are the readers for whom I wrote.[3]

During this entire period, my didactic concerns were closely associated with my struggle to assume responsibility for the ways in which both my critical interpretations and my teaching affect others.[4] This cross-fertilization between ethical and pedagogical preoccupations led me to pay more attention to the didactic aspects of my practice of critical biblical studies. After all, the way I present the results of my interpretations, whether in publications or in the classroom, is shaped by didactic goals; I attempt to teach something to my readers and hearers. Even though critical biblical studies might aim at teaching many different things, there are always didactic goals that shape the way the subject matter is presented.

These didactic concerns are not an afterthought in critical biblical studies. Rather, they consciously or subconsciously motivate our entire critical practice, set its ultimate goals, and thus shape it from its inception. Each given critical biblical study has a didactic character. In addition to being a *critical* discourse and an *interpretive* discourse about the Bible, a critical study also is a *didactic* discourse. Acknowledging this didactic character of our work as biblical scholars opens the way to rethinking the relationship between critical biblical studies and faith-interpretations of the Bible as Scripture and to envisioning the possibility of a critical study of the Bible as Scripture — scriptural criticism.

Critical Biblical Studies as Didactic Discourses

What is a critical biblical study? I define it most generally as "an interpretation of a biblical text that strives to make explicit the interpretive processes and the evidence upon which the conclusions are based." This broad definition keeps in mind that scholars see biblical criticism as an ongoing quest for transparency (and thus strive to make explicit how they interpret). I believe that most scholars can agree with this definition, even though each of us works with a more precise definition reflecting the specificity of our projects.

What does it mean that a critical biblical study has a didactic character? That it is a didactic discourse? Consulting the dictionary is a good starting point.[5] According to Webster's most general definition, "teach" "applies to any manner of imparting information or skill so that others may learn." More specifically, still according to Webster's, "learn" has a threefold object: it is "to gain *knowl-*

edge or *understanding* of or *skill* in" (my italics) something that the learners do not know, or do not understand, or in which they do not have skill. Thus, a teaching (i.e., what is taught) is necessarily new for learners.[6] For instance, according to this definition, a teaching about the Sermon on the Mount somehow transforms either the learners' knowledge of this text, or their understanding of it, or their skill in it (way of practicing discipleship according to it).

Moving beyond Webster's definition, we can note that this definition of teaching implies that learners are not *tabulae rasae;* what is new for them can only be apparent by contrast with something old they already have. Readers of the Sermon on the Mount come to this text with all their previously gained knowledge and life experience. Similarly, I expect that my readers come to my comments about the Sermon on the Mount with their own (pre)understandings of this text and its teaching for believers today. This means that a critical biblical study as didactic discourse somehow takes into account who the learners are, what they already know and understand, and what skills they already have. Obviously, we do not present in the same way a critical biblical study to biblical scholars, to undergraduate students, to participants in an adult Sunday school class, and to seminarians.

These general characteristics of teaching leave us free to orient our critical biblical studies as didactic discourses in many different directions. A basic choice concerns the primary kind of transformation we seek to bring about in the learners: Is it an *informational* transformation of the learners' knowledge of the biblical text? Or is it a *hermeneutical* transformation of their understanding of this text? Or is it a *pragmatic* transformation of their skill in applying this text to their lives? Which transformation is preponderant?

By raising the latter question I signal that I presuppose that (1) each critical biblical study as didactic discourse involves these three kinds of transformation, and (2) any one of these three kinds of transformation may, eventually, be preponderant.

Even though many critical biblical studies might have a primarily informational didactic goal, studies that are no less critical might have primarily hermeneutical or pragmatic didactic goals. Each is critical, because it strives to make explicit its interpretative processes — the condition for being truly critical. In so doing, such a critical study cannot help but acknowledge that the informational, hermeneutical, and pragmatic goals of the teaching of a text are closely intertwined. Thus, any critical study ends up teaching about the three, whatever its specific focus, as will become apparent as soon as we take an example.

Informational Critical Biblical Studies Aimed at Teaching Something about the Text

Let us first consider those critical biblical studies that are primarily concerned with conveying some kind of knowledge or information about the text. Most critical biblical studies seem to have such an informational didactic goal.

Many kinds of knowledge about a biblical text can be communicated. This knowledge might be, for instance, about textual, historical, literary, structural, rhetorical, ideological, or social-scientific features of the text. A critical study strives to make explicit the kind of information it provides about the text. Thus, it specifies how it focuses attention on certain textual features by means of its *analytical frame*, which can take the form of a particular methodology or analytical procedure — for instance, the critical categories and procedures of textual, historical, literary, structural, rhetorical, ideological, or social-scientific criticism.[7] Yet, even if the primary didactic purpose of a study is the communication of information about the text, when the subject matter is a text that Christian believers regard as Scripture, the didactic-critical study cannot help but take into account the two other didactic dimensions.

It has to take into account how this new knowledge transforms the understanding — or better, comprehension — of the scriptural text, that is, how it transforms the fusion of the reader-believers' horizon with the horizon of the text and how it modifies the *hermeneutical frame* that facilitates this fusion through its *theological categories* — here, conceptualizations of discipleship, ethics, Scripture, and authority. A critical biblical study is shaped by such a hermeneutical frame, even when it denounces the theological categories of this frame as inappropriate projections of wrongheaded believer-readers.

Similarly, as a didactic discourse, an informational critical biblical study must take into account how this new knowledge transforms the skill in applying the biblical text to life, which believers use as they pragmatically identify the teaching of this scriptural text for them. In so doing, the critical biblical study is also shaped by a *contextual frame* with its *bridge-categories*, which believers use to relate life and text, including their perceptions of needs and problems in their lives that the text can address. A contextual frame is always present even when the didactic goal of this study is to reject a particular contextual frame.

Illustrations for each of these points can readily be found in my discussion of the five types of readings of the Sermon on the Mount in the preceding chapters. Even though I re-present them in a different way, it is clear that at least three of these — Readings A, C, and D (and at times, Reading B) — are based on *informational* critical biblical studies (commentaries), whose primary didactic concern is the communication of new information about the text. Nevertheless, as I show in these chapters, all of them display at least some hermeneutical-theological and contextual-pragmatic concerns, which I choose to foreground.

Before explaining why I choose to foreground hermeneutical-theological and contextual-pragmatic didactic concerns, I will summarize the preceding discussion by noting that as a part of their didactic thrust critical biblical studies make explicit the positive or negative roles of three frames through which the text is seen and read. (Cristina Grenholm and I have developed this threefold conceptualization of the critical task for studying the relationship between receptions of Paul's letter to the Romans through history and cultures and critical studies of this letter.)[8]

- An *analytical frame* with its *critical categories* (or codes) focuses the reading upon certain features of the text identified as particularly significant, such as the textual, historical, literary, structural, rhetorical, ideological, or social-scientific textual components, as well as the voices and themes of the text.

- A *hermeneutical frame* with its *theological categories* focuses the reading on those textual features that allow the fusion or clash of horizons of the readers and of the text. More generally, it is through the hermeneutical frame and its theological categories that readers make sense of the biblical text as a religious text. Thus, views of discipleship, ethics, Scripture, divine authority, revelation, and the kingdom function as theological categories in many interpretations of the Sermon on the Mount.

- A *contextual frame* with its *bridge-categories* focuses the reading on the relationship between life and text; it is through bridge-categories (which originate in the readers' context because of their pragmatic character) that readers address questions to the text regarding their lives. Thus, bridge-categories include the readers' perceptions of their needs and problems. For instance, anti-Semitism and anti-Judaism may function as bridge-categories in the context of Jewish-Christian dialogue in a post-Holocaust period; feminism and patriarchalism as bridge-categories in a context where the consciousness about the status of women in society and the church needs to be raised or issues about their status urgently need to be addressed; political questions as bridge-categories in a context of political oppression, etc.

Because of their specific didactic goals, critical biblical studies emphasize one or the other of these frames of the interpretive process. Thus, as we will see below, one can speak of critical studies with informational didactic goals (which are *text-centered* as they focus on the analytical frame), critical studies with hermeneutical didactic goals (which are *fusion-centered* as they focus on the hermeneutical frame), and critical studies with pragmatic didactic goals (which are *life-centered* as they focus on the contextual frame).

The Didactic Goals I Pursue through Critical Biblical Studies

In the introduction to this book, I repeatedly emphasize that my didactic goal is to help my readers bring to critical understanding their faith-interpretations of the Sermon on the Mount. More generally, I invite them to participate in a critical study of this biblical text as Scripture. This invitation reflects options that foreground the hermeneutical and pragmatic goals of our readings of the Sermon on the Mount.

In this study my primary didactic goal is not, therefore, to communicate new information about the Sermon on the Mount, as the type of study discussed above does. Yet, the informational didactic goal is not absent. I expect that through this study many of my readers will gain new knowledge about various aspects of the Sermon on the Mount. In the process of pursuing my own goals, I present many features of the Sermon on the Mount in terms of critical categories corresponding to different analytical frames through which the text is read. This kind of informational teaching continues to be important even when other didactic options are emphasized.

In my view, informational teaching should not be, in the present context, the primary didactic goal of critical biblical studies. An informational pedagogy is appropriate in elementary schools and in classes on a subject matter that is totally new for learners. But it is not appropriate when we teach adults about the Bible (whether they are college students, seminarians, or members of adult Sunday school classes). This conclusion is grounded on both ethical and pragmatic concerns.

First, a teaching primarily characterized by the communication of knowledge about the Bible to adults is ethically inappropriate, because it would represent a "banking" model of pedagogy.[9] The teacher adds to the learners' existing knowledge of the Bible new pieces of information. A transformation does take place, but it is only the transformation of the sum total of the learners' cognitive possessions. The ethical problem is that this banking model of pedagogy reduces adults to the role of ignorant children, as if they did not know how to read, and as if they did not already have a valuable knowledge of the Bible. As Freire pointed out, it is an oppressive and alienating kind of education in which learners are supposed to be passive receivers of knowledge bestowed upon them as a gift by teachers, who alone possess "true" knowledge. The teachers are the depositors who alone are in a position to bring forth new and valuable knowledge. Learners are deemed ignorant about essential aspects of the subject matter; they are more or less empty bank accounts whose role is limited to receiving, filing, and storing deposits. Because of its demeaning hierarchical structure, this model of education condones, and often contributes to, all kinds of cultural, social, and economic oppression. Thus, if one follows Freire (and I believe one should, as I discuss below), this view of teaching is ethically problematic. Second, and decisively, conceiving of the communication of new information about the Bible as the primary didactic goal of critical biblical studies is inappropriate, because it is unrealistic. Such a teaching fails to address the actual needs of the learners. Gaining knowledge about the Bible is rarely (if ever) an end in itself for people who want to learn about the Bible — especially when the learners are believers — because no one can truly forget that this text is held as Scripture by believers. Therefore, especially if the learners are Christian believers, a teaching exclusively concerned with the communication of information about the Sermon on the Mount never fully addresses their concern for the role that this part of Christian Scripture might play as it transforms either their understanding of the Christian faith (through a hermeneutical fusion of horizons) or their practice of this faith (through a pragmatic "reading" of their life in terms of the text).

In sum, in this book I deliberately reverse the didactic priorities found in many critical biblical studies that have informational didactic goals, and this in an attempt to meet more directly the needs of "ordinary" readers of the Bible.

Consequently, the pedagogy of this book is aimed at transforming what student-readers already know, instead of offering new knowledge to them. My primary goal is to help them gain a better understanding — a critical understanding — of the interpretations of the Sermon on the Mount that they already have or that they can formulate on their own. Since from a hermeneutical perspective, understanding a text involves the fusion (or clash) of the readers' horizon with that of the text, it is not simply a transformation of the amount of information they have about the text (according to the banking model), but also and primarily a transformation of their modes of being in the world. Their existing vision of human existence is transformed. This becomes even clearer from a pragmatic perspective, in the case of a text that is read as Christian Scripture. From this perspective, readers who learn, in the sense of gaining skill in, are affected and thus transformed in their contextual experience as they seek to practice the Christian faith, because with the help of bridge-categories, the text "reads" their experience, which then appears in a different light.

It is this reversal of didactic priorities that I seek to convey by saying that my primary didactic goal is this: *to help my readers bring to critical understanding their faith-interpretations of the Sermon on the Mount by inviting them to participate in a critical study of this biblical text as Scripture.*

This goal calls for a much more interactive pedagogy. The primary subject matter of my teaching is no longer information about the Bible (which I would have and which my student-readers would not have). It is rather the ways in which believers are affected by the text, experiences to which my student-readers have direct access, whether or not they are themselves believers. Thus, I have much to learn from my student-readers even as they have much to learn from me. As I try to make clear in the introduction, I am a facilitator in a collective learning process rather than a learned lecturer who dispenses knowledge. Yet, I have much to teach, because through my scholarly training I am aware of the great diversity of existing interpretations of the biblical text under study.[10]

I need to explain why this particular didactic approach is plausible from both a hermeneutical and a pragmatic perspective. Yet, before doing so, I need to explain my ethical reasons for advocating a didactic approach that calls for a "critical study of the Bible as Scripture," a phrase that, for most biblical scholars, is an oxymoron. Throughout this discussion it needs to be remembered that this approach is not an oxymoron for conscientious preachers who, because they have to prepare sermons, are led to practice scriptural criticism somewhat haphazardly by consulting critical commentaries, envisioning the contextual needs of their congregations, and entering into dialogue with the text about given theological issues — thus framing their interpretation in analytical, contextual, and hermeneutical ways.

Ethical Reasons for Reexamining the Relationship of Critical Studies and Faith-Interpretations

As I argued in *Ethics of Biblical Interpretations*, critical biblical scholars and believers cannot afford to ignore each other.[11] Yet, in most instances we do, and at great cost. A practice of biblical scholarship that overlooks faith-interpretations and other "interested" interpretations unfortunately leads to the dramatic excesses of biblical interpretations that, by passing on unexamined faith-interpretations, condone, and at times promote, anti-Semitism, racism, patriarchalism and sexism, colonialism, imperialism, apartheid, and/or related injustices, oppressions, and horrors.[12] I do not need to repeat these essential points, even though we are always tempted to minimize them by pretending they merely concern "potential problems." Suffice it to say that these problematic effects of our scholarly interpretations signal that our choice among alternative didactic practices of biblical scholarship is far from being inconsequential.

Conceiving the Relationship between Critical Studies and Faith-Interpretations in Terms of What the Text Meant and What the Text Means

Biblical scholars — and especially we male European-American scholars — are primarily responsible for building the wall separating our critical interpretations from believers' faith-interpretations. This separation is at the heart of our practice of biblical scholarship when we construe it in terms of a clear distinction between "what the text meant" (the subject matter of critical studies primarily driven by informational didactic goals) and "what the text means."[13] From this perspective, what the text means (hermeneutical and theological interpretations for believers today) must be grounded in, and therefore subordinated to, (informational) critical studies.

For this traditional practice of biblical scholarship, it is self-evident that the main interpretive problem is the historical gap separating modern people from the biblical texts; modern people lack the historical knowledge that would allow them to have an appropriate understanding of the text for their lives. From this perspective, the task of critical biblical scholarship is to bridge this gap by ascertaining what the text meant (a knowledge),[14] because it is further presupposed that the teaching of the text for believers today (what it means) is the application of the original meaning in today's new context.

This conception of the relationship between critical interpretations and faith-interpretations of biblical texts is obviously plausible, as is demonstrated by its use during more than two centuries. Yet, we should remember that it is a construct, that there are alternative plausible models for describing this relationship, and therefore, that we have a choice. Consequently, we must consider the ethical implications of adopting the traditional conception of the relationship between critical and faith-interpretations. Where there is choice there is moral responsibility, and ethical questions should be first addressed,[15] especially in biblical interpretation.

Ethical Implications of Conceiving Critical Studies in Terms of What the Text Meant and What the Text Means

Conceiving the relationship between critical interpretations and faith-interpretations in terms of what the text meant and what the text means has the effect of insulating critical biblical studies from "ordinary" faith-interpretations by believers. Accordingly, in our traditional didactic practices, both in classrooms and publications, we present our scholarly interpretations as totally independent from faith-interpretations, and we portray ourselves as detached interpreters who stand above the subjectivism of faith-interpretations.[16]

Of course we have good reasons for conceiving our didactic practice in this way. One of our goals is (and has been for two centuries) to free the Bible from the dogmatic straightjacket in which tradition, fundamentalism, and/or ecclesiastical hierarchy imprison it and, consequently, to facilitate responsible readings of the Bible by members of the churches. We aim at overcoming alienating interpretations, and thus at addressing the ethical problems mentioned above. Fine.

But let us consider what happens when we practice critical biblical studies as if scholarly interpretation should be conducted completely apart from faith-interpretations, as if a faith-interpretation could not be legitimate in and of itself, and/or as if a scholarly interpretation is a necessary condition for a legitimate faith-interpretation. In such cases, our scholarly interpretations arbitrarily reject as illegitimate all faith-interpretations that are not subordinated to them.

Then we wonder why our practice of biblical scholarship does not seem to be effective! We are painfully surprised when Jews, African-Americans, and women, as well as Christians from the Two-Thirds World, point out to us that our practice of critical biblical studies not only fails to overcome alienating interpretations of which they are the victims, but contributes to the problem!

Can we at least claim to have succeeded in facilitating responsible readings of the Bible by ordinary believers, lay members of the churches? Alas, no! As I have argued elsewhere, in most instances our practice of biblical scholarship has exactly the opposite effect.[17] Even though we might repeatedly exhort students and church members to read the Bible, our didactic practice signals to them in the strongest possible way, "Do *not* read the Bible!" How? Simply by teaching them that they cannot reach legitimate conclusions about the teaching of a text without our help.

This negative effect of our work is confusing for us, because we have good intentions and because each aspect of our scholarly approach — our linguistic skills, our methods — is in and of itself "just and good."[18] But each of these good things becomes a devastating means of oppression as it participates in the alienating logic of our didactic practice.

Consider how this logic unfolds. For instance, it is obviously good to learn Greek and Hebrew and to use these linguistic skills in our interpretations. Then, is it not appropriate to insist, as we do, that in order to have a true understanding of a biblical text one needs to read it in its original language? Similarly, as we proceed with our interpretation of a biblical text it is good to have a solid knowledge of its historical background, its literary features, and its structural characteristics. Then, is it not appropriate to insist, as we do, that in order to have a true understanding of a biblical text one must have this historical, literary, and structural knowledge?

It is certainly appropriate to train new scholars.

The problem arises when we confuse the training of scholars — future teachers — and the teaching of critical biblical studies to other people. The vast majority of our students (including future pastors and priests) and most members of the churches do not have the luxury of devoting a lifetime to scholarly endeavors. But because we have presented scholarly interpretations as the only truly legitimate interpretations, we have cast the majority of the readers of the Bible in the role of inept interpreters who are totally unable to read the Bible correctly by themselves. The more sophisticated our teaching, the more we convince students and members of the churches that they cannot read the Bible by themselves and that they have no alternative but to rely on readings by experts. Thus, instead of reading the biblical text itself (a useless exercise, since they would end up with a wrong interpretation!), they read commentaries and other secondary sources. We encourage our students to do so by sending them to the library.

Of course, once again, there is nothing wrong in recommending — and even demanding — that our students make use of the resources of the library. The problem is that, in the logic of our didactic practice, we send our students to the library so that they might find the interpretations of experts who have read the text for them, because by themselves they cannot read it correctly. In this way, personally or collectively, we, biblical scholars, present ourselves as experts who read the biblical text for our students, and thus, who read it instead of them. This means that we treat them as children, or as subalterns, as Gayatri Spivak would say.[19] We patronize them.

The devastating effect of this didactic practice appears. There were people who, before encountering critical biblical studies in our classes and/or publications, were reading the Bible by themselves. Among these people were ordinary believers and lay members of the churches who read the Bible with the confidence that their faith-interpretations appropriately grounded in the text the teachings for their lives that they identified in it. After this encounter with critical biblical studies, we are left with subalterns and childish people who cannot read the Bible by themselves.

The chilling fact is that after two centuries of such a didactic practice of critical biblical studies we have been quite successful. The "silence of the Bible in the church" is no longer a strange phenomenon resulting from the gap between the Bible and the modern world (as if this gap did not exist before!).[20] Instead of being part of the solution, our critical practice is part of the problem. We reached many with our critical studies, either directly or indirectly, through our students, including pastors and priests who duplicate our efforts. The tragedy is that most of those we reached have stopped reading the Bible. Is this not clear in Europe, where the churches are now mostly empty? And in North America, where most members of the mainline churches no longer read the Bible (except in groups led by an "expert")? Furthermore, through this didactic practice, we male Western scholars convinced women that they should not read the Bible except from our androcentric perspective, so much so that we reinforced the common prejudice that the only teaching of the Bible is a patriarchal teaching. Similarly, we, European-American scholars, convinced many people from other cultures that the only legitimate way of reading the Bible is to read it from a Western perspective, so much so that we convinced many of them that the only teaching of the Bible is a colonialist, imperialistic teaching that demands the rejection of any non-European culture as wrong, infantile, childish, pagan, and/or sinful.

Were we at least successful in our efforts to free the Bible from the dogmatic straitjacket in which tradition, fundamentalism, and/or ecclesiastical hierarchy imprisoned it? Did we facilitate responsible readings of the Bible by members of the churches? In my view, not at all.[21] Of course, those who are no longer reading the Bible are no longer misinterpreting it! But they are not reading it responsibly either! Conversely, most Protestant fundamentalists and Catholic integrists simply ignore critical biblical studies on the ground that these studies at the very least fail to account for faith-interpretations and frequently deny their legitimacy. Thus, fundamentalist, integrist, and other alienating dogmatic biblical interpretations persist and even flourish.

Reconceiving the Relationship between Critical Biblical Studies and Faith-Interpretations

In view of the ethical cost of maintaining a distinction between what the text meant and what the text means, it is clear that we need to avoid conceiving the relationship between critical biblical studies and faith-interpretations in this way. But what alternative do we have?

The above comments on the didactic goals of critical biblical studies suggest another possibility. Critical biblical studies, as they carry out their vocation of making explicit the interpretive processes, do not need to have as their primary didactic goal the communication of information about what the text meant (which is then set in a hierarchical relationship with what the text means).[22] They can have as their primary didactic goal the fusion-centered hermeneutical dimension of interpretation and/or the life-centered pragmatic features of interpretation.[23] Thus, believers' faith-interpretations (in either a hermeneutical or a pragmatic mode) are as much the subject matter of critical studies as scholarly interpretations are.

Why should these hermeneutical and pragmatic uses of the biblical text (commonly foregrounded in faith-interpretations) be the object of critical biblical studies? Why should making explicit the interpretive processes of these hermeneutical and pragmatic aspects of biblical interpretation be viewed as a necessary part of critical biblical studies?

As already implied, my answer is that any interpretation of the Bible, even if it appears to be entirely focused upon informational features and totally devoted to an assessment of what the text meant, necessarily also includes the features that are foregrounded in faith-interpretations, namely the hermeneutical and pragmatic features. Thus, in the same way that critical exegeses make explicit the interpretive processes that lead them to their informational conclusions, interpretations, in order to be truly critical, must make explicit the interpretive processes that lead them to their hermeneutical and pragmatic conclusions, even when (especially when!) these conclusions are not spelled out and remain subconscious.

Granted that these hermeneutical and pragmatic interpretive features are found in believers' faith-interpretations of the Bible as Scripture, are they truly a part of every interpretation of the Bible? Including critical biblical interpretations? The above reflections on the didactic goals of critical biblical studies already suggest an affirmative response. I propose to develop it further by considering biblical interpretation from the perspective of hermeneutical theories (a common practice since the nineteenth century) and pragmatic theories (a rarer practice).

Hermeneutical Reasons for a Critical Study of the New Testament as Scripture: Schneiders's Proposal

Schneiders: Interpreting the New Testament as Sacred Scripture

The hermeneutical reasons for a critical study of the New Testament as Scripture are admirably presented by Sandra Schneiders in *The Revelatory Text: Interpreting the New Testament as Sa-*

cred Scripture, a monograph steeped in the works of Heidegger, Gadamer, and Ricoeur.[24] In it, Schneiders confronts the widespread view that believers' faith in the Bible as Scripture is beyond the scope of critical biblical studies by scholars, even if the scholars are themselves believers. She shows how difficult it is to maintain that scholarly interpretations are detached from faith concerns. For this purpose, she reviews the main aspects of the interpretation process, emphasizing at each stage the difference it makes to approach the text with the conviction that it is revelatory. Thus, before illustrating her approach by presenting her interpretation of John 4:1–42 as a revelatory text for women (chap. 7), she offers detailed discussions of hermeneutical theories (chap. 1), various views of the Bible as Word of God (chap. 2), and Scripture as "church book" in relation to tradition (chap. 3). She also develops a threefold methodology, successively focused on "the world behind the text" (chap. 4), "the world of the text" (chap. 5), and ultimately, "the world before the text," namely, the "transformative appropriation of the meaning of the text" (chap. 6).

Without attempting to summarize her argument (a summary could not do justice to the flow of her insightful presentation of each of these important issues), I want to call attention to key questions she raises about hermeneutical theories and Scripture as Word of God.

Regarding hermeneutical theories, Schneiders stresses that, before embarking on an elucidation of the meaning of the New Testament, it is essential to clarify "the meaning of meaning" by recognizing its two dimensions (she leaves aside the pragmatic dimension that I discuss below): (1) meaning as information (what the text says [sense] and what it is about [reference, i.e., a historical event, theological argument, or other content]) and meaning as hermeneutical transformation ("what is understood" or "expands our human being" and thus transforms us because, as Heidegger and Gadamer have emphasized, understanding is "our characteristically human way of being, our fundamental mode of being-in-the-world").[25] Thus, one begins to recognize that it is disingenuous to claim that biblical scholars as readers and believers are not transformed as they study and thus "understand" the text.

Regarding Scripture as Word of God, in a particularly insightful discussion, Schneiders emphasizes that saying "the Bible is Word of God" is using a metaphor, which (like any metaphor) keeps in tension an "is" and an "is not." As Word of God the Bible is revelatory — powerfully disclosive of the divine — for believer-readers.

Yet, simultaneously, it is not literally generated by God's vocal cords and mouth; it is expressed in human words, written down by human authors. Thus, she concludes that the Bible is Scripture, Word of God, in a sacramental sense, as the mystery of divine revelation in human texts (which, like any sacramental object, can be distorted into a magical object or idol). If, therefore, the Bible is "the sacrament of the Word of God," its revelatory character cannot be apprehended without faith (defined as openness to the transcendent). "Just as one who did a laboratory analysis of the eucharistic bread would find real — and only — bread, so the Bible is really a human text that can be analyzed and understood as such without reference to the transcendent."[26] But then one cannot recognize the transcendent reality that it mediates. Unless one wants to deny that the subject matter of the Bible is religious experience, one has to conclude that

> The answer to the question about the relationship of faith to interpretation is twofold. Faith as a fundamental openness to the religious truth claims of the text is a requirement for even minimally valid interpretation of the text as *text*; faith as thematic Christian commitment is necessary for interpretation of the Bible as *scripture*. Obviously, if one holds that this text *is* scripture, then an adequate interpretation, one that takes full account of the text in terms of its own nature and purpose, requires its interpretation *as* scripture.[27]

In subsequent chapters, Schneiders proceeds to demonstrate that the study of the world behind the text shows that the subject matter of the text (what it refers to) is the revelatory character of the person and message of Jesus; yet, this world behind the text is a dynamic image involving a plurality of revelatory moments in Jesus and in early Christian communities.

Similarly, the study of the world of the text shows that it bears witness to Jesus in his life, death, and resurrection, a witnessing that involves truth claims about the revelatory character of Jesus, and is also itself a revelatory event; this text as language is a written discourse, which by its very nature always involves a multiplicity of potential meanings, because a text always expresses more than any given interpretation can grasp due to its "surplus of meaning."

In sum, both stages of the study of the New Testament as text, whether focused on the world behind the text or on the world of the text, deal with revelatory events.

The hermeneutical appropriation of the meaning of the text as Scripture by reader-believers — the world before the text — is another revelatory moment that involves a "transformative understanding of the subject matter of the text."[28]

The Fusion-Centered Hermeneutical Dimension of Interpreting a Text as Scripture

The above remarks show that from Schneiders's hermeneutical perspective, a critical study of the New Testament can ignore neither the revelatory character of the world behind the text (the person and message of Jesus) nor the revelatory character of the world of the text (as revelatory witnessing). Yet, she also makes clear that biblical study as critical study must not ignore hermeneutical appropriations of the New Testament — what I call faith-interpretations and Schneiders terms "appropriations of the revelatory text" in "the world before the text."

This is to say that Schneiders bridges the gap between scholarly interpretations and faith-interpretations by moving from what is behind and in the text to the transformative appropriation before the text in the hermeneutical moment. It is "a fusion of horizons" (although, I would add, it can also be a "clash of horizons").[29] "The world horizon of the reader fuses with the horizon of the world projected by the text."[30] A believer's interpretation is "neither a mastery of the text by the reader (an extraction of its meaning by the application of method) nor a mastery of the reader by the text (a blind submission to what the text says) but an ongoing dialogue with the text about its subject matter."[31]

Thus Schneiders emphasizes that a critical study of the Bible as Scripture demands that we renounce the traditional view of critical biblical study as exegesis — an extraction of the meaning of the text — and as a mastery of the text by the reader. It must recognize the hermeneutical features of the interpretation process and its fusion of horizon as another object of critical biblical studies. In our terminology with Grenholm, a critical biblical study must elucidate the role of the hermeneutical frame and its theological categories that preside over the fusion (or clash) of horizons in each interpretation.

Some might object that this fusion (or clash) of horizons cannot be part of critical biblical studies, because it involves reading into the text what is not there ("eisegesis"), namely, the reader-believers' life horizon (with its religious or secular components), which is brought to and (con)fused with that of the text. Such objections are another occasion to emphasize that, for me (as discussed above) as well as for Schneiders and the hermeneutical studies she reviews, reducing critical biblical studies to exegesis as the analytical study and description of what the text meant is an unwarranted and reductionistic view of critical biblical studies. It reduces meaning to what the text says (sense) and to what it is about (reference), ignoring the many different ways in which a text affects its readers, especially when it is a rich religious text with a great surplus of meaning. This undue reduction of critical biblical studies to the information dimension of interpretation (and thus to a critical exegesis that makes explicit its analytical frame) leads to conceiving critical biblical scholarship as the production of new or better interpretations of a biblical text — the problematic practice that reduces others to the position of subalterns.[32]

Against this caricatural reduction, I want to emphasize with Schneiders (who follows Heidegger, Gadamer, and Ricoeur), that the production of meaning occurring in the world before the text is part of the interpretive process that critical biblical studies must account for and make explicit. Otherwise critical studies will end up not only with ethically problematic didactic effects, but also with a very truncated view of the text. Only a critical study that makes explicit the interpretive processes taking place in a fusion of horizons is in a position to perceive the textual features that contribute to this fusion, or that "expands our human being" by transforming "our fundamental mode of being-in-the-world."[33]

In addition, and going beyond any of Schneiders's suggestions, I believe that critical biblical studies also need to account for and to make explicit the interpretive processes of the pragmatic dimension of reading.

Pragmatic Reasons for a Critical Study of the New Testament as Scripture

The Life-Centered Pragmatic Dimension of Interpretation: Allowing the Scriptural Text to Read One's Life

The pragmatic features of interpretation are apparent in those devotional readings of the Bible in which believers deliberately bring to Scripture their concrete lives with the expectation that the text will have a teaching for them in these situations. The Word of God for them is a new way of perceiving specific aspects of their lives (Scripture "reading" their lives) and/or what they should do in their situation. The same is true in faith-interpretations that emphasize theological issues in church life or moral issues in the believers' life, as well as social, economic, political, and/or cultural issues in society.

This brief evocation of faith-interpretations is enough to illustrate that the pragmatic focus of reading, which they foreground, is neither text-centered (as an informational interpretation is), nor fusion-centered (as a hermeneutical interpretation is), but life-centered. It is the aspect of a reading of the Bible as Scripture through which readers allow the text to "read" their life-experiences. The pragmatic focus of interpretation involves a reading of the text through a contextual frame and its bridge-categories.

The Scope of Critical Biblical Studies from the Perspective of Semiotic Theories and Pragmatic Philosophies

Why should these pragmatic uses of the biblical text be the object of critical biblical studies? It is even farther away from exegesis than hermeneutical appropriation as fusion of horizons. Why should making explicit the interpretive processes of this pragmatic aspect of biblical interpretation be viewed as a necessary part of critical biblical studies?

My answer is that the pragmatic aspects of interpreting the Bible as Scripture are an integral part of any reading of a biblical text, as soon as one is aware that there are believers who hold this text as Scripture. More generally, I would point out that interpretation of any text necessarily includes a pragmatic dimension, as semiotic theories and pragmatic philosophies have long argued.

This is not the place for a detailed discussion of semiotic theories and pragmatic philosophies. Allusions to a few of their main tenets will be enough to ground our critical study of the Bible as Scripture.

In *The Religious Dimensions of Biblical Texts*,[34] I have underscored, following Greimas, the different ways in which several dimensions of biblical texts are revelatory — communicate religious meaning — along three axes. What I say in that book applies to critical biblical studies and other biblical interpretations as discourses. Along the *syntactic* axis, one finds a set of textual dimensions that refers to or denotes religious entities (events, persons, or theological and moral ideas) and the focus of informational biblical interpretations. Along the *semantic* axis, one finds a set of textual dimensions that represent, or connote, semantic or symbolic worlds and values and which is the focus of hermeneutical biblical interpretations. Along the *discoursive* axis, one finds a set of textual dimensions that reflects the process of enunciation or rhetorical force ascribed to these religious entities and semantic or symbolic worlds and values. This third set of dimensions is the hinge by which the text is connected with the readers and their lives.

By opening in this way the question of the role of actual readers in the reading process, I have begun to draw attention to the pragmatic dimension of the reading process. In brief, to make sense of the markings on a page, readers must "textualize" them, that is, transform them into a meaningful text. This is not to say that the text is a random, "meaning-less" inkblot upon which readers are invited to project meaning. On the contrary, the problem is that it is a "meaning-full" text, indeed, a polyvalent text with a surplus of meaning (as Schneiders emphasizes, following Ricoeur). Therefore, to make sense of a text, the reader needs to choose what is most significant in it.

More specifically, to account for an entire written message in a responsible reading, one makes sense of it in terms of one of its dimensions, since each is manifested throughout the message. Thus, Greimas suggests that readers textualize the markings on a page by focusing attention on whichever of its many textual dimensions is posited as most significant.

This textualization as the process of producing meaning with the text is part of the complex pragmatic dimension of reading, through which readers allow a text to transform their lives as the text "reads" their lives and as they bring to the text the concerns and interests related to their life-situations. This process is made much more explicit in those semiotic theories that from the start seek to account for the pragmatic dimension of reading, such as that of Charles Sanders Peirce.[35]

From a pragmatic perspective (that is in terms of pragmatic philosophy, especially pragmatic semiotics, as represented by Peirce, and also of neopragmatism, which continues this tradition), one "resist[s] the positivist dichotomy of facts and values in [one's] explanations of human life and actions."[36] Thus, as Anderson says, a reading process that would "not make cognitive and moral sense of the world and of human experience" even as it makes sense of the text is simply inconceivable. In Peirce's terminology, a reading is meaningful (there is *semiosis*) only insofar as a text as "sign" is read in terms of its dynamic interaction both with its "object" (what it says) and with its "interpretant" (a reader in a concrete context). Peirce insists that "this tri-relative influence [is not] in any way resolvable into actions between pairs."[37] In other words, without the dynamic interaction between reader (interpretant) and both the text (sign) and what the text says (its object), there is no meaningful reading.

When we apply Peirce's pragmatic perspective to biblical scholarship, we realize that the attempt to reduce critical biblical study to an analytical description of the interaction between the text (sign) and what the text says (its object) — as positivistic exegeses pretend to do, by exclusively focusing upon the informational character of interpretation — cannot result in a meaningful reading. But in view of the fact that these exegeses actually do result in meaningful readings, we can infer that even in such interpretations the dynamic relationship with the interpretant-reader is present, though in an occulted way. In sum, the meaningful interpretation of a text always includes a life-centered pragmatic dimension through which interpretant-readers read the text in terms of a contextual frame and its bridge-categories, thus allowing the text to "read" their life.

Foregrounding the pragmatic features of reading to make them explicit in critical studies is so easy that we biblical scholars often neglect to do it. It is simply a matter of acknowledging the didactic character of our critical studies (as I emphasized in the first part of this appendix), and then noticing that among our student/readers there are at least a few believers who come to our class/book with their own faith-interpretations of the text read as Scripture. Such faith-interpretations, by their very nature, emphasize the pragmatic dimension of reading. Therefore, a critical study of the Bible as Scripture does not need to speculate about the pragmatic dimension; it does not even need to produce faith-interpretations. All that we biblical scholars have to do is recognize that faith-interpretations already exist and that implicitly we have presupposed in our own interpretations one or several of these faith-interpretations, which shape our critical studies even if it is primarily by motivating us to find a better interpretation!

The Place and Role of Faith-Interpretations in Critical Biblical Studies: Assessing Their Legitimacy, Plausibility, and Relative Value

From the perspective of pragmatic semiotic theories we can now recognize that, in most instances, far from being inept, faith-interpretations (as interpretations emphasizing the pragmatic interpretive dimension) are legitimate and plausible. The fact that they are life-centered (and that their primary concern is to allow the text to "read" the believers' life-experiences) does not mean that they necessarily betray the text. On the contrary, we can expect believers to be quite careful to ground in the text their pragmatic interpretations, because their life depends on it.[38] It is therefore often the case that believers account for significant features of the text that informational and hermeneutical readings neglect; and thus, they end up contributing to our knowledge of the text.

Consequently, in agreement with Schneiders, I would like to affirm that having a faith commitment through which faith-interpretations are produced cannot be detrimental to critical study and can actually be most helpful. Conversely, I want to insist that such a faith commitment is not required of biblical scholars, even though a "faith openness" sensitive enough to recognize genuine religious experience and thus genuine faith-interpretations is required. This is so because, in the same way that a critical study of the Bible as Scripture requires an assessment of the legitimacy of the textual evidence that grounds the interpretation of what the text says (informational textual features) and an assessment of the plausibility of the formulation of the horizon of the text that has fused with that of the readers (hermeneutical textual features), likewise the critical study of the Bible as Scripture requires an assessment of the pragmatic value of the interpretation, that is, of the pragmatic dimension of the interpretation through which reader-believers are affected in their religious experience by this religious text.

The Practice of Scriptural Criticism

A critical study that accounts for the pragmatic dimension of interpretation does not neglect the other dimensions of interpretations. It simply becomes a more complete practice of critical biblical study, scriptural criticism. Because scriptural criticism starts with faith-interpretations and aims at bringing them to critical understanding, it needs to account for all the aspects of the interpretive process.[39]

The ultimate goal of scriptural criticism is the assessment of the relative value (pragmatic value) of each faith-interpretation. The value of a faith-interpretation finds expression in the way the biblical text (the sign) and its horizon (the object of a religious text) affect reader-believers in the concreteness of their lives — a teaching bringing something new for or about their lives. Consequently, assessing whether or not a faith-interpretation is genuine involves determining if the text and its horizon have features with the potential of "marking" believers and their experience in this way (as the sharp edge of a special chisel chosen by a sculptor marks wood in a specific way).

For this purpose, scriptural criticism asks at the outset: What is the teaching of this text for these believers? What transformation did the encounter with the text bring about for believers (since, by definition a teaching transforms in some way the one who is taught)? This is why I begin by asking my readers to formulate what is, according to them, the teaching of this text for believers, and by formulating my own.[40] Beyond this one needs to look for — listen for — different kinds of teachings for believers expressed or implied by other interpretations. Scholarly interpretations also imply teachings for believers, even though, because they rarely make them explicit, one needs to formulate these teachings on the basis of clues that they give in passing remarks, illustrations, introductory or closing comments.

Then, a practice of scriptural criticism proceeds to verify that each of these faith-interpretations is legitimate, in the sense of being grounded in textual evidence, and more specifically grounded in a specific textual dimension that is viewed as particularly significant because of the particular analytical frame (with its critical categories) that the interpreters have implicitly or explicitly used in their reading. A partial taxonomy of potential analytical frames with corresponding analytical methodologies can then be proposed.

Similarly, as it progresses, a practice of scriptural criticism verifies that each of these faith-interpretations is plausible, in the sense that the hermeneutical frame, through which the horizons of the text and of the readers are set into a dialogical relationship, is both appropriately grounded in textual evidence (the text must directly or indirectly refer to theological categories comparable to those of the interpretations) and appropriately related to actual features of the readers' lives. For instance, in chapters 5, 6, and 7 I examine the variety of teachings about Scripture expressed by the text and the views of Scripture embodied by faith-interpretations; as a result, I could propose a partial listing of ways in which different functional views of Scriptural authority implicitly or explicitly frame interpretations.

Finally, scriptural criticism provides each interpreter with the possibility of truly raising about each alternative faith-interpretation the ethical question: What is its relative value? Why choose this faith-interpretation rather than another one? This question requires the critic to consider how this particular interpretation affects reader-believers, how it is related to their convictions, and how it affects other people around them.

Such a practice of scriptural criticism invites readers to assume responsibility for their interpretations, by becoming aware that each interpretation results from a series of choices among equally legitimate and plausible options, and by recognizing the ways in which their choices are determined by their convictions and how they affect other people. As a result of bringing to critical under-standing their faith-interpretations such readers are in a position to self-consciously decide whether or not they want to claim a given interpretation as the best for believers today or, in the case of Christian interpreters, to confess, "I believe (*credo*) it is Word of God for us today."

Notes

Introduction

1. See Mahatma Gandhi and Leo Tolstoy, *Letters*, ed. B. Srinivasa Murthy (Long Beach Calif.: Long Beach Publications, 1987). As Laurence Welborn pointed out to me, the same could be argued about Franz Kafka and Walter Benjamin.

2. Through this practical dimension of reading, readers bridge the gap between the text and their life in a particular situation or context. Consequently, I will call *bridge-categories* the life problem or issue that the reader brings to the text with the conviction that the text can address it. This practical dimension of reading is the concern of pragmatic theories as discussed in the appendix.

3. For the pedagogical purpose of this book, I do not need to develop these points here. Yet, since teachers might want to discuss them with their more advanced classes, I expand on such issues in the appendix.

4. Note that, by definition, the teaching of a scriptural text is new for believers; it transforms our understanding of our experience and of the way we live. From this practical perspective, when we merely find in the text a confirmation of what we already know and believe, we show that we have not yet allowed the text to teach us anything. Repeating what the text says does not express what the teaching of the biblical text is for us. I will reemphasize this point in the following chapters.

5. See Saint Anselm, *Proslogion,* trans. M. J. Charlesworth (Notre Dame, Ind.: Notre Dame University Press, 1979), 110–15 (note Charlesworth's comments on pp. 33–34).

6. See the appendix, where these issues are further discussed.

7. The history of reception is summarized in Ulrich Luz, *Matthew 1–7: A Commentary* (Minneapolis: Augsburg, 1989), 203–460.

8. It is appropriate to develop a new scholarly interpretation of a text in terms of existing faith-interpretations of believers, as Blount does in a remarkable way on the basis of preaching in the black church today. See Brian K. Blount, *Go Preach! Mark's Kingdom Message and the Black Church Today* (Maryknoll, N.Y.: Orbis, 1998); *Cultural Interpretation: Reorienting New Testament Criticism* (Minneapolis: Augsburg/Fortress, 1995).

9. Here and elsewhere I summarize points that I have documented in *Discipleship According to the Sermon on the Mount: Four Legitimate In-*

terpretations, Four Plausible Views of Discipleship, and Their Relative Values (Valley Forge, Pa.: Trinity Press International, 1996).

10. Reading a text has also been usefully compared to "reading" a tapestry with multiple significant textures by Robbins, who emphasizes the *inner texture, intertexture, social and cultural texture,* and *ideological texture.* See Vernon K. Robbins, *The Tapestry of Early Christian Discourse: Rhetoric, Society and Ideology* (London and New York: Routledge, 1996).

11. This example was suggested by Revelation Velunta, a Vanderbilt University Ph.D. candidate and my research assistant.

Chapter One

1. Throughout this chapter (and the rest of this book) the focus is on "the teaching of Scripture for believers and/or would-be believers today." It is this complete phrase that is meant by the shortened phrase "the teaching of Scripture for believers today."

2. "Enjoying favorable circumstances." See Johannes P. Louw and Eugene A. Nida, eds., *Greek-English Lexicon of the New Testament: Based on Semantic Domains* (New York: United Bible Societies, 1988 (=Louw and Nida).

3. A primary meaning in the Hellenistic world. Henry George Liddell and Robert Scott, *A Greek-English Lexicon* (Oxford: Clarendon, 1948) (=Liddell-Scott).

4. "Clear of shame" is a primary meaning in the Hellenistic world (see Liddell-Scott).

5. Dietrich Bonhoeffer, *The Cost of Discipleship*, trans. R. H. Fuller (New York: Simon & Schuster, 1995).

6. Reading A (both A1 and A2) is represented by Georg Strecker, *The Sermon on the Mount: An Exegetical Commentary*, trans. O. C. Dean Jr. (Nashville: Abingdon, 1988), and Jack D. Kingsbury, *Matthew as Story* (Minneapolis: Fortress, 1986).

7. Reading B is inspired by Richard A. Edwards, "Uncertain Faith: Matthew's Portrait of the Disciples," in *Discipleship in the New Testament*, ed. F. F. Segovia (Minneapolis: Fortress, 1985). See also Edwards, *Matthew's Story of Jesus* (Minneapolis: Fortress, 1985); *Matthew's Narrative Portrait of Disciples: How the Text-Connoted Reader Is Informed* (Valley Forge, Pa.: Trinity Press International, 1997).

8. Reading C is represented by Ulrich Luz, *Matthew 1–7: A Commentary* (Minneapolis: Augsburg, 1989), and by W. D. Davies and D. C. Allison Jr., *A Critical and Exegetical Commentary on the Gospel According to Saint Matthew*, vol. 1, International Critical Commentary (Edinburgh: T. & T. Clark, 1988).

9. Reading D is represented by Daniel Patte, *The Gospel According to Matthew: A Structural Commentary on Matthew's Faith* (Minneapo-

lis: Fortress, 1987; reprint, Valley Forge, Pa.: Trinity Press International, 1996).

10. Reading E is represented by Carlos Bravo Gallardo, "Matthew: Good News for the Persecuted Poor," in *Subversive Scriptures: Revolutionary Readings of the Christian Bible in Latin America*, ed. Leif E. Vaage (Valley Forge, Pa.: Trinity Press International, 1997), 173–92. Bravo Gallardo's original article (in Spanish) was written before the following book, which provides an interpretation that readily supports its conclusions about the teaching of the beatitudes: Michael H. Crosby, *House of Disciples: Church, Economics and Justice in Matthew* (Maryknoll, N.Y.: Orbis, 1988), especially pp. 147–95.

11. I am indebted to Noel L. Baybay, when he was an M.Th. candidate, Southeast Asia Graduate School of Theology, for his insights in developing this reading in terms of solidarity with the poor and oppressed in a paper he wrote for a class I taught at Union Theological Seminary, Philippine Christian University, Manila and Dasmariñas.

12. Noel Baybay proposed this twofold reading of the beatitudes.

13. As proposed by Alice Walker in her extraordinary rendition of the beatitudes, entitled "the Gospel of Shug," in *The Temple of My Familiar* (New York: Pocket Books, 1990), 287–89.

14. Bravo Gallardo, "Matthew: Good News for the Persecuted Poor," 183.

15. Bravo Gallardo, "Matthew: Good News for the Persecuted Poor," 187; see pp. 184–87 for many insights summarized in this paragraph.

Chapter Two

1. These two sets of questions have been formulated by D.Min. students at Union Theological Seminary, Philippine Christian University (Manila campus) in an extraordinary three-hour discussion of their conclusions regarding the teaching of the beatitudes for believers today in the Philippines. The way I address these questions below owes much to their way of framing them and to Revelation Velunta's perceptive help in making sense of them.

2. Obviously, these issues primarily concern interpretations by believers (thus *faith*-interpretations). Yet, this discussion applies to all interpretation of the teaching of this text for believers, whether or not the interpreter is a Christian believer.

3. See the appendix, and also, Daniel Patte, *The Ethics of Biblical Interpretation: A Reevaluation* (Louisville, Ky.: Westminster John Knox, 1995).

4. A phrase used by Luke Timothy Johnson in his article "Learning Jesus," *Christian Century* 115, no. 33 (1998). This phrase captures well key concepts of Gabriel Marcel and Emmanuel Lévinas.

5. See Susan L. Nelson, *Healing the Broken Heart: Sin, Alienation*

and the Gift of Grace (St. Louis: Chalice Press, 1997), and in an African context regarding the healing of international relations as well as communal and personal relations, Musa W. Dube, "Divining the Texts for International Relations (Matt. 15:21–28)," in *Transformative Encounters: Jesus and Women Re-viewed*, ed. Ingrid Rosa Kitzberger, Biblical Interpretation Series (Leiden: Brill, 1999).

6. See Wilfred Cantwell Smith, *What is Scripture? A Comparative Approach* (Minneapolis: Fortress, 1993).

7. See Elisabeth Schüssler Fiorenza, *Bread Not Stone: The Challenge of Feminist Biblical Interpretation* (Boston: Beacon Press, 1984).

8. See Kwok Pui-lan, *Discovering the Bible in the Non-Biblical World* (Maryknoll, N.Y.: Orbis, 1995), and Mary John Mananzan, *Challenges to the Inner Room: Selected Essays and Speeches on Women* (Manila: Institute of Women's Studies, 1998). The "talking book" metaphor is suggested by Kwok Pui-lan (which I will relate to "empowering word" in chapter 7).

9. See Theophus Smith, *Conjuring Culture: Biblical Formations of Black America* (New York and Oxford: Oxford University Press, 1994), and Brian K. Blount, "Righteousness from the Inside: The Transformative Spirituality of the Sermon on the Mount," in *The Theological Interpretation of Scripture: Classic and Contemporary Readings*, ed. Stephen E. Fowl (Cambridge, Mass. and Oxford: Blackwell, 1997), 262–84.

10. I allude to the title of the book edited by Kitzberger, *Transformative Encounters*.

11. I prefer to use the more general phrase "subversive thrust," rather than the "subversive story" proposed by Elaine Wainwright, because I believe it better represents the textual dimension she sees as most significant in Matthew from her feminist perspective. This dimension is not limited to narrative features. Wainwright's work on Matthew is the most systematic and self-conscious reading of that Gospel with a subversive-thrust analytical frame: "The Gospel of Matthew," in *Searching the Scriptures*, vol.2, *A Feminist Commentary*, ed. Elisabeth Schüssler Fiorenza (New York: Crossroad, 1994), 635–77.

12. Borrowing from the title of the book edited by R. S. Sugirtharajah, *Voices from the Margin: Interpreting the Bible in the Third World* (Maryknoll, N.Y.: Orbis, 1991).

Chapter Three

1. See Jonathan Magonet, *A Rabbi's Bible* (London: SCM, 1991), 15–25 (especially p. 25).

2. A deontological ethical theory emphasizes the importance of intersubjective relations as the structure of the moral life as expressed in basic principles that take the form of laws. I follow here and below Ogletree's excellent summary presentation of different preunderstandings of the

moral life. See Thomas W. Ogletree, *The Use of the Bible in Christian Ethics: A Constructive Essay* (Philadelphia: Fortress, 1983), 15–45.

3. Hans Dieter Betz, *Essays on the Sermon on the Mount*, trans. L. L. Welborn (Minneapolis: Fortress, 1985), 35.

4. Strecker, *Sermon*, 28–47. Of course, the ethical character of the beatitudes is also recognized by other commentators, even if they focus on another significant dimension of the text. See, e.g., Luz, *Matthew*, 224–46; Davies and Allison, *Matthew*, 429–67.

5. Jacques Dupont, *Les béatitudes*, vol. 3 (Paris: Gabalda, 1973), 457–71; Georg Strecker, "Die Makarismen der Bergpredigt," *New Testament Studies* 17 (1970): 262; Strecker, *Sermon*, 30–34.

6. Rudolph Bultmann, "πένθος, πενθέω," *Theological Dictionary of the New Testament*, ed. G. Kittel and G. Friedrich; trans. G. W. Bromiley (Grand Rapids: Eerdmans, 1964–1974), 6:40–43.

7. Strecker, *Sermon*, 34–35. See James 4:9.

8. This interpretation underscores that the translation "meek" is misleading because it suggests a nonviolent attitude that the Greek word does not have (Strecker, *Sermon*, 35–36). Of course, other interpretations affirm the nonviolent connotation, by noting that the beatitudes need to be read in terms of their relationship to other parts of the Sermon on the Mount—5:5 needs to be interpreted in terms of 5:39 ("Do not resist an evildoer").

9. A behavior, and not, in this perspective, a longing for righteousness as something to be given by God (God's justice), as in Reading E (Strecker, *Sermon*, 36–38).

10. Strecker, *Sermon*, 39.

11. Ibid., *Sermon*, 42.

12. When interpreted in terms of 5:10, although it can also be interpreted as being persecuted for proclaiming Jesus (Strecker, *Sermon*, 43–45). It is only insofar as one practices such an ethical behavior that one can truly claim to be a disciple. Strecker (*Sermon*, 33) also notes that these features of the beatitudes are comparable to "the cultic list of virtues of the Old Testament."

13. Strecker, *Sermon*, 33–34. This "ethicization" of the beatitudes is seen by Strecker as a part of the general ethicization of Jesus' teaching by Matthew. See Georg Strecker, "The Concept of History in Matthew" in *The Interpretation of Matthew*, ed. Graham Stanton (Philadelphia: Fortress, 1983), 67–84; "Die Makarismen," 255–75.

14. Kingsbury, *Matthew as Story*, 104–10.

15. Luz, *Matthew*, 167. This is Luz's comment upon Matt. 3:2, which is in direct contrast with his interpretation of the beatitudes as "non-realized eschatology" (*Matthew*, 235, 245–46).

16. Kingsbury, *Matthew as Story*, 129.

17. Thus, Strecker (*Sermon*, 35) concludes, "The passive of the eschatological future [in Matt. 5:4, 6, 7, 9] speaks of God's action, which will be revealed at the end of the world but is already happening in the present."

18. Strecker, *Sermon*, 29.

19. Kingsbury, *Matthew as Story*, 129.

20. Ogletree, *Use of the Bible*, 20.

21. *The Philosophy of John Stuart Mill*, ed. Marshall Cohen (New York: Modern Library, 1961), and David Lyons, *The Form and Limits of Utilitarianism* (New York and London: Oxford University Press, 1965). See Ogletree, *Use of the Bible*, 21, 42 n. 9.

22. Ogletree, *Use of the Bible*, 18.

23. The title of one of Eberhard Arnold's central books, *Salt and Light: Talks and Writings on the Sermon on the Mount* (Rifton, N.Y.: Plough Publishing House, 1977).

24. From Moore's preface to Eberhard Arnold, *God's Revolution: Justice, Community, and the Coming Kingdom* (Farmington, Pa.: Plough Publishing House, 1997), xii.

25. Arnold, *God's Revolution*, 32.

26. Arnold (*Salt and Light*, 5) expresses this in a gender-exclusive language common in his time: "We want to become true men. We want to dedicate ourselves entirely to all men."

27. Bonhoeffer, *The Cost of Discipleship*, 57–78; the quotations to follow are from pp. 107, 108, 114.

28. Clarence Jordan, *Sermon on the Mount*, rev. ed. (Valley Forge, Pa.: Judson Press, 1993), 8. See also Jordan, *The Cotton Patch Version of Matthew and John* (Clinton, N.J.: New Wine Publishing, 1970), 22.

29. Jordan, *Sermon on the Mount*, 7–21; see also Jordan, *Cotton Patch Version*, 22.

30. Jordan, *Sermon on the Mount*, 15.

31. The story dimension would be called by Greimas, "narrative syntax," and by Bal, "fabula." See A. J. Greimas and J. Courtès, *Semiotics and Language: An Analytical Dictionary*, trans. L. Crist, D. Patte, et al. (Bloomington: Indiana University Press, 1982), 332–34, and Mieke Bal, *Narratology: Introduction to the Theory of Narrative*, trans. C. van Boheemen (Toronto: University of Toronto Press, 1985), 11–47.

32. Note that in Matthew (by contrast with the other Gospels) the disciples do not go into mission during Jesus' ministry, although they receive extensive teaching about going to mission (Matthew 10).

33. In contrast to Reading A, where the authoritative Jesus commands his disciples. Here, we note that, at this point of the unfolding of the plot, Jesus does not yet have the authority he will have as the resurrected Lord (28:18). Actually, according to 7:21–27, calling Jesus "Lord, Lord" may lead to a false confidence. Yet, acknowledging his authority, as the crowds do in 7:28–29, is appropriate.

34. The effect of the beatitudes upon the crowds is that of a call to discipleship, because, despite obvious differences, the beatitudes and the call of the four fishers are similar kinds of utterances. Jesus' call of the four fishers (Matt. 4:19) has three features:

1. A command, "Come with me," that expresses what they should do (yet, this is not an unconditional command that by itself would establish their will).
2. A promise, "I will make you fishers of people," that establishes their will to do what is commanded (they want to be made fishers of people).
3. An expression of the authority-trustworthiness of Jesus (their positive response expresses that they trust Jesus' promise).

Each of the beatitudes also has these three components:

1. It expresses what disciples should do (be poor in spirit, mourn, etc.); each beatitude demands that the disciples commit themselves to a specific way of life.
2. Each beatitude includes a promise: "theirs is the kingdom of heaven," "they shall be comforted," etc.
3. Each beatitude expresses the authority-trustworthiness of Jesus; as blessing, a beatitude is a word that has the power to bring about a new reality — blessedness. By uttering beatitudes, Jesus presents himself as one who is in a position to make such a promise in the name of God.

Chapter Four

1. See William Finnegan, *Cold New World: Growing Up in a Harder Country* (New York: Random House, 1998). This book and Beaudoin's (see the next note) were called to my attention by the excellent review article of Charles R. Foster, "Paying Attention to Youth Culture," *Christian Century* 115, no. 34 (1998): 1185–87.

2. See Tom Beaudoin, *Virtual Faith: The Irreverent Spiritual Quest of Generation X* (San Francisco: Jossey-Bass, 1998).

3. That discipleship requires faith is not unique to this interpretation, but what constitutes faith varies radically. In Reading A (a deontological interpretation), faith is a belief in the extraordinary authority of Jesus as the exalted Lord — a necessary condition for receiving the Sermon on the Mount as the expression of God's eternal will. In Reading B (a consequentialist interpretation), faith includes a belief in Jesus' promises, and thus in his authority, but it is primarily a belief-trust in the goodness of God and of God's will.

4. More specifically, the declarations of blessing ("blessed") are present manifestations of God's loving care comparable to the blessings and beatitudes in cultic, wisdom, and apocalyptic texts of the Hebrew Bible and its Greek translation, the Septuagint. See Davies and Allison, *Matthew*, 431–34. These blessings include those uttered by the Levites upon those who "obey the voice of the Lord" (Deut. 28:1–14, particularly relevant, because of the ethical descriptions of the blessed ones). These blessings are preceded (Deut. 27:15–26) and followed (Deut. 28:15–68) by curses upon those who "do not obey the voice of the Lord." This feature is important, even though Matthew, unlike Luke (6:20–26), does not directly associate blessings with curses (woes); the negative counterpart of the beatitudes is found in the conclusion of the Sermon, Matt. 7:24–27.

As a religious word of blessing uttered by someone who has religious authority, namely, Jesus, such a blessing is a word that has the power of positing a new reality, as a curse also does. See William F. Beardslee, *Literary Criticism of the New Testament*, Guides to Biblical Scholarship (Minneapolis: Fortress, 1971), 27–39.

5. In agreement with the Jewish *anawim* piety. See Davies and Allison, *Matthew*, 442–43; Betz, *Essays*, 33–34.

6. Luz, *Matthew*, 232–34; Betz, *Essays*, 34.

7. Luz, *Matthew*, 431.

8. A righteousness belonging to another order of law ("the order of law of the kingdom") as compared with the usual kind of righteousness of this world. See Luz, *Matthew*, 269–70, 273, passim.

9. See Wayne A. Meeks, *The Moral World of the First Christians* (Philadelphia: Westminster, 1986), 13–14.

10. As Stanley Hauerwas puts it, "For the Greeks the term virtue, *arete*, meant that which causes a thing to perform its function well. *Arete* was an excellence of any kind that denotes the power of anything to fulfill its function." See Hauerwas, *A Community of Character: Toward a Constructive Social Ethic* (Notre Dame, Ind.: University of Notre Dame Press, 1981), 111.

11. Note the present tense of the promise in Matt. 5:3, 10, and its future tense in all the other beatitudes.

12. Luz, *Matthew*, 211–13. See also Davies and Allison (*Matthew*, 590–617), who end up with the same overall structure of the Sermon as does Luz, even though they are more cautious.

13. As emphasized by Luz, *Matthew*, 203–4, 211.

14. See Luz, *Matthew*, 203–4; Davies and Allison, *Matthew*, 724–25, who note the repeated mentions of teaching by Jesus (4:23; 5:2; and 7:28–29), of the great crowds following Jesus (4:25; 5:1; and 7:28; 8:1), and of climbing and descending the mountain (5:1; 8:1).

15. With Luz, *Matthew*, 212–13.

16. Luz, *Matthew*, 216–17.

17. Disciples cannot literally duplicate Jesus' ministry. Models of discipleship are not (realistic) examples that disciples/church members can readily and completely emulate (as the examples and teachings identified and emphasized in Readings A and B). Models of discipleship are ideals toward which people can and should orient their life in order to envision their discipleship in terms of them. Disciples are people who have been formed or conformed to these models (note the passive verb forms). People are made fishers of people; that is, disciples are made, not self-made.

18. This distance between Jesus and the disciples and the high christology it involves are accentuated, according to the symbolic interpretation (and also a historical-realistic interpretation), in chapters 1–4 of the Gospel. See, for instance, Luz (*Matthew*, 215): "Jesus the Son of God speaks" (in the Sermon on the Mount).

19. Davies and Allison, *Matthew*, 423–27; Luz, *Matthew*, 224, 455–56.

20. There is discontinuity between Jesus and Moses as suggested by the clear opposition between the authority of Jesus and the authority of the scribes (7:29); the law of the old covenant (taught by the scribes) is set in tension with the law of the new covenant taught by the Mosaic Messiah (5:21–48). But there is also continuity between Moses and Jesus, when one reads 7:29 in light of 5:17 as an expression that Jesus' teaching does not invalidate Moses and the old law.

21. By speaking of such an eschatological horizon, I begin to show that, on the basis of our discussion of Matt. 4:18–22, I conceive of the teaching of the Sermon on the Mount on discipleship as a vision of discipleship or, better, as a symbolic world in which disciples have to be socialized. See chapter 6.

22. Davies and Allison, *Matthew*, 439–40.

23. Ibid., 467. Thus, Luz (*Matthew*, 408) stresses that Jesus as presented in the Gospel according to Matthew served as the model for "early Christian itinerant radicals."

24. Ogletree, *Use of the Bible*, 31.

25. Review in note 10 what Hauerwas says about virtue.

26. The phrase "to practice virtues" is, of course, tautological.

27. See Patte, *Matthew*, 60–62.

28. See Patte, *Matthew*, 100; also p. 408, where the formal oppositions are listed.

29. Here and in what follows I paraphrase my conclusions regarding the significance of the beatitudes (Patte, *Matthew*, 101) in the clearer perspective provided by an interpretation that already presupposes the interpretation of Matt. 7:21–27 and its emphasis on moral discernment.

30. This is most directly expressed by women of the Two-Thirds World who are the victims of at least a twofold oppression. See Dorothy Ramodibe, "Women and Men Building Together the Church in Africa," in *With Passion and Compassion: Third World Women Doing Theology*, ed. Virginia Fabella and Mercy Amba Oduyoye (Maryknoll, N.Y.: Orbis, 1988), 14–21. She writes, "Is it possible for women and men together to build the church in Africa when there is exploitation, oppression, and domination of women by men? . . . To me, this sounds like the same apartheid drums that I hear at home, where people (particularly P. W. Botha) call upon whites and blacks to build together the 'nation' of South Africa while apartheid remains intact. . . . I am going to argue that for reconciliation to be possible we must do away with evil, injustice, and sin" (pp. 14–15). See also, in the same volume (pp. 173–80), the essay by Elsa Tamez, "Women's Rereading of the Bible." Tamez emphasizes the need to read the Bible with the poor as a point of departure.

31. This could be as in Reading D, when one discerns in the poor, the oppressed, and the powerless, models of righteousness/justice to be lifted up.

32. Enrique Dussel, *Ethics and Community*, trans. Robert Barr (Maryknoll, N.Y.: Orbis, 1988). After emphasizing that "the radical principle of Christian ethics is the face-to-face of the person-to-person relationship in the concrete, real, satisfied, happy, *community*, in the gladness of being *one* with God... and one with our brothers and sisters, the members... of the community" (p. 16), Dussel proceeds not only to identify evil (the breach of this "face-to-face"), but also to elucidate the systemic mechanisms of evil, in order to advocate a praxis of liberation that is both historical and eschatological.

33. George M. Soares-Prabhu, "Class in the Bible: The Biblical Poor a Social Class?" in *Voices from the Margin: Interpreting the Bible in the Third World*, ed. R. S. Sugirtharajah (Maryknoll, N.Y.: Orbis, 1991), 147–71.

34. See Jean-François Collange, *De Jésus à Paul: L'éthique du Nouveau Testament*, Le champ éthique 3 (Geneva: Labor et Fides, 1980). In this study of New Testament ethics, the author shows that a primary kind of ethical teaching found in the New Testament "from Jesus to Paul" presupposes that the basic human predicament is being unable to do the good that one knows one should do, and that one wants to do.

35. This systemic sin and evil of oppression in political, social, economic, cultural, and religious forms is repeatedly emphasized in Dussel, *Ethics and Community*, as well as in the authors of the prophetic essays in Fabella and Oduyoye, eds., *With Passion and Compassion*. See in particular in that volume Aruna Gnanadason, "Women's Oppression: A Sinful Situation" (pp. 69–76), and Mary John Mananzan and Sun Ai Park, "Emerging Spirituality of Asian Women" (pp. 77–88) (who emphasize the holistic nature of spirituality, which necessarily encompasses the concreteness of struggle against oppression and discrimination in any form). This systemic sin and evil is strongly emphasized in the trilogy of Walter Wink, *Naming the Powers: The Language of Power in the New Testament* (Philadelphia: Fortress, 1984); *Unmasking the Powers: The Invisible Forces That Determine Human Existence* (Philadelphia: Fortress, 1986); *Engaging the Powers: Discernment and Resistance in a World of Domination* (Minneapolis: Fortress, 1992).

36. Soares-Prabhu ("Class in the Bible," 157–61) speaks of "the poor of the Bible as a dialectical group."

37. Michael H. Crosby, *House of Disciples: Church, Economics, and Justice in Matthew* (Maryknoll, N.Y.: Orbis, 1988); regarding the Sermon on the Mount, see especially pp. 49–75, 147–95.

38. The quotations of Crosby that follow are from *House of Disciples*, 153–70.

39. Alice Walker, *The Temple of My Familiar* (New York: Pocket Books, 1990), 287–89.

40. Luise Schottroff, *Let the Oppressed Go Free: Feminist Perspectives on the New Testament* (Louisville, Ky.: Westminster John Knox, 1993), 24.

41. Bravo Gallardo, "Matthew: Good News for the Persecuted Poor," 183.

42. Wainwright, "The Gospel of Matthew," 636.

43. If faith-interpretations are genuine (truly transformative teachings for believers), there is a high probability that they are legitimately grounded on the text, because the reader-believers have much at stake in their reading.

Chapter Five

1. See Christopher Rowland and Mark Corner, *Liberating Exegesis: The Challenge of Liberation Theology to Biblical Studies* (Louisville, Ky.: Westminster John Knox, 1989), 35–84; Blount, *Go Preach!* 202; see also pp. 199–215.

2. See in chapter 2 the mention of a few other metaphors, including several that originated and make sense in non-Western settings.

3. The mild adversative *de* does not necessarily have the force of "but." This follows the translation by Pinchas Lapide, *The Sermon on the Mount: Utopia or Program of Action?* (Maryknoll, N.Y.: Orbis, 1986), 44–45.

4. A frequent textual variant adds "without cause."

5. This alternate translation paraphrases the Authorized Version.

6. Here also, Reading A (both A1 and A2) is represented by Strecker, *Sermon;* Kingsbury, *Matthew as Story.*

7. According to Reading A, the correspondence between scriptural text and life can be represented as follows.

IN BIBLICAL TIME		IN BELIEVERS' PRESENT
Revelation of God's will made complete by Jesus		Revelation of God's will made complete by Jesus
Life in Jesus' context or Matthew's context	=	Life in believers' present contexts

8. I provide the metaphor "good news" for this function of Scripture. Although Reading B is inspired by three of Edwards's works ("Uncertain Faith"; *Matthew's Story of Jesus; Matthew's Narrative Portrait of Disciples*), these do not make explicit the teaching of the text for believers today about Scripture.

9. According to Reading B, the correspondence between the scriptural text and life can be represented as follows:

IN BIBLICAL TIME		IN BELIEVERS' PRESENT
Good news that God's will is good to do as challenge of		Good news that God's will is good to do as challenge of
Way of life offered by the world in Jesus' or Matthew's situation	=	Way of life offered by the world in believers' present situations

10. I provide the metaphor "family album" for this function of Scripture. Though Reading C is represented by Luz (*Matthew*) and by Davies and Allison (*Matthew*), neither commentary makes explicit the teaching of the text for believers today about Scripture.

11. According to Reading C, the correspondence between the scriptural text and life can be represented as follows:

In Biblical Time		In Believers' Present
Renewed vision of human relations in terms of the kingdom and the Father's care as embodied by Jesus		Renewed vision of human relations in terms of Jesus as model of life in the kingdom and under the Father's present care
Common vision of human relations that failed to ground itself on past revelations	=	Disintegrating vision of human relations in modern societies

12. The metaphor "corrective glasses" for this function of Scripture goes back to John Calvin's *Institutes of the Christian Religion.* Although Reading D is represented by my commentary (Patte, *Matthew*), I did not make explicit there the teaching of the text for believers today about Scripture.

13. According to Reading D, the correspondence between scriptural text and life can be represented as follows:

In Biblical Time		In Believers' Present
Expressions of God's will in Jesus' or Matthew's situation		Expressions of God's will in believer's present situations
All of life in Jesus' or Matthew's cultural context	=	All of life in believers' present cultural contexts

14. I propose the metaphor "empowering word" for this function of Scripture. By this metaphor, I seek to express the threefold function of the gospel for believers according to Bravo Gallardo ("Matthew: Good News for the Persecuted Poor"): (1) "consolation for the excommunicated and persecuted," i.e., the poor and marginalized; (2) revelation about God, Christ, and primarily that the poor are "the true people of God in whose favor God reigns"; (3) "the operative projection of a *new justice*" ("the gospel of new Christian praxis").

15. Scripture conjuring a new reality is related to the metaphor of empowering word and is proposed by Blount ("Righteousness from the Inside," 262–84) out of African-American traditions.

16. This series of quotations is from Bravo Gallardo, "Matthew: Good News for the Persecuted Poor," 190–91. On the "spirituality of resistance," see Evelyn Mattern, *Blessed Are You: The Beatitudes and Our Survival* (Notre Dame, Ind.: Ave Maria), 15–24 and, indeed, the entire book.

17. Reading E emphasizes the transforming power of Scripture. The correspondence between the scriptural text and life can be represented as follows:

IN BIBLICAL TIME		IN BELIEVERS' PRESENT
Scripture conjured manifestations of the kingdom and of God's justice in Jesus' ministry in favor of the powerless: "God reigned for them"		Scripture conjures manifestations of the kingdom and of God's justice in their present situations: "God reigns for the powerless" today
Powerless people were empowered to struggle for the kingdom and God's justice	=	Powerless people are empowered to struggle for the kingdom and God's justice

Chapter Six

1. Ernst Käsemann, "The Beginnings of Christian Theology," in *New Testament Questions of Today* (Minneapolis: Fortress, 1969), 87.

2. See Strecker, *Sermon*, 95. Cf. Gerhard Barth, "Matthew's Understanding of the Law," in G. Bornkamm, G. Barth, and H. J. Held, *Tradition and Interpretation in Matthew,* trans. P. Scott. (Philadelphia: Westminster, 1963), 75–85.

3. Strecker, *Sermon*, 61–95.

4. Ibid., 75.

5. Ibid., 71.

6. Ibid., 83.

7. Ibid., 81–85.

8. Ibid., 85.

9. As Matthew's scribes and Pharisees (not to be confused with the historical scribes and Pharisees) do, according to the story.

10. Jordan, *Sermon on the Mount*, 40.

11. See Patte, *Matthew*, 263–66.

12. Dietrich Bonhoeffer, *The Cost of Discipleship*, 141.

13. Ibid., 141–42. Note that Bonhoeffer wrote this before World War II (it was published in 1937). Later he expressed a quite different view through his actions (plotting against Hitler) and his writings. See Bonhoeffer, *Letters and Papers from Prison*, ed. Eberhard Bethge (New York: Macmillan, 1972).

14. Arnold, *God's Revolution*, 47.

15. Jordan, *Sermon on the Mount*, 30.

16. Arnold, *God's Revolution,* 159.

17. Jordan, *The Sermon on the Mount*, 48.

18. Bonhoeffer, *The Cost of Discipleship*, 144–45. By emphasizing that this teaching is not secular, Bonhoeffer does not mean that it would apply only to a religious aspect of life. He explicitly rejects (p. 143) the Reformers' distinction between personal suffering of Christians (to which this teaching would apply) and suffering in the exercise of public duties (where violence could be used to resist evildoers). Bonhoeffer, as well as Arnold and Jordan and the interpretive tradition they represent, emphasizes the opposite. It is not so much in personal life, but in public life, that this teaching applies.

19. I summarize here Luz, *Matthew*, 255–73.

20. Luz, *Matthew*, 279.

21. Ibid., 284 (italics mine), 295, and notes. See Davies and Allison, *Matthew*, 511–21, 522.

22. Against Luz (*Matthew*, 285), who here is inconsistent with the rest of his symbolic interpretation, this is not devaluating the law of the civic order, but rather increasing the value of the moral demands (with Davies and Allison, *Matthew*, 507, 521, 522).

23. Luz, *Matthew*, 285–86.

24. Davies and Allison, *Matthew*, 508.

25. Luz, *Matthew*, 431 (cf. pp. 328–29, 341–42). Luz makes this observation about other antitheses, but it also applies here.

26. Luz, *Matthew*, 350.

27. Especially when it is actualized by Matthew, who identifies the enemies as persecutors of the community (5:44).

28. Luz, *Matthew*, 346.

29. As Luz (*Matthew*, 298–310) and Davies and Allison (*Matthew*, 527–32) note.

30. Luz, *Matthew*, 306.

31. As Luz (*Matthew*, 322) says about the next antithesis.

32. I believe that this formulation accounts for "how the faithfulness in marriage demanded by God remains free without becoming relative," which should be the teaching of these verses according to Luz (*Matthew*, 310).

33. Luz, *Matthew*, 326, and notes. See also Davies and Allison, *Matthew*, 543–48.

34. See examples in Hellenistic and Jewish literature in Luise Schottroff, "Gewaltverzicht und Feindesliebe in der urchristlichen Jesustradition (Mt 5,38–48; Lk 6,27–36)," in *Jesus Christus in Historie und Theologie*, ed. G. Strecker (Tübingen: Mohr, 1975), 207–11.

35. Matthew 5:40 is clearly parodic, since, if one followed it literally, one would go away naked! See J. D. Crossan, "Jesus and Pacifism," in *No Famine in the Land*, ed. J. W. Flanagan and A. W. Robinson (Atlanta: Scholars Press, 1975), 195–208.

36. Matthew 5:42 echoes the injunction in 5:23–26 to reconcile oneself with others at all costs, including economic costs — cf. "until you have paid the last penny."

37. This is particularly true in the United States, as Robert Jewett has shown in *Paul, The Apostle to America: Cultural Trends and Pauline Scholarship* (Louisville, Ky.: Westminster John Knox, 1994), and *Saint Paul at the Movies: The Apostle's Dialogue with American Culture* (Louisville, Ky.: Westminster John Knox, 1993), especially pp. 19–30, 43–53, 105–47.

38. Mattern, *Blessed Are You*. The quotations that follow are from pp. 57–67.

39. Thus, "blessed are the meek" is interpreted by Mattern (*Blessed Are You*, 57), "Blessed is the one who knows when it is appropriate to feel and express anger."

40. Mattern, *Blessed Are You*, 60–61. Of course, King was not always meek. As Lewis V. Baldwin notes, King did not embrace nonviolence before 1959 (after encountering Gandhi's thought). Prior to this, in Montgomery he applied for a permit to carry a handgun (which he did not receive.) See Baldwin's trilogy: *There Is a Balm in Gilead: the Cultural Roots of Martin Luther King, Jr.* (Minneapolis: Fortress, 1991); *To Make the Wounded Whole: the Cultural Legacy of Martin Luther King, Jr.* (Minneapolis: Fortress, 1992); *Toward the Beloved Community: Martin Luther King, Jr. and South Africa* (Cleveland: Pilgrim, 1995).

41. Mattern, *Blessed Are You*, 60.

Chapter Seven

1. The three previous readings are focused on particular aspects of the content of these verses as expressions of God's will: knowledge of the admonitions and prohibitions that disciples should implement (Reading A), or the good news that establishes the disciples' will to do these commandments (Reading B), or the faith-vision without which a life of discipleship does not make any sense (Reading C).

2. The "implied readers" are the readers inscribed in the text, by contrast with actual readers, who never fully correspond to this ideal reader.

3. I am identifying the "inverted parallelisms" of the "thematic units" as part of an interpretation focused upon the "transformative encounter" dimension (or more technically the "thematic dimension") of a text. See Daniel Patte, *Structural Exegesis for New Testament Critics*, 2d printing (Valley Forge, Pa.: Trinity Press International, 1996) and *The Gospel According to Matthew: A Structural Commentary on Matthew's Faith*, 3d printing (Valley Forge, Pa.: Trinity Press International, 1996).

4. This alternate translation paraphrases the Authorized Version, which at this point is closer to the Greek than the New Revised Standard Version (for the sake of a smoother English sentence, it alters the syntax and does not translate "therefore").

5. But the principle of judgment (of Reading A) does not apply here. From the perspective of Reading D, judgment and kingdom are the horizon in terms of which one needs to discern the expressions of God's will in the present — that is, those who belong to the kingdom and will withstand the judgment.

6. Among whom are evangelicals, as defined in the North American context. See Robert K. Johnston, *Evangelicals at an Impasse: Biblical Authority in Practice* (Atlanta: John Knox, 1979).

7. Since Matthew himself applies this teaching, one can also say that *Matthew* formulates what God's will was for the disciples *in his time*.

8. Dr. Apilado, president of Union Theological Seminary, Philippine Christian University, and professor of church history, made this suggestion as he discussed with me his research about Filipino traditions and church history.

9. Revelation Velunta, *"Ek Pisteōs eis Pistin* and the Filipinos' Sense of Indebtedness" in *Seminar Papers of the Society of Biblical Literature, 1998,* ed. Kent Richards (Atlanta: Scholars Press, 1998), 33–54. See Mariano Apilado, *Revolutionary Spirituality: A Study of the Protestant Role in the American Colonial Rule of the Philippines, 1898–1928* (Quezon City, Philippines: New Day, 1999.)

10. See Patte, *Matthew*, 80.

11. The connection between the Sermon on the Mount and pastoral care was suggested by Richard Lischer, "The Sermon on the Mount as Radical Pastoral Care," in Fowl, ed. *The Theological Interpretation of Scripture*, 294–306. Lischer's interpretation is closely related to Reading C rather than to Reading D.

12. James B. Nelson and Sandra P. Longfellow, *Sexuality and the Sacred: Sources for Theological Reflection* (Louisville, Ky.: Westminster John Knox, 1994), xiv.

13. Paul F. Palmer, "Christian Marriage: Contract or Covenant?" in *Theological Studies* 33 (1972): 619.

14. The definition proposed by Larry K. Graham, *Care of Persons, Care of Worlds* (Nashville: Abingdon, 1992), 44.

15. Joretta L. Marshall, *Counseling Lesbian Partners* (Louisville, Ky.: Westminster John Knox, 1997); see especially chapter 3, "Covenants of Love, Justice, and Mutuality." The preceding quotations are found on pp. 21, 49, 57.

16. Patte, *Matthew*, 82.

17. Although I am not focusing on the structure of authority in the household, as Michael H. Crosby does, the following reading reaches similar conclusions. Yet, Crosby does not focus his attention on the teaching about Scripture when dealing with these verses. See Crosby, *House of Disciples*, especially pp. 179–87.

18. These statements do not need to be read as antitheses, "You have heard...*but* I tell you." They can be read as expressing the fulfillment of the biblical text, following the possible translation: "You have heard...*and* I tell you." This point is also made by Crosby, *House of Disciples*, 183.

19. Bravo Gallardo, "Matthew: Good News for the Persecuted Poor," 183.

20. This metaphor is particularly appropriate for the role of Scripture in the women-church. See Elisabeth Schüssler Fiorenza, *Bread Not Stone*.

21. See διαλλάσσω in dictionaries of classical Greek.

22. Elaine Wainwright provides an excellent example of a study that pays close attention to the tensions in order to perceive the subversive dimension of the text and to hear the voices from the margin. See Wainwright, "The Gospel of Matthew," 635–38.

23. The hermeneutical category "solidarity with the poor" as necessarily linked with a ministry of "empowerment" and "subversive memory" was shaped for me by the prophetic outlook of the United Church of Christ in the Philippines made accessible to us in the well-documented work by Melanio La Guardia Aoanan, *Ecumenical and Prophetic: The Witness of the United Church of Christ in the Philippines* (Quezon City, Philippines: Claretian Publications, 1998), 67–76.

24. These quotations are from Bravo Gallardo, "Matthew: Good News for the Persecuted Poor," 190–91. On the "spirituality of resistance," see Mattern, *Blessed Are You*, 15–24, and indeed, the entire book.

25. Elsa Tamez, "Women's Rereading of the Bible," 67. See also Tamez, *Bible of the Oppressed* (Maryknoll, N.Y.: Orbis, 1982).

26. Tamez, "Women's Rereading of the Bible," 67–68. Note that by contrast with some (European-American) feminist interpretations, Tamez calls neither for a rejection of the biblical text as patriarchal and oppressive nor even for a reading of the text "against the grain." Both of these views would presuppose that the text "has" a particular meaning. By contrast, Tamez recognizes that meaning is always appearing in contextual interpretations. Thus, the problem is not with the biblical text, but with the interpretations. To be nourished by the "gospel of life," one needs to distance oneself from patriarchal and oppressive interpretations of the text. Similarly, below, Kwok Pui-lan emphasizes the multiplicity of potential meanings of the biblical text.

27. Tamez, "Women's Rereading of the Bible," 68.

28. Kwok Pui-lan, *Discovering the Bible*, 44–56.

29. Ibid., 55–56. Kwok Pui-lan's comments on "dialogue" and "internal dialogization" are explained in terms of Bakhtin's semiotic theory of communication.

30. Blount, "Righteousness from the Inside," 262–84. Blount uses Halliday's work on "social semiotic" regarding the social interpretation of language together with African-American perspectives as the hermeneutical frame for his interpretation.

31. Here Blount refers to Smith's study of the "conjuring" African-American hermeneutic, through which the presence of God and the biblical world is made real, as for instance in Martin Luther King Jr. performing the role of Moses in his last speech in which he refers to his Moses-like mountaintop experience. See Theophus Smith, *Conjuring Culture: Biblical Formations of Black America* (New York: Oxford University Press, 1994).

32. Blount, "Righteousness from the Inside," 277–78.

33. One of the scholars whose critical study of the New Testament most

directly brings together the plight of women and the plight of the poor is Luise Schottroff. See especially Schottroff, *Lydia's Impatient Sisters: A Feminist Social History of Early Christianity* (Louisville, Ky.: Westminster John Knox, 1994).

34. For instance, see Amy-Jill Levine, "Matthew," in *The Women's Bible Commentary*, ed. Carol Newsom and Sharon Ringe (Louisville, Ky.: Westminster John Knox, 1992), 255; Wainwright, "The Gospel of Matthew," 645.

35. Luz, *Matthew*, 298–310; "The Disciples in the Gospel According to Matthew," in *The Interpretation of Matthew*, ed. Graham Stanton (Philadelphia: Fortress, 1983), 300.

36. Against scholars who "suggested that the injunction against divorce establishes for women an economically secure position," Levine ("Matthew," 255) underscores that the marriage contract and the possibility of divorce with a certificate of divorce gave Jewish women a relatively secure position, both economically and emotionally (in case of abusive relationships). She then suggests that this is a false problem: the real issue is the question of the relationship between woman and man (as it existed before the fall).

37. Kwok Pui-lan, *Discovering the Bible*, 56.

38. My thanks (*maraming salamat*) to Revelation Velunta and Melinda Grace Aoanan for their insightful comments on a first draft of this section that radically transformed (corrected!) my interpretation of these verses as empowering word.

39. The tragedy of the debts of Two-Thirds World countries can be illustrated by taking the case of the Philippines, which is a relatively good situation. From reports in the *Philippines Daily Inquirer* one learns that, even though the Philippines devoted (and continues to devote) 40 percent of its income to debt servicing (and thus paid $29 billion to the World Bank and the International Monetary Fund during the presidency of Corazon Aquino), during the same period the debt dramatically increased (from $26 billion to $42 billion), due to compounded interest.

40. A general comment by John P. Meier concerning the Sermon on the Mount (*The Vision of Matthew: Christ, Church and Morality in the First Gospel* [New York: Paulist, 1979], 54), quoted by Crosby (*House of Disciples*, 184). Meier concludes that the only realistic teaching is in 5:42: sharing is already a manifestation of the kingdom.

41. Bonhoeffer's actions and interpretations of the Sermon on the Mount in the period between 1940 and 1944 (as reflected in his *Letters and Papers from Prison*) had evolved dramatically since the pre-World War II writing of his commentary on the Sermon on the Mount, published in 1937 (see *The Cost of Discipleship*, 141).

Chapter Eight

1. This is one of the central issues raised in chapters 1 and 2 of Patte, *Ethics of Biblical Interpretation.*

2. Our perception of a contextual problem is the result of our interpretation of a specific situation. Therefore, our perception of this concrete situation is also framed by pragmatic issues (our concrete experience of the way in the situation affects us provides "the contextual frame of our contextual frame"), as well as by an analysis of the situation (analytical frame) and by our convictions concerning, for instance, evil (hermeneutical frame).

3. This the interpretation of the Lord's Prayer of Strecker, *Sermon,* 113–21.

4. My personal reasons for my choice of this type of interpretation are discussed at some length in my essay "The Guarded Personal Voice of a Male European-American Biblical Scholar," in *Personal Voices in Biblical Scholarship,* ed. Ingrid Rosa Kitzberger (London: Routledge, 1998), 12–23.

5. John P. Burgess, *Why Scripture Matters: Reading the Bible in a Time of Church Conflict* (Louisville, Ky.: Westminster John Knox, 1998). Unfortunately, I could not enter into dialogue with this important book for the present volume, because it became available only after the final stage of my manuscript.

Appendix

1. This is also the occasion to acknowledge my indebtedness to the pioneers in the development of a critical study of the Bible as Scripture. Brevard S. Childs, *Introduction to the Old Testament as Scripture* (Philadelphia: Fortress Press, 1979) and *The New Testament as Canon: An Introduction* (Philadelphia: Fortress Press, 1985), first raised the issue for me, even though I end up going in a very different direction, in part because I take into account the "functional" definition of Scripture provided by Wilfred Cantwell Smith, *What Is Scripture? A Comparative Approach* (Minneapolis: Fortress, 1993), in contrast with the "knowledge" (informational) emphasis of Shlomo Biderman, *Scripture and Knowledge: An Essay on Religious Epistemology* (Leiden: E. J. Brill, 1995). As is clear from the discussion below, Sandra M. Schneiders, *The Revelatory Text: Interpreting the New Testament as Sacred Scripture* (San Francisco: HarperSanFrancisco, 1991) was most helpful to me. I adopt her proposal, even as I set it in a broader context because of didactic and ethical considerations, including those raised by Kwok Pui-lan, *Discovering the Bible in the Non-Biblical World* (Maryknoll, New York: Orbis, 1995). In order to address Kwok Pui-lan's call to "demythologize the sacred authority that is associated with the Bible" and to "demystify the ways the Bible has been used to reinforce unequal relationship between the East and the

West, women and men, and the rich and the poor" (p. 30), we cannot but include in critical biblical studies an investigation of the pragmatic dimension of biblical interpretation, namely the believers' faith-interpretations. Although it took me a long time to understand how we should account for the pragmatic dimension of interpretation in critical biblical studies, this issue was constantly with me since I was confronted with it in the work of J. Severino Croatto, *Biblical Hermeneutics: Toward a Theory of Reading as the Production of Meaning*, trans. Robert R. Barr (Maryknoll, N.Y.: Orbis, 1987) (see especially his chapter on "Praxis and Interpretation"), and Gerald O. West, *Contextual Bible Study* (Pietermaritzburg, South Africa: Cluster Publications, 1993) and *Biblical Hermeneutics of Liberation: Modes of Reading the Bible in the South African Context*, rev. ed. (Pietermaritzburg, South Africa: Cluster Publications; Maryknoll, N.Y.: Orbis, 1995).

2. Daniel Patte, *Discipleship According to the Sermon on the Mount: Four Legitimate Interpretations, Four Plausible Views of Discipleship, and Their Relative Values* (Valley Forge, Pa.: Trinity Press International, 1996). This book makes a contribution, on the one hand, to the study of the Sermon on the Mount through its critical analysis of four kinds of scholarly interpretations of this text and a study of their interrelationship and, on the other hand, to the methodology for critically assessing the legitimacy, plausibility, and ethical values of scholarly interpretations.

3. Several groups of students have made use of drafts of this book, which they improved, either by their constructive proposals, as is reflected in the footnotes, or by their questions, which helped to clarify certain points (as happened more often than I could acknowledge).

4. See Daniel Patte, *Ethics of Biblical Interpretation: A Reevaluation* (Louisville, Ky.: Westminster John Knox, 1995).

5. I quote from *Webster's Seventh New Collegiate Dictionary* (Springfield, Mass.: G. & C. Merriam, 1970). I will not use unduly technical language here. Yet, these reflections are based on an examination of didactic discourses in terms of semiotic categories. From this perspective, the didactic character of a discourse is an aspect of its pragmatic dimension (called by Greimas, the enunciative or discoursive dimension), one of the three broad dimensions of a discourse (besides the syntactic and semantic dimensions) that semiotic theories help us to distinguish. I allude to Greimas's and Peirce's semiotic theories as discussed in Herman Parret, *Semiotics and Pragmatics: An Evaluative Comparison of Conceptual Frameworks* (Amsterdam and Philadelphia: John Benjamins, 1983). See also Daniel Patte, *Elements of a Semiotic of Didactic Discourse: Analysis of 1 Thessalonians*, Documents de Travail (Urbino, Italy: Centro Internazionale di Semiotica e di Linguistica, 1981); "Method for a Structural Exegesis of Didactic Discourses. Analysis of 1 Thessalonians," *Narrative and Discourse in Structural Exegesis: John 6 and 1 Thessalonians*, ed. D. Patte, Semeia 26 (Chico, Calif.: Scholars Press, 1983), 85–129; *The Re-*

ligious Dimensions of Biblical Texts: Greimas's Structural Semiotics and Biblical Exegesis, SBL Semeia Studies (Atlanta: Scholars Press, 1990).

6. This is why I have insisted throughout that "the teaching of a biblical text for believers" is new for them.

7. Here, and until the end of this appendix, I make use of the conceptualization of the relationship between, on the one hand, theological and other receptions of biblical texts and, on the other hand, scholarly interpretations of these texts that Cristina Grenholm and I have developed for the study of the book of Romans in the series "Romans through History and Culture." This includes the conceptualization of what we call the "analytical frame," "theological frame," and "contextual frame," as well as their respective components and the informational, hermeneutical, and pragmatic interpretive goals to which they are related. All the features of this conceptualization of the components of biblical interpretation are progressively introduced in the rest of this appendix. See our introduction in Cristina Grenholm and Daniel Patte, eds., *Reading Israel in Romans: Legitimacy and Plausibility of Divergent Interpretations*, Romans through History and Cultures, vol. 1 (Harrisburg, Pa.: Trinity Press International, 2000). As is clear, the entire critical study of the Sermon on the Mount as Scripture presented in this book is based upon this conceptualization and therefore owes much to Cristina Grenholm's works, including *Romans Interpreted: A Comparative Analysis of the Commentaries of Barth, Nygren, Cranfield and Wilckens on Paul's Epistle to the Romans*, Studia Doctrinae Christianae Upsaliensa 30 (Uppsala: Acta Universitatis Upsaliensis, 1990); *The Old Testament, Christianity and Pluralism* (Tübingen: J C. B. Mohr/Paul Siebeck, 1996); and her insightful contributions to our joint publication project.

8. This is a more direct presentation of the conceptualization of the components of biblical interpretations presented in the introduction of Grenholm and Patte, eds., *Reading Israel in Romans*.

9. The "banking concept of education" is described and criticized by Paulo Freire, *Pedagogy of the Oppressed*, trans. Myra Bergman Ramos (New York: Herder and Herder, 1971), 57–74.

10. It is clear that my understanding of pedagogy owes much to Freire, *Pedagogy of the Oppressed*, and his followers, especially Gerald West, *Contextual Bible Study* (Pietermaritzburg, South Africa: Cluster Publications, 1993), and Bell Hooks, *Teaching to Transgress: Education as the Practice of Freedom* (New York and London: Routledge, 1994).

11. Patte, *Ethics of Biblical Interpretation*, 73–107.

12. Patte, *Ethics of Biblical Interpretation*, 17–30, passim. I further develop these issues in *Discipleship According to the Sermon on the Mount*, 351–96.

13. This is the distinction advocated in Krister Stendahl, "Biblical Theology, Contemporary" in *The Interpreter's Dictionary of the Bible*, vol. 1 (Nashville: Abingdon, 1962), 418–32. This distinction originates with

Johann P. Gabler's 1787 distinction between biblical theology (a descriptive historical task) and dogmatics; Cristina Grenholm appropriately called this distinction "Gabler's Gap." See Grenholm, *The Old Testament, Christianity and Pluralism,* 264–280.

14. The conception of critical biblical studies as the elucidation of what the text meant presupposes a banking model of pedagogy.

15. As Emmanuel Lévinas emphasized. See, for instance, Lévinas, *Ethics and Infinity,* trans. R. Cohen (Pittsburgh: Duquesne University Press, 1985); *Time and the Other,* trans. R. Cohen (Pittsburgh: Duquesne University Press, 1987); and his explicit post-Holocaust reflections in *Entre nous: Essais sur le penser-à-l'autre* (Paris: Bernard Grasset, 1991).

16. This separation of critical interpretations from faith-interpretations is a matter of didactic practices, because it exclusively finds expression in the way we present the results of our studies and the way we portray ourselves. As our discussion of the hermeneutical questions related to these issues will show, by its very nature critical biblical interpretation cannot and does not remain separate from faith-interpretations. The separation is in the way we present our studies and ourselves.

17. Patte, *Ethics of Biblical Interpretation,* 73–107.

18. I describe my own confusion, when I was confronted with this reality, in *Ethics of Biblical Interpretation,* 17–30.

19. Gayatri Chakravorty Spivak, "Can the Subaltern Speak?" in *Marxism and the Interpretation of Culture,* ed. G. Nelson and L. Grossberg (London: Macmillan, 1988), 277–313.

20. I allude to James D. Smart, *The Strange Silence of the Bible in the Church: A Study in Hermeneutics* (Philadelphia: Westminster, 1970). Smart sounded an early alarm and formulated appropriate "warnings against blind alleys and false approaches to the problem" (p. 164). Though, as we will see below, a hermeneutical solution cannot, by itself, address the problem, Smart already perceived that a reexamination of the relationship between critical biblical studies and reading the Bible as Scripture was necessary. See also Carl E. Braaten and Robert W. Jenson, eds., *Reclaiming the Bible for the Church* (Grand Rapids: Eerdmans, 1995); John P. Burgess, *Why Scripture Matters: Reading the Bible in a Time of Church Conflict* (Louisville, Ky.: Westminster John Knox, 1998).

21. I make this point in *Ethics of Biblical Interpretation,* 79–83.

22. Consequently, they do not need to limit themselves to making explicit the interpretive processes of scholarly interpretations, as is the case in the preceding model in which scholarly interpretations are the only ones worthy of critical attention because they are assumed to be the only ones with the potential to be legitimate. Then critical biblical studies become the exclusive (segregated) domain of biblical scholars. All others are excluded from the conversation.

23. Then critical studies cannot be limited to making explicit the interpretive processes of the scholarly interpretations (see the preceding note),

because interpretations by systematic theologians and pastoral counselors, as well as by ordinary believers, are as likely to be plausible and valid as those by biblical scholars.

24. Sandra M. Schneiders, *The Revelatory Text: Interpreting the New Testament as Sacred Scripture* (San Francisco: HarperSanFrancisco, 1991).

25. Ibid., 14–15, 17.

26. Ibid., 60.

27. Ibid., 61 (Schneiders's italics).

28. Ibid., 169–78.

29. In Schneiders's presentation, this fusion of horizons still gives priority to one of the two horizons — the one found behind and in the text — and therefore to the scholarly interpretations that elucidate it. Thus, implicitly (and against several of her key points), she is not quite free of the problematic dichotomy between what the text meant and what the text means.

30. Schneiders, *The Revelatory Text*, 172.

31. Ibid., 177. For Schneiders the subject matter of the dialogue is that of the text, because for her a faith-interpretation is an "appropriation of the meaning of the text" (p. 177). Yet, following her repeated claim that one needs to begin with the questions of the interpreter (because there is "a potentially innumerable multiplicity of interpretations" due to "the surplus of meaning," [p. 152]), I would emphasize that there is no reason to freeze the fusion and the dialogue into one-way relationships. In the hermeneutical revelatory moment, the reader's dialogue with the text moves back and forth between the two partners. The subject matter of the dialogue is therefore the subject matter proposed by the text and the subject matter proposed by the believer-reader; or a combination of the two — the point at which they overlap in the fusion (or clash) of the world of the text and the world of the readers — if one wants to speak of a single subject matter of the dialogue. This is why I emphasize that the hermeneutical didactic goal is fusion-centered rather than text-centered (as the informational didactic goal is).

32. One needs to make explicit the interpretive processes of a single interpretation, one's own, because it is the "better" interpretation, which, hopefully, will replace all others, which by definition are wrong!

33. Schneiders, *The Revelatory Text*, 17.

34. Daniel Patte, *The Religious Dimensions of Biblical Texts: Greimas's Structural Semiotics and Biblical Exegesis* (Atlanta: Scholars Press, 1990).

35. On the close relationship between Peirce's pragmatic semiotics and Greimas's structural semiotics (arising out of the theory of Danish linguist Louis Hjelmslev and influenced by Russian semiotics), see Parret, *Semiotics and Pragmatics*.

36. Victor Anderson, *Pragmatic Theology: Negotiating the Intersections of an American Philosophy of Religion and Public Theology* (Albany: State University of New York Press, 1998), 3–4. Throughout this book,

see his clear and concise presentation of pragmatism as it relates to religion.

37. "By 'semiosis' I mean...an action, or influence, which is, or involves, a cooperation of *three* subjects, such as a sign, its object, and its interpretant, this tri-relative influence not being in any way resolvable into actions between pairs" (quoted in Parret, *Semiotics and Pragmatics*, 34).

38. An important point underscored by Gary A. Phillips and Danna Nolan Fewell in "Ethics, Bible, Reading As If," in *Bible and Ethics of Reading*, ed. Danna Nolan Fewell and Gary A. Phillips, Semeia 77 (Atlanta: Scholars Press, 1997), 1. They make this point by referring to Jonathan Magonet (*A Rabbi's Bible* [London: SCM, 1991]), who recounts the story of young Czech Jews whose sophisticated reading of the newspaper "as if your life depended on it" trained them to read the Bible with "a keen eye for textual nuances and a remarkable feel for the Bible's underlying concerns."

39. Robbins has the same concern, even though he uses slightly different categories. Because he focuses on the study of the text (though understood as interpretation of the text), he emphasizes the "inner texture," "intertexture," "social and cultural texture," and "ideological texture." There is a clear correspondence with the categories that Grenholm and Patte developed through the study of interpretations of the text: the "analytical frame," "hermeneutical frame," and "contextual frame," with their components. See Vernon K. Robbins, *The Tapestry of Early Christian Discourse: Rhetoric, Society and Ideology* (London and New York: Routledge, 1996).

40. I ask my readers/students to formulate the teaching of the text for believers today rather than their own faith-interpretations, both to make clear that nonbelievers can do it and to help Christian believers take some distance from their faith-interpretations (as is explained in the introduction and in chapter 2).

Bibliography

Anderson, Victor. *Pragmatic Theology: Negotiating the Intersections of an American Philosophy of Religion and Public Theology.* Albany: State University of New York Press, 1998.

Aoanan, Melanio La Guardia. *Ecumenical and Prophetic: The Witness of the United Church of Christ in the Philippines.* Quezon City, Philippines: Claretian Publications, 1998.

Arnold, Eberhard. *Salt and Light: Talks and Writings on the Sermon on the Mount.* Rifton, N.Y.: Plough Publishing House, 1977.

———. *God's Revolution: Justice, Community, and the Coming Kingdom.* Farmington, Pa.: Plough Publishing House, 1997.

Bal, Mieke. *Narratology: Introduction to the Theory of Narrative.* Trans. C. van Boheemen. Toronto: University of Toronto Press, 1985.

Baldwin, Lewis V. *There Is a Balm in Gilead: The Cultural Roots of Martin Luther King, Jr.* Minneapolis: Fortress, 1991.

———. *To Make the Wounded Whole: The Cultural Legacy of Martin Luther King, Jr.* Minneapolis: Fortress, 1992.

———. *Toward the Beloved Community: Martin Luther King, Jr. and South Africa.* Cleveland: Pilgrim, 1995.

Barth, Gerhard. "Matthew's Understanding of the Law." In G. Bornkamm, G. Barth, and H. J. Held, *Tradition and Interpretation in Matthew,* trans. P. Scott. Philadelphia: Westminster, 1963.

Beardslee, William F. *Literary Criticism of the New Testament.* Guides to Biblical Scholarship. Philadelphia: Fortress, 1971.

Beaudoin, Tom. *Virtual Faith: The Irreverent Spiritual Quest of Generation X.* San Francisco: Jossey-Bass, 1998.

Betz, Hans Dieter. *Essays on the Sermon on the Mount.* Trans. L. L. Welborn. Minneapolis: Fortress, 1985.

Biderman, Shlomo. *Scripture and Knowledge: An Essay on Religious Epistemology.* Leiden: E. J. Brill, 1995.

Blount, Brian K. *Go Preach! Mark's Kingdom Message and the Black Church Today.* Maryknoll, N.Y.: Orbis, 1998.

———. "Righteousness from the Inside: The Transformative Spirituality of the Sermon on the Mount." In *The Theological Interpretation of Scripture: Classic and Contemporary Readings,* ed. Stephen E. Fowl. Cambridge, Mass. and Oxford: Blackwell, 1997.

Bonhoeffer, Dietrich. *Letters and Papers from Prison.* Ed. Eberhard Bethge. New York: Macmillan, 1972.

———. *The Cost of Discipleship.* New York: Simon & Schuster, 1995.

Braaten, Carl E., and Robert W. Jenson, eds. *Reclaiming the Bible for the Church.* Grand Rapids: Eerdmans, 1995.

Bultmann, Rudolph. "πένθος, πενθέω" In *Theological Dictionary of the New Testament.* Ed. G. Kittel and G. Friedrich; trans. G. W. Bromiley. Vol. 6. Grand Rapids: Eerdmans, 1964–1974.

Burgess, John P. *Why Scripture Matters: Reading the Bible in a Time of Church Conflict.* Louisville, Ky.: Westminster John Knox, 1998.

Childs, Brevard S. *Introduction to the Old Testament as Scripture.* Philadelphia: Fortress, 1979.

———. *The New Testament as Canon: An Introduction.* Philadelphia: Fortress, 1985.

Cohen, Marshall, ed. *The Philosophy of John Stuart Mill.* New York: Modern Library, 1961.

Collange, Jean-François. *De Jésus à Paul: L'éthique du Nouveau Testament.* Le champ éthique 3. Geneva: Labor et Fides, 1980.

Croatto, J. Severino. *Biblical Hermeneutics: Toward a Theory of Reading as the Production of Meaning.* Trans. Robert R. Barr. Maryknoll, N.Y.: Orbis, 1987.

Crosby, Michael. *House of Disciples: Church, Economics and Justice in Matthew.* Maryknoll, N.Y.: Orbis, 1988.

Crossan, John Dominic. "Jesus and Pacifism." In *No Famine in the Land,* ed. J. W. Flanagan and A. W. Robinson. Atlanta: Scholars Press, 1975.

Davies, W. D., and D. C. Allison Jr. *A Critical and Exegetical Commentary on the Gospel According to Saint Matthew.* International Critical Commentary, vol. 1. Edinburgh: T. & T. Clark, 1988.

Dube, Musa W. "Divining the Texts for International Relations (Matt. 15:21–28)." In *Transformative Encounters: Jesus and Women Reviewed,* ed. Ingrid Rosa Kitzberger. Biblical Interpretation Series. Leiden: Brill, 1999.

Dupont, Jacques. *Les béatitudes.* 3 vols. Paris: Gabalda, 1969–1973.

Dussel, Enrique. *Ethics and Community.* Trans. Robert Barr. Maryknoll, N.Y.: Orbis, 1988.

Edwards, Richard A. *Matthew's Story of Jesus.* Minneapolis: Fortress, 1985.

———. "Uncertain Faith: Matthew's Portrait of the Disciples." In *Discipleship in the New Testament,* ed. F. F. Segovia. Minneapolis: Fortress, 1985.

———. *Matthew's Narrative Portrait of Disciples: How the Text-Connoted Reader Is Informed.* Valley Forge, Pa.: Trinity Press International, 1997.

Fabella, Virginia, and Mercy Amba Oduyoye, eds. *With Passion and Compassion: Third World Women Doing Theology.* Maryknoll, N.Y.: Orbis, 1988.

Finnegan, William. *Cold New World: Growing Up in a Harder Country.* New York: Random House, 1998.

Foster, Charles R. "Paying Attention to Youth Culture." *Christian Century* 115, no. 34 (1998): 1185–87.

Freire, Paulo. *Pedagogy of the Oppressed.* Trans. Myra Bergman Ramos. New York: Herder and Herder, 1971.

Gallardo, Carlos Bravo. "Matthew: Good News for the Persecuted Poor." In *Subversive Scriptures: Revolutionary Readings of the Christian Bible in Latin America,* ed. Leif E. Vaage. Valley Forge, Pa.: Trinity Press International, 1997.

Gnanadason, Aruna. "Women's Oppression: A Sinful Situation." In *With Passion and Compassion: Third World Women Doing Theology,* ed. Virginia Fabella and Mercy Amba Oduyoye. Maryknoll, N.Y.: Orbis, 1988.

Goppelt, Leonhard. *Theology of the New Testament.* 2 vols. Grand Rapids: Eerdmans, 1981–1982.

Graham, Larry K. *Care of Persons, Care of Worlds.* Nashville: Abingdon, 1992.

Greimas, A. J., and J. Courtès. *Semiotics and Language: An Analytical Dictionary,* trans. L. Crist, D. Patte, et al. Bloomington: Indiana University Press, 1982.

Grenholm, Cristina. *Romans Interpreted: A Comparative Analysis of the Commentaries of Barth, Nygren, Cranfield and Wilckens on Paul's Epistle to the Romans.* Studia Doctrinae Christianae Upsaliensa 3. Uppsala: Acta Universitatis Upsaliensis, 1990.

———. *The Old Testament, Christianity and Pluralism.* Tübingen: J. C. B. Mohr/Paul Siebeck, 1996.

Grenholm, Cristina, and Daniel Patte, eds. *Reading Israel in Romans: Legitimacy and Plausibility of Divergent Interpretations.* Romans through History and Cultures, vol. 1. Harrisburg, Pa.: Trinity Press International, 2000.

Hauerwas, Stanley. *A Community of Character: Toward a Constructive Social Ethic.* Notre Dame, Ind.: University of Notre Dame Press, 1981.

Hooks, Bell. *Teaching to Transgress: Education as the Practice of Freedom.* New York and London: Routledge, 1994.

Jewett, Robert. *Saint Paul at the Movies: The Apostle's Dialogue with American Culture.* Louisville, Ky.: Westminster John Knox, 1993.

———. *Paul, The Apostle to America: Cultural Trends and Pauline Scholarship.* Louisville, Ky.: Westminster John Knox, 1994.

Johnson, Luke Timothy. "Learning Jesus." *Christian Century* 115, no. 33 (1998): 1142–46.

Johnston, Robert K. *Evangelicals at an Impasse: Biblical Authority in Practice.* Atlanta: John Knox, 1979.

Jordan, Clarence. *The Cotton Patch Version of Matthew and John.* Clinton, N.J.: New Wine Publishing, 1970.

———. *Sermon on the Mount.* Rev. ed. Valley Forge, Pa.: Judson Press, 1993.

Käsemann, Ernst. *New Testament Questions of Today.* Minneapolis: Fortress, 1969.

Kingsbury, Jack D. *Matthew as Story.* Minneapolis: Fortress, 1986.

Kitzberger, Ingrid Rosa, ed. *Transformative Encounters: Jesus and Women Re-viewed.* Biblical Interpretation Series. Leiden: Brill, 1999.

———. *Personal Voices in Biblical Scholarship.* London: Routledge, 1998.

Lapide, Pinchas. *The Sermon on the Mount: Utopia or Program of Action?* Maryknoll, N.Y.: Orbis, 1986.

Lévinas, Emmanuel. *Ethics and Infinity.* Trans. R. Cohen. Pittsburgh: Duquesne University Press, 1985.

———. *Time and the Other.* Trans. R. Cohen. Pittsburgh: Duquesne University Press, 1987.

———. *Entre nous: Essais sur le penser-a-l'autre.* Paris: Bernard Grasset, 1991.

Levine, Amy-Jill. "Matthew." In *The Women's Bible Commentary*, ed. Carol Newsom and Sharon Ringe. Louisville, Ky.: Westminster John Knox, 1992.

Lischer, Richard. "The Sermon on the Mount as Radical Pastoral Care." In *The Theological Interpretation of Scripture: Classic and Contemporary Readings*, ed. Stephen E. Fowl. Cambridge, Mass. and Oxford: Blackwell, 1997.

Luz, Ulrich. *Matthew 1–7: A Commentary.* Minneapolis: Augsburg, 1989.

———. "The Disciples in the Gospel according to Matthew." In *The Interpretation of Matthew*, ed. Graham Stanton. Philadelphia: Fortress, 1983.

Lyons, David. *The Form and Limits of Utilitarianism.* New York and London: Oxford University Press, 1965.

Magonet, Jonathan. *A Rabbi's Bible.* London: SCM, 1991.

Mananzan, Mary John. *Challenges to the Inner Room: Selected Essays and Speeches on Women.* Manila: Institute of Women's Studies, 1998.

Mananzan, Mary John, Sun Ai Park. "Emerging Spirituality of Asian Women." In *With Passion and Compassion: Third World Women Doing Theology*, ed. Virginia Fabella and Mercy Amba Oduyoye. Maryknoll, N.Y.: Orbis, 1988.

Marshall, Joretta L. *Counseling Lesbian Partners.* Louisville, Ky.: Westminster John Knox, 1997.

Mattern, Evelyn. *Blessed Are You: The Beatitudes and Our Survival.* Notre Dame, Ind.: Ave Maria, 1994.

Meeks, Wayne A. *The Moral World of the First Christians.* Philadelphia: Westminster, 1986.

Meier, John P. *The Vision of Matthew: Christ, Church and Morality in the First Gospel.* New York: Paulist, 1979.

Nelson, James B., and Sandra P. Longfellow. *Sexuality and the Sacred: Sources for Theological Reflection.* Louisville, Ky.: Westminster John Knox, 1994.

Nelson, Susan L. *Healing the Broken Heart: Sin, Alienation and the Gift of Grace.* St. Louis: Chalice Press, 1997.

Ogletree, Thomas W. *The Use of the Bible in Christian Ethics: A Constructive Essay.* Philadelphia: Fortress, 1983.

Palmer, Paul F. "Christian Marriage: Contract or Covenant?" *Theological Studies* 33 (1972): 619–25.

Parret, Herman. *Semiotics and Pragmatics: An Evaluative Comparison of Conceptual Frameworks.* Amsterdam and Philadelphia: John Benjamins, 1983.

Patte, Daniel. *Elements of a Semiotic of Didactic Discourse: Analysis of 1 Thessalonians.* Documents de Travail. Urbino, Italy: Centro Internazionale di Semiotica e di Linguistica, 1981.

———, ed. *Narrative and Discourse in Structural Exegesis: John 6 and 1 Thessalonians.* Semeia 26. Chico, Calif.: Scholars Press, 1983.

———. *The Gospel According to Matthew: A Structural Commentary on Matthew's Faith.* Minneapolis: Fortress, 1987; reprint, Valley Forge, Pa.: Trinity Press International, 1996.

———. *Structural Exegesis for New Testament Critics.* Guides to Biblical Scholarship. 2nd printing. Valley Forge, Pa.: Trinity Press International, 1996.

———. *The Religious Dimensions of Biblical Texts: Greimas's Structural Semiotics and Biblical Exegesis.* SBL Semeia Studies. Atlanta: Scholars Press, 1990.

———. *Ethics of Biblical Interpretation: A Reevaluation.* Louisville, Ky.: Westminster John Knox, 1995.

———. *Discipleship According to the Sermon on the Mount: Four Legitimate Interpretations, Four Plausible Views of Discipleship, and Their Relative Values.* Valley Forge, Pa.: Trinity Press International, 1996.

Peirce, Charles S. *Collected Papers of Ch. S. Peirce.* Ed. C. Hartshorne and P. Weiss. Cambridge, Mass: Belknap/Harvard University Press, 1931–63.

Phillips, Gary, and Danna Nolan Fewell, eds. "Ethics, Bible, Reading As If." In *Bible and Ethics of Reading.* Semeia 77. Atlanta: Scholars, 1997.

Pui-lan, Kwok. *Discovering the Bible in the Non-Biblical World.* Maryknoll, N.Y.: Orbis, 1995.

Ramodibe, Dorothy. "Women and Men Building Together the Church in Africa." In *With Passion and Compassion: Third World Women Doing Theology,* ed. Virginia Fabella and Mercy Amba Oduyoye. Maryknoll, N.Y.: Orbis, 1988.

Robbins, Vernon K. *The Tapestry of Early Christian Discourse: Rhetoric, Society and Ideology.* London and New York: Routledge, 1996.

Rowland, Christopher, and Mark Corner. *Liberating Exegesis: The Challenge of Liberation Theology to Biblical Studies.* Louisville, Ky.: Westminster John Knox, 1989.

Schneiders, Sandra M. *The Revelatory Text: Interpreting the New Testament as Sacred Scripture.* San Francisco: HarperSanFrancisco, 1991.

Schottroff, Luise. "Gewaltverzicht und Feindesliebe in der urchristlichen Jesustradition (Mt 5,38–48; Lk 6,27–36)." In *Jesus Christus in Historie und Theologie,* ed. G. Strecker. Tübingen: Mohr, 1975.

————. *Let the Oppressed Go Free: Feminist Perspectives on the New Testament.* Louisville, Ky.: Westminster John Knox, 1993.

————. *Lydia's Impatient Sisters: A Feminist Social History of Early Christianity.* Louisville, Ky.: Westminster John Knox, 1994.

Schüssler Fiorenza, Elisabeth. *Bread Not Stone: The Challenge of Feminist Biblical Interpretation.* New York: Beacon Press, 1984.

Smart, James D. *The Strange Silence of the Bible in the Church: A Study in Hermeneutics.* Philadelphia: Westminster, 1970.

Smith, Theophus. *Conjuring Culture: Biblical Formations of Black America.* New York and Oxford: Oxford University Press, 1994.

Smith, Wilfred Cantwell. *What is Scripture? A Comparative Approach.* Minneapolis: Fortress, 1993.

Soares-Prabhu, George M. "Class in The Bible: The Biblical Poor a Social Class?" In *Voices from the Margin: Interpreting the Bible in the Third World,* ed. R. S. Sugirtharajah. Maryknoll, N.Y.: Orbis, 1991.

Spivak, Gayatri C. "Can the Subaltern Speak?" In *Marxism and the Interpretation of Culture,* ed. G. Nelson and L. Grossberg. London: Macmillan, 1988.

Stanton, Graham, ed. *The Interpretation of Matthew.* Philadelphia: Fortress, 1983.

Strecker, Georg. "Die Makarismen der Bergpredigt." *New Testament Studies* 17 (1970): 255–75.

————. "The Concept of History in Matthew." In *The Interpretation of Matthew,* ed. Graham Stanton. Philadelphia: Fortress, 1983.

————. *The Sermon on the Mount: An Exegetical Commentary.* Trans. O. C. Dean Jr. Nashville: Abingdon, 1988.

Stendahl, Krister. "Biblical Theology, Contemporary." In *The Interpreter's Dictionary of the Bible,* ed. George A. Buttrick. Vol. 1. Nashville: Abingdon, 1962.

Sugirtharajah, R. S., ed. *Voices from the Margin: Interpreting the Bible in the Third World* Maryknoll, N.Y.: Orbis, 1991.

Tamez, Elsa. "Women's Rereading of the Bible." In *Voices from the Margin: Interpreting the Bible in the Third World,* ed. R. S. Sugirtharajah. Maryknoll, N.Y.: Orbis, 1991.

————. *Bible of the Oppressed.* Maryknoll, N.Y.: Orbis, 1982.

Velunta, Revelation. "*Ek Pisteōs eis Pistin* and the Filipinos' Sense of Indebtedness." In *Seminar Papers of the Society of Biblical Literature, 1998*, ed. Kent Richards. Atlanta: Scholars Press, 1998.

Walker, Alice. *The Temple of My Familiar.* New York: Pocket Books, 1990.

Wainwright, Elaine. "The Gospel of Matthew." In *Searching the Scriptures.* Vol. 2, *A Feminist Commentary*, ed. Elisabeth Schüssler Fiorenza. New York: Crossroad, 1994.

West, Gerald. *Contextual Bible Study.* Pietermaritzburg, South Africa: Cluster Publications, 1993.

————. *Biblical Hermeneutics of Liberation: Modes of Reading the Bible in the South African Context.* Rev. ed. Pietermaritzburg, South Africa: Cluster Publications; Maryknoll, N.Y.: Orbis, 1995.

Wink, Walter. *Naming the Powers: The Language of Power in the New Testament.* Philadelphia: Fortress, 1984.

————. *Unmasking the Powers: The Invisible Forces That Determine Human Existence.* Philadelphia: Fortress, 1986.

————. *Engaging the Powers: Discernment and Resistance in a World of Domination.* Minneapolis: Fortress, 1992.